Database Management Systems

2nd edition

D1315058

FASTTRACK

DATABASE MANAGEMENT SYSTEMS
2nd edition

Patricia Ward

COURSE TECHNOLOGY
CENGAGE Learning™

Australia • Brazil • Japan • Korea • Mexico • Singapore • Spain • United Kingdom • United States

 COURSE TECHNOLOGY
CENGAGE Learning

Middlesex
University
PRESS

**Database Management Systems,
2nd Edition**

Patricia Ward

Series Editor: Walaa Bakry, Middlesex University

Publishing Partner: Middlesex University Press

Publishing Director: John Yates

Publisher: Patrick Bond

Managing Editor: Celia Cozens

Development Editor: Matthew Lane

Content Project Editor: Leonora Dawson-Bowling

Manufacturing Manager: Helen Mason

Senior Production Controller: Maeve Healy

Marketing Manager: Rossella Proscia

Typesetter: Keyline Consultancy, Newark

Cover design: Matthew Ollive

Text design: Design Deluxe, Bath

For product information and technology assistance,
contact **emea.info@cengage.com**
For permission to use material from this text or product,
and for permission queries,
email **clsuk.permissions@cengage.com**

British Library Cataloguing-in-Publication Data
A catalogue record for this book is available from the British Library.
ISBN: 978-1-4080-0768-6

Cengage Learning EMEA
High Holborn House, 50-51 Bedford Row
London WC1R 4LR

Cengage Learning products are represented in Canada by Nelson Education Ltd.

Printed in Croatia by Zrinski d.d.
1 2 3 4 5 6 7 8 9 10 – 10 09 08

Contents

The FastTrack Series

Cengage Learning and Middlesex University Press have collaborated to produce a unique collection of textbooks which cover core, mainstream topics in an undergraduate computing curriculum. FastTrack titles are instructional, syllabus-driven books of high quality and utility. They are:

- **For students**: concise and relevant and written so that you should be able to get 100% value out of 100% of the book at an affordable price
- **For instructors**: classroom tested, written to a tried and trusted pedagogy and market-assessed for mainstream and global syllabus offerings so as to provide you with confidence in the applicability of these books. The resources associated with each title are designed to make delivery of courses straightforward and linked to the text.

FastTrack books can be used for self-study or as directed reading by a tutor. They contain the essential reading necessary to complete a full understanding of the topic. They are augmented by resources and activities, some of which will be delivered online as indicated in the text.

How the series evolved

Rapid growth in communication technology means that learning can become a global activity. In collaboration, Global Campus, Middlesex University and Cengage Learning have produced materials to suit a diverse and innovating discipline and student cohort.

Global Campus at the School of Computing Science, Middlesex University, combines local support and tutors with CD Rom-based materials and the Internet to enable students and lecturers to work together across the world.

Middlesex University Press is a publishing house committed to providing high-quality, innovative, learning solutions to organisations and individuals. The Press aims to provide leading-edge 'blended learning' solutions to meet the needs of its clients and customers. Partnership working is a major feature of the Press's activities.

Together with Middlesex University Press and Middlesex University's Centre for Learning Development, Global Campus developed FastTrack books using a sound and consistent pedagogic approach. The SCATE pedagogy is a learning framework that builds up as follows:

- **Scope:** Context and the learning outcomes
- **Content:** The bulk of the course: text, illustrations and examples
- **Activity:** Elements which will help students further understand the facts and concepts presented to them in the previous section. Promotes their active participation in their learning and in creating their understanding of the unit content
- **Thinking:** These elements give students the opportunity to reflect and share with their peers their experience of studying each unit. There are *review questions* so that the students can assess their own understanding and progress
- **Extra:** Further online study material and hyperlinks which may be supplemental, remedial or advanced.

Database Management Systems

This book introduces you to the major concepts and issues in the field of database systems. You will learn how to model databases using a number of techniques and approaches. You will also learn how to write SQL code to query data in a database and to write some more sophisticated coding using Oracle's PLSQL. In addition, you will be made aware of certain issues and trends connected with database software.

The book covers the areas of:

- Relational, object-oriented and object-relational models
- Entity relationship modelling and normalisation
- The standard query language SQL
- Oracle's procedural language, PL/SQL
- Query optimisation
- Transaction management and concurrent access
- Database recovery
- Distributed database systems
- Web database connection.

Using this book

There are several devices which will help you in your studies and use of this book. **Activities** usually require you to try out aspects of the material which have just been explained, or invite you to consider something which is about to be discussed. In some cases, a response is provided as part of the text that follows – so it is important to work on the activity before you proceed! Usually, however, a formal answer will be provided in the final section of the chapter in which the activity appears.

The **time bar** indicates *approximately* how long each activity should take:

short < 10 minutes

medium 10-45 minutes

long > 45 minutes

 Review questions are (usually) short questions at the end of each chapter to check you have remembered the main points of a chapter. They are a useful practical summary of the content, and can be used as a form of revision aid to ensure that you remain competent in each of the areas covered. Answers are provided at the back of the complete book

Where computer code is encountered, it is displayed in a different typeface and, where practical, is also provided online (see **About the Website**) – so you are not required to key in very long pieces of code. Do note, however, that the act of keying code is a useful discipline, and your keying errors are a valuable lesson in their own right. If your code does not run, do check the obvious – there is often little visual difference between l,1, I (small 'L', figure one, capital letter 'I' or between 0 and O.

About the author

Patricia Ward

Patricia Ward is a Senior Lecturer in the School of Computing Science at Middlesex University. She completed her undergraduate studies at the University of Edinburgh and earned an MSc in Computing at the University of North London. She has worked in UK universities for more than twenty-five years, initially as a Research Fellow and then as a Lecturer. Her research interests include database design and programming and green computing.

Acknowledgements

The author and publishers would like to acknowledge the contribution made by Mark Ward who died during the writing of the second edition, and also to Wendy Wu for her contribution in respect of chapter 10. The author would like to thank the reviewers, and also her colleague Lindsey Brodie for her suggestions.

Visit the accompanying website at **www.cengage.co.uk/fasttrack** and click through to the appropriate booksite to find further teaching and learning material including:

For students

- Activities
- Multiple choice questions for each chapter
- Source code
- Tools & resources.

For lecturers

- Downloadable PowerPoint slides
- Questions (exam style) with outline answers and grading guidelines
- Discussion topics.

CHAPTER 1

Introduction

OVERVIEW

This chapter introduces the basic concepts of database systems for more detailed discussion in subsequent chapters. We start with a brief **history of database systems** and then establish definitions of some **basic concepts**, namely database, a database system and a database management system. A database system consists of a number of **components** including data, computer hardware and software and users; we look particularly at the software that manages and controls access to the database, namely the **database management system** (DBMS). We examine how the DBMS interacts with both the operating system and the database itself and study the functions that a typical DBMS will provide; some functions are explored in detail in subsequent chapters. In this chapter we look at one particular component: 'categories of users' which include **end users**, **database designers** and the **database administrator**.

Different groups of users of a database may wish to have access to different parts of the database, i.e. users may require **different views** of the same database depending on their requirements. Other users may be more concerned with how the data is actually stored: for example, if access to the database is to be made more efficient. We introduce the idea of **abstract and physical views**, as seen by users of a database.

Finally, we introduce the process of designing a database system, particularly the development of a **conceptual data model** of the real world which is of interest and relevant to an application. We also look at how the design of database systems fits into the development of complete information systems for an organisation.

Learning outcomes　　On completion of this chapter, you should be able to:

- Explain the main developments in the history of database systems
- Distinguish between a database, a database system and a database management system
- Describe the components of the database system environment
- Describe the structure of a typical DBMS and the key functions it must support
- Distinguish between abstract and physical views of data
- Identify the main tasks involved in database development.

1.1 A brief history of database systems

From paper to shared computer files

Database systems developed because of the need to store large amounts of data and retrieve that data quickly and accurately. For example a university library stores details about the books held and loans taken out by students. Not very long ago this information about the books and loans might have been stored in a box card index. Nowadays, only a few decades later, students are able to view their loans online using a web browser and see if any books are overdue. They can check to see if a book is available and reserve it. The library staff can quickly access statistics on overdue books, popular books and books which never leave the shelves.

Another example would be a company that accepts customer orders – for instance, orders for spare parts for electrical goods. Originally, orders might have been created when customers telephoned the company to place their orders. If information about a customer already existed in a **paper file,** then his/her details would be retrieved; otherwise, customer details would be requested and recorded. For each order, an order form would have been filled in and copied: one copy would be stored in a filing cabinet; the other sent to the warehouse. To complete an order, information on stock held in the warehouse would need to be accessed. In turn, this would lead to purchase orders being raised to replenish the stock ordered by the customers and to invoices being raised to bill the customers for their orders.

Eventually the order entry system was likely to be computerised so that by the early 1960s the data about customers and orders might have been stored in a **computer file** - a magnetic tape file and then later magnetic disk. These files were processed by computer programs — i.e. **application software**. Other applications programs were developed which could create invoices, purchase orders to suppliers and so on. Although different applications would at times require similar data, the data would be kept in different files. The diagram below shows, for a typical company which sells goods to customers, the different applications each with their own copy of the files they use.

Figure 1.1: File-based approach to data

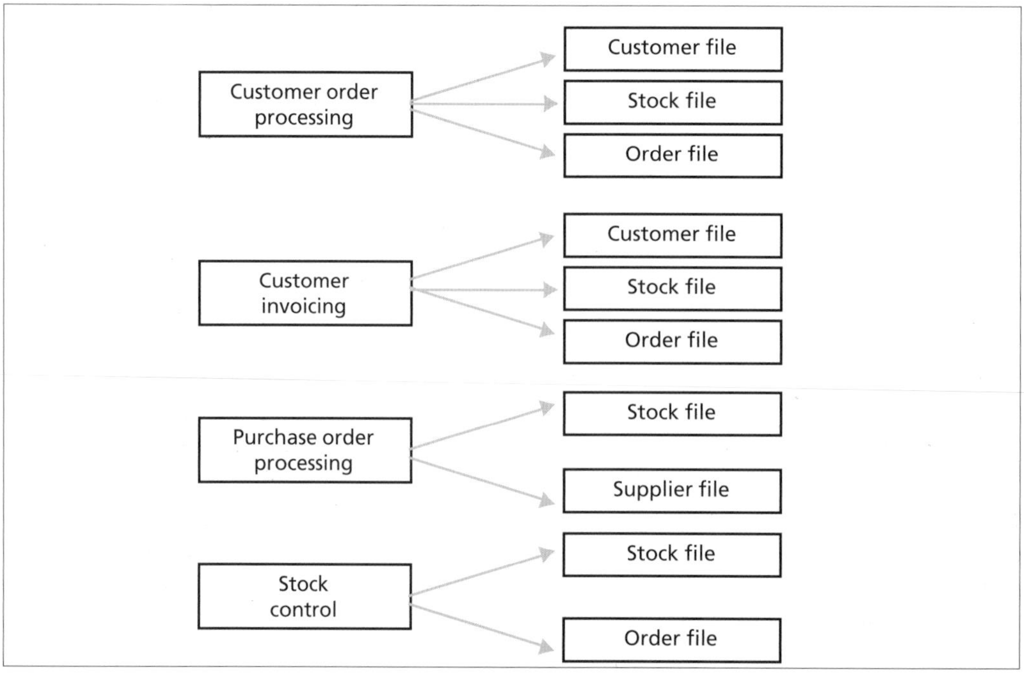

In both types of system, the paper one and the **computerised file system**, processing was slow and problems of inconsistencies of data could easily develop. If an item of data in one file needs updating (for example, the customer addresses in the customer file) then it will need to be updated in all the relevant files: otherwise, inconsistencies will develop. The introduction of **shared files**, whereby different applications shared some of the same files, solved some of the problems, and was good for providing routine data. For example, a customer order application and an invoicing application might use both the customer and stock files, and in addition their own files. As only one copy of each file was made available, the inconsistencies were avoided. This method was however not efficient, as a shared file would only be available to one application at a time. Shared file systems were also not effective in providing data for planning and control of an organisation.

Early database systems

In the 1960s, **database systems** began to emerge, improving on the shared file system (described above). Such systems allowed simultaneous access to the data by a number of different users and provided facilities for querying, security and integrity of the data.   The IBM product, IMS, was an early system where the user viewed the data as a **hierarchical** tree. By the late sixties, database systems based on a different **data model** had been developed. This time the **user view** of the data was a **network** of data records. In both cases (hierarchical and network models) skilled programmers were required to write the programs to create, access and change the data in the database. The users of these database systems tended to be large organisations.

The database approach was an improvement on the shared file solution as the software which was used (the **database management system – DBMS**) to control the data (the **database**) was quite powerful. The database management system consisted (and still consists) of a number of components, which as mentioned provided facilities for querying data, data security and integrity and the ability to access the data simultaneously by different users. Another characteristic of database systems is that the underlying structure of the data is isolated from the actual data itself. The description of the structure of the entire database is called a **conceptual schema**. There are various levels of schema: these levels will be discussed later in this chapter. If there is a requirement to change the logical structure of the data (for example to add a new characteristic) the change will be made at the conceptual level. Such changes are independent of both the physical storage level and the level seen by individual users.

Relational database systems

Returning to our brief history, by the 1970s the study of database systems had become a major academic and research area. The **relational model** was first proposed in 1970 by E F Codd with his series of pioneering papers. Codd was a British computer scientist who at the time was working for IBM at their research centre in San Jose, California. Gradually, relational database systems replaced the earlier hierarchical and network-based systems. The theory underpinning relational databases is derived from the mathematical principles of set theory and predicate logic. The model is based on the familiar concepts of tables, rows and columns. So for example, a university library database which is based on the relational model would consist of tables of borrower data, book data and loan data among others.

The manipulation of these tables is achieved through a collection of simple and well-understood set theory operators, such as union and intersection. The **Structured Query Language** (SQL), based on these set theory operators, was developed in the 1970s by IBM to support its relational products.

Since then, many other features of SQL have been added which go beyond the original relational operators and it has now become the most important query language for relational databases.

The first commercial relational product, **Oracle**'s DBMS, was released in 1980. The relational model has been successfully adopted for **transaction processing** in numerous organisations and supports most of the major database systems in commercial use today. Its ability to handle efficiently simple data types, its powerful query language, and its good protection of data from programming errors make it an effective model. Commercial relational database management systems available today have incorporated all these things and a lot more. For example, Oracle and many of its competitors have expanded far beyond the original DBMS software. The DBMS is now usually part of a suite of software products which also includes fourth-generation tools such as form, report and application generators, data warehousing software and data casting over the Web.

Most of the remaining chapters in this book place a strong emphasis on the relational approach. Chapter 2 introduces the reader to relational database theory and later in Chapters 5 and 6 the reader will be introduced to the query language, developed for relational databases, SQL.

Post-relational database systems

Relational databases, although widely adopted, do have a number of weaknesses which led, in the 1990s, to attention shifting to **object-oriented databases**. We shall see that these databases became successful for applications which require more complex data structures than simple tables. Examples of such applications include computer-aided design (CAD) and computer-aided manufacturing (CAM). Some of these ideas (such as user-defined types and routines) were adopted by vendors of relational database systems (e.g. Oracle). New features were integrated into their products and these became known as **object-relational databases**.

In the mid 1990s, the first databases which could be accessed over the **Word Wide Web** began to appear. The Web created a need to extend traditional database technologies and to develop new ones. We will see in Chapter 12 how a number of different approaches have been developed to integrate database systems with the Web. Nowadays the growth of databases supporting websites continues exponentially.

In the late 1990s vendors began to integrate **XML** into their products. XML is a web-based standard for describing many different kinds of data. It is primarily used to facilitate the sharing of data across different systems connected via the Internet. Traditional database systems, such as relational and object-oriented ones, are only good for handling data where the data's structure is constant and rarely changes. On the other hand, XML is used to describe **semi-structured data** – i.e. data which has a wide variation in structure and does not fit neatly into a rigid database schema. We shall look at some examples of XML in Chapter 12.

1.2 Data, database and database management system

It is assumed that most people reading the above section on the history of database systems will have a rough idea of what a database is. We will now examine the term more fully. Before defining 'database' let us first be clear about what we mean by the term '**data**'. It can be defined as numerical, character or other symbols which can be recorded in a form suitable for processing by a computer, such as the names and addresses of users of the university library described above.

The term '**database**' is not just a technical expression but is now part of our everyday language. It generally means a collection of related data (such as data for a library) arranged for speedy search and retrieval. In computing terms we have to add that it is a set of related data that is created and managed by a piece of software called a **database management system** (DBMS). Nowadays the data in a database may take a number of forms including text, numbers, images, sound and video.

Also the data in our database will be stored on a computer storage medium in a common pool for access by different applications – i.e. the applications accessing the data share the same **integrated data**. Put another way, there is generally only one copy of each item of data in the database. To go back to our university library example, it is likely that this application is one of many in the university. For example there will also be a student records system and a personnel system for staff. The applications will share the same integrated data: for example, both the library application and the student records system will have access to student names, addresses and so on. For one particular student, John Smith for example, there will exist only one copy of John's name, address, etc in the database associated with a particular student.

In fact, the database does not only contain the actual data. Stored with the data will be a description of the data items held: the **catalog** or data dictionary. The data itself will probably be stored as a set of files. However, the users of the database and the application programs which access the database do not need to be aware of the **physical storage**. The programs do not directly access the data – instead the DBMS uses the system catalog to retrieve the information from the appropriate place in the database. The data is therefore stored so it is independent of the programs that use the data.

Another characteristic of a database is that the data will be stored for some time after it is created, i.e. it is **persistent**. This contrasts with non-persistent data such as input and output data (for example, data entering the system for the first time from a workstation or data which is sent out to workstations to be printed on a report). Non-persistent data is also data that exists only while an application program is running – for example, in the form of temporary variables used by a program.

A definition of 'database' to include all the characteristics mentioned could be:

> A database is a collection of persistent, related data stored on computer storage medium and arranged for speedy search and retrieval. It is created and managed by a piece of software called a database management system (DBMS). The data in a database will be stored in a common pool for access by many applications – i.e. the applications accessing the data share the same integrated data. The data will be stored so they are independent of programs which use the data. Generally there is only one copy of each item of data although there may be controlled repetition of some of the data.

1.3 The components of a database system

There are various components that make up a **database system**. They include the data (the database); the description of the data items held (the catalog); the people involved in designing, creating, maintaining and using the system; the computer hardware and the software. The latter is made up of the database management system and the application programs written by programmers to create, update and query the database.

The components can be shown diagrammatically as in figure 1.2.

Figure 1.2: Simplified database system environment

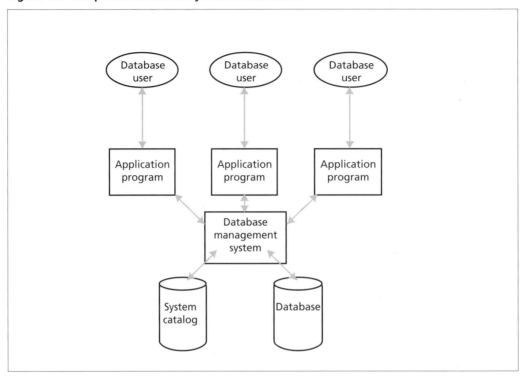

Centralised and distributed databases

We shall assume initially that the data comprising a database is held together in one place – i.e. it is **centralised**. Later in this book you will see that the database can be **distributed** over a number of computers or sites in different locations. With a centralised database configuration a **back-end** computer (the Database Server) will control access to the database. Other computers, the **front-end** will run that part of the DBMS software (such as report and form generators), which interfaces with the users of the application. This two-tier architecture describes what is known as a **client/server architecture** and this together with distributed database systems will be discussed further in Chapter 11.

The system catalog

An important component of database systems is the system catalog (sometimes called the data dictionary). This contains the **metadata**, which describes all the data in our database (the **schemas**) plus information about the users and the applications that use the database. Typically schema information is the definitions of the data (including names, data types and the size of database items), the relationships between these items, integrity constraints and allowable operations on data items. The catalog is also used to help the DBMS find the actual record in physical storage when there is a request to access data in the database. We shall see that there are various **levels of schemas** in our database and the system catalog is responsible for maintaining data about these.

The users of the database system

The users of the database system are the people involved in using, designing, creating and maintaining the database. Some of these categories of users are described here:

- The people who utilise the database are called **end users** – in our university library example end users would be library staff, students, lecturers and so on. It is likely that these users will have access to a menu-driven interface which includes forms and reports
- The **database designer** specifies the structure or logical design of the database. The structure should support the requirements of the applications. For example in a university library application the database should be designed to enable the details of overdue books to be made available. The database designer also specifies the physical design of the database by detailing how the database is to be physically realised (for example in terms of the tables to be created and the access methods)
- The **application programmers** are responsible for writing the application software to create, update and query the database, i.e. the programs which implement the required functionality for the end users
- Another category of user is the **database administrator** (DBA) who is responsible for control of the database at a technical level. The role of the DBA is discussed below.

The database administrator

The database administrator (DBA) is in overall control of the database and the DBMS at a technical level. The role may be carried out by one person or a group of people. The DBA is responsible for a particular database or databases and the applications that use them. Areas of responsibility include:

- **Development, implementation** and **operation** of the physical database
- **Creation of the system catalog** and modifications to its structure to accommodate any required changes
- Optimising database **performance**
- Monitoring and controlling database **security** and **authorisation**: defining and/or implementing access controls to the database to permit authorised users and prevent any unauthorised access to data
- Setting up controls to ensure the **quality** and **integrity** of data
- Ensuring the **availability** of the database and instigating **backup** and **recovery procedures**: the aim being to guard against failures due to hardware or software problems; creating and testing backup copies and system logs and ensuring that the database is able to recover if a failure should occur.

1.4 The database management system

Many of the topics in this book look in detail at particular functions of the database management system (DBMS) so a fuller description of this piece of software is given here. We will look at the structure of a typical DBMS and the key functions that a DBMS must support. A simple definition is given:

> A DBMS is a collection of programs that allow users to specify the structure of a database, to create, query and modify the data in the database and to control access to it.

The DBMS and the operating system

In fact, figure 1.2, a simplified database system environment, does not show the need for the DBMS to interact with both the operating system and the database.

An operating system is the key software component of any computing system: it manages the computer's hardware and software resources. Examples of operating systems are Windows Vista, Server 2008, Unix, Linux and Mac OS X. The elements of the operating system that are critical are shown below.

Figure 1.3: The DBMS and the operating system

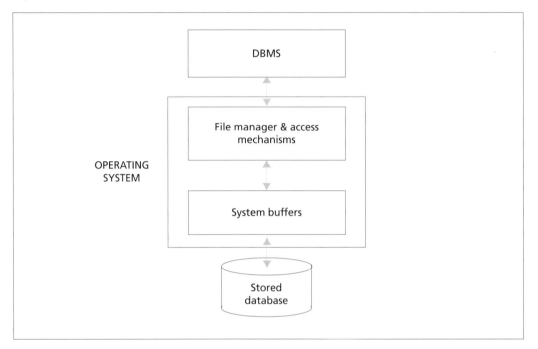

Access to the database is controlled by the host operating system. The DBMS accepts requests for data from the application program and then informs the operating system to transfer the appropriate data. This is done via the file manager which keeps track of the location of the underlying database files in secondary storage. The system buffers (in particular, database buffers) are temporary locations for storing and manipulating data. Reading and writing of data is performed via these buffers. Memory is organised in pages and these pages are read from secondary storage into the buffer in main memory and then written back.

Functions of a DBMS

Originally, database management systems were large and expensive and were run on large computers. Nowadays they appear as a common tool for even small machines. Despite this, modern DBMSs are complex pieces of software and, although the architecture will vary, there are a number of functions that a typical DBMS will support. These include:

- **A Data Definition Language (DDL)** to define a database. A DBMS must allow users to create database definitions. DDL statements in the SQL query language will be examined in Chapter 5
- **A Data Manipulation Language (DML)** to insert, update, delete and query data in the database. Note that both the DDL statements and DML statements will be written in the definition language of the target DBMS software. DML statements in SQL will be examined in Chapters 5 and 6
- **Buffer management:** this function is responsible for transferring data to and from main memory and secondary storage

- **Query processing and optimisation:** query processing transforms queries into low-level instructions which are then optimised. Query optimisation determines the optimum strategy for a query execution. This will be looked at in detail in Chapter 7
- **Concurrency control:** this allows shared access to the database, with multiple transactions being executed at the same time and scheduled in a safe manner. This will be looked at in detail in Chapter 9
- **Recovery:** the DBMS must take steps to ensure that, if the database fails, it remains in a consistent state. This will be looked at in detail in Chapter 10
- **Security control:** the DBMS should prevent unauthorised access to the database
- **Data integrity:** the DBMS must include the facility for enforcing integrity constraints whenever a change is made to the database to ensure the data is consistent and correct. This will be examined in Chapter 2
- **System catalog:** a DBMS includes a repository for storing metadata. Metadata is data about the data held and includes the structure of the data items, information about the relationships between the data items, integrity constraints and authorisation privileges.

As detailed above a number of the DBMS functions are discussed in more detail in subsequent chapters in this book.

1.5 Abstract and physical views of the data

Earlier we discussed how the system catalog records the **metadata** of the database system. The catalog describes all the data in our database including the **conceptual schema** and **user views** – these are the **abstract views** of the data in terms of the data requirements and are independent of how the requirements are to be met and how the data is physically stored. For a university library such a view might include a description of the items of data held in the database, such as book, loan, student and lecturer (i.e. the entities), the characteristics of each entity, such as student number and student name and the relationships between the various entities.

As far as the abstract view of the data is concerned, users do not always require the same data, so **multiple abstract views** may exist. In addition it will be necessary to have a complete abstract view of the whole database (the conceptual schema as described earlier in this chapter) as seen by the organisation and in particular the database administrator.

The system catalog will also contain a **physical storage** view (physical schema) of the data. Metadata held to describe the physical storage of the database will include file names, organisation and access methods. This part of the catalog is used to help the DBMS speedily find required data in physical storage. A major aim of database systems is to hide the physical view, of how the data is stored and manipulated, from the users of the database.

Figure 1.4 illustrates the well-established ANSI-SPARC (American National Standards Institute - System Planning and Requirements Committee) three-tier architecture. It was proposed in 1975 as a general architecture which fits most database systems.

Figure 1. 4: The three-tier architecture

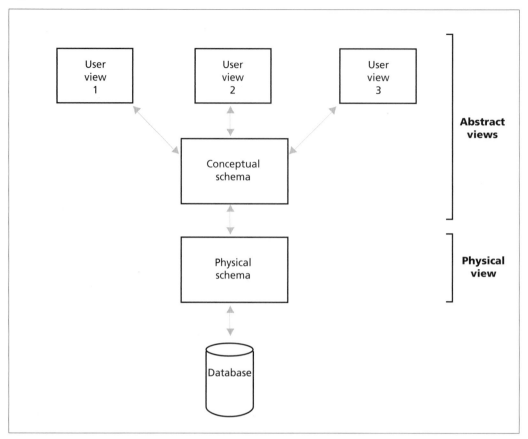

The diagram illustrates that there are **three levels of abstraction**, i.e. three separate levels at which data in the database can be described. Notice that there is one single conceptual schema and one physical schema but many user views. The conceptual schema defines the complete abstract structure in terms of how the organisation views the data – the details of the physical data are hidden from the users. The user views describe how different classes of users each see a subset of the database. Users should be allowed to see only data that is of interest to them and be unaware of those parts of the database which are irrelevant to them. The physical schema describes how the data is physically stored and accessed in the database.

A simple example of the three levels of abstraction is given in the next figure, for the university library database system. Note that schemas are defined using a language which is generally known as **data definition language** (DDL).

Figure 1.5: Example of three levels of abstraction (University Library)

Conceptual schema
   Student (student id: string, student name: string, address: string, date of
   birth: date, course: string)
   Lecturer (lecturer id: string, lecturer name: string, department: string, extension:
   string)
   Book (ISBN: string, title: string, author: string, value: number)
   Loan (student id: string, ISBN: string, loan-date: date, due-date: date)

User view1
   Student-loan (student id: string, student name: string, ISBN: string, title: string,
   loan-date: date, due-date: date)
User view2
   Lecturer-department (lecturer id: string, lecturer name: string, department:
   string)

User view3 ....

Physical schema
   Student
      Storage method - unordered file
      Access method - index on student id
   Lecturer ....

Data independence

The way the metadata in the system catalog is organised (i.e. using the three-level architecture described above) means that the structure of the data is transparent to both the users of the database and the applications programs which access it. This insulation of the data is known as data independence. There are two forms of data independence, one between the conceptual schema and user view and the other between the conceptual schema and physical schema:

- **Logical data independence:** the protection of existing user views to changes made to the conceptual schema. So for example in figure 1.5 we can add a new data item such as 'email address' to Student in the conceptual schema without affecting the existing user views

- **Physical data independence:** the insulation of the conceptual schema to changes made to the physical schema. What this means is that the physical storage of the data can be modified without the need to alter the conceptual schema or the existing applications. So for example in the physical schema in figure 1.5 we can change the storage and access methods for 'Student' in order to make access faster. However, the conceptual schema or the existing applications which use the student data will not need to change. Database users therefore do not have to be aware of the underlying physical structure of the data in the database.

Both logical and physical data independence are major aims of database systems.

1.6 Database design

Stages in database design

From the outset, decisions have to be made about the data to be stored in a database to satisfy the requirements of a particular application, such as the university library system described earlier. The successful design of a database system is extremely important in achieving speedy and accurate search and retrieval. Also the designer must allow for future changes in requirements while avoiding future, major changes to the design.

We have already used the term 'data model' earlier in this chapter when we discussed various approaches to storing data. Examples of different 'architectural' data models include hierarchical and relational models. The term 'data model' can be confusing as it is also widely used to refer to the model used to represent the data required in the design of a database application, as in 'a data model for a University library'.

The main stages in the database design process can be categorised under the following headings (but beware that some database practitioners and textbooks use the terms 'conceptual' and 'logical data modelling' synonymously):

- **Conceptual data modelling:** a concise description of the data requirements of an application. It is high-level model which is not concerned with what type of database system is used nor concerned with storage requirements. It is discussed in more detail below and in Chapter 3
- **Logical modelling:** this stage involves mapping the conceptual model to one suitable for implementation using a particular DBMS (such as a relational one). It is also discussed in Chapter 3
- **Physical modelling:** a data model for an application expressed in terms of internal storage structures and access methods. Physical data modelling is discussed briefly in Chapter 3.

Conceptual data modelling

The identification of the information to be recorded and how it is structured in the conceptual schema is part of the database design process and is known as conceptual data modelling. The conceptual data model must be understood by different users of the system so is often in the form of easily understood diagrams and narrative. It is a high-level description of the information to be stored – the model is not concerned with the low-level, physical storage details. The model is different to the conceptual schema example in figure 1.5 – the latter is written in the data definition language for a particular DBMS.

A conceptual data model can be defined as a representation of the real world which is of interest and relevant to an organisation. There are a number of approaches to developing a conceptual data model. A top-down approach to designing databases is **entity-relationship modelling** and is the most important method used. With this technique the designer establishes the entities (elements of interest in an organisation), the attributes (properties of the entities) and relationships between the entities. We will examine this method in Chapter 3.

The entity-relationship model was proposed in 1976 by Peter Chen. Since then his basic approach has been extended to include additional semantic concepts. We will look at one of the most important extensions, the **enhanced entity-relationship model** in Chapter 8.

Another data modelling method, a bottom-up one known as **normalisation** is examined in Chapter 4. These modelling methods map easily to relational databases, where data is viewed as a set of relations or tables. Relational databases are discussed in Chapter 2. Other models discussed in this book map more easily to object-oriented and object-relational databases, which we discuss later in this book in Chapter 8, where we will show how entity-relationship modelling can be adapted for object-oriented database design.

1.7 Overview of database development

Conceptual data modelling is one of a number of tasks involved in the development of a database system. Here we put the tasks involved in database development into the context of the complete information system life cycle. We identify the major activities which are typically carried out as follows:

- Fact finding and requirements analysis
- Database design which includes:
    - conceptual data modelling
    - logical data modelling
    - physical data modelling
- Process modelling
- User interface design (menu, form, report and web page design)
- Prototyping
- Implementation and testing
- Monitoring, tuning and maintenance.

The development may start with a fact-finding investigation which involves the identification of the nature and use of the current data in the organisation. Fact-finding techniques include interviewing end users and other interested parties, and conducting surveys through questionnaires. The reading of relevant organisational documentation and observing how the system currently operates is also carried out at this stage. The requirements analysis involves the identification of the requirements for the new database system. The information gleaned at this stage of the development forms the basis of the conceptual data model which is subsequently translated or mapped into a logical data model and then to a physical data model suitable for use by a particular DBMS architecture. These three models are described in section 1.6. The end result of the data design activity will be the DBMS-specific logical and physical schemas and user views.

The next activity listed above, process modelling, is likely to take place in tandem with database design and involves the design of programs that use and process the data in the database.

The design of user interfaces, i.e. menu, forms, reports and web pages, is also carried out as part of the design process. Forms are used by users to input and display database items, such as a form to display student information and all the books borrowed by that student. Additionally, items in the databases can be updated or deleted using a form as the interface. Reports are intended for printing and involve formatted data including that which is extracted from the database. An example might be a listing of all books which have not been borrowed in the last year.

The design of programs and user interfaces may entail the creation of prototypes. A prototype is a 'mock-up' of a system for the purposes of demonstrating to end users what the system will look like and how it will work. If problems are found, then a refinement of the design may be necessary.

After these activities are carried out, the application programs are created. As well as the creation of the database definitions in the system catalog, implementation may also involve the conversion and loading of data from the old system (if it exists) to the new system. The database system will then be tested against the original requirements for accuracy and any errors will be rectified.

As time goes on, new requirements may be identified. These may be incorporated into the database system and some changes to the database design may be necessary. If logical data independence exists, such restructuring should not affect the existing applications, and users should be unaware of any changes. After the system is in operation it will be continually monitored for defects or inefficiencies. Where inefficiencies occur, some tuning of the database may be necessary. Tuning might involve, for example, changes to access methods for files in the database and hence the physical design would need to be altered to reflect these changes. Physical data independence should ensure that there is no impact on the conceptual schema.

1.8 Summary

This chapter introduced the reader to database systems. A brief history of database systems was examined: from the origins in shared file systems; to early hierarchical and network database systems; leading to the relational and object-oriented approaches and later to web-enabled databases. The chapter also focused on basic concepts and terminology.

Database systems and their components were examined as was the important piece of database software, the database management system (DBMS). The ANSI-SPARC three-tier architecture was introduced and the importance of the design of one of the tiers, the conceptual data model, was discussed. The life cycle of a database system was briefly outlined, from requirements analysis, through conceptual and physical design to implementation and maintenance.

1.9 Review questions

Review question 1.1   Re-read section 1.1 on the history of database systems and then draw a time-line to show the main events in the history. The time-line has been started for you below:

early 60s
Computer files
used to store data

Review question 1.2   With the advent of shared file systems an application was now able to have access to files used by other applications. What are the advantages of sharing files? What are the disadvantages which led to the development of database systems?

Review question 1.3   Re-draw figure 1.1 'File-based approach to data' to illustrate a shared file approach.

Review question 1.4   List the kinds of information that the following organisations might want to store in a database:

- A library

- A hospital

- A university

- A manufacturing company.

Review question 1.5   Distinguish between the terms 'data', 'database' and 'database system'.

Review question 1.6   Use a search engine to find definitions of the following terms:

- Abstraction
- Metadata
- Conceptual schema

- Data model
- System catalog

Review question 1.7   Re-read functions of a DBMS within section 1.4 . Investigate a DBMS of your choice such as Oracle 11g or MS Access 2007 and establish whether the functions listed are provided by that DBMS.

Review question 1.8   It is an aim of database systems to provide both physical data independence and logical data independence. Distinguish between physical and logical data independence.

CHAPTER 2

The relational model

OVERVIEW

We begin our discussion of data modelling with the most popular type of database architecture and one which the reader may already have experienced, the relational data model. This chapter provides an overview of the relational data model and introduces the standard relational features. We concentrate on the underlying concepts of relational databases including structure, constraints and manipulation. We introduce the languages used to create, manipulate and query data in a relational database, looking in particular at relational algebra, a language for retrieving data from the database. This sets the scene for the query language, SQL, in Chapters 5 and 6. This chapter looks also at the advantages and disadvantages of relational databases, when compared with other means of storing data.

Learning outcomes

On completion of this chapter, you should be able to:

- Appreciate some important theoretical issues related to the structure of the relational model, and explain some basic concepts, including relation, attribute, null value, primary key and foreign key

- Understand the key features of data integrity in the relational data model

- Describe the relational algebra operators

- Understand the advantages and weaknesses of relational database management systems.

2.1 Introduction

Relational database systems remain by far the most popular database systems used in organisations today. The relational model has become widely accepted because of its conceptual simplicity and its sound theoretical basis. As we saw in Chapter 1 when we examined the history of database systems, the relational model was developed by E F Codd in the early 1970s with his series of pioneering papers. The theory underpinning relational databases is derived from the mathematical principles of set theory and predicate logic. The model is based on the familiar concepts of tables, rows and columns, and the manipulation of data stored in these tables achieved through a collection of well-understood set theory operators. A relational database is a collection of these tables.

Commercial systems based on the relational model began to appear in the late 1970s. Since then the model has become by far the most dominant, superseding the earlier network and hierarchical models. At the present time there are several hundred relational DBMSs and most computer vendors support 'relational' software. Examples of well-known products include Oracle, IBM's DB2, Sybase, MySQL, Microsoft SQLServer and Microsoft Access. Although relational databases remain dominant, we will see (Chapter 8) that some database management systems have incorporated 'post-relational' object-oriented features.

The relational model

Relational databases are based on the relational model of data. Codd defined the term 'data model' to consist of three elements:

- Definitions of the structure of the data
- Definitions of the types of operations allowed on the data
- Integrity constraints used to ensure the data is as accurate as possible. For example, constraints can be specified to ensure that data falls within a set of values.

We shall examine in this chapter (and also in Chapters 5 and 6) how the three elements above of structure, manipulation, and integrity of data are applied to the relational model.

2.2 Relational concepts

Some terminology

The model uses terminology taken from mathematics, particularly set theory and predicate logic. With relational databases, users perceive the data to be stored as tables (or relations, to give the mathematical term). In other types of database systems, the conceptual view of the data is different – for example, the conceptual view of the data might be a hierarchical structure (hierarchical and object-oriented databases) or a network structure (network databases). Basic terminology used in relational theory includes:

- A **relation** is a table or flat file with columns and rows which has certain properties
- A **tuple** is a row of a relation and represents an instance of a relation
- An **attribute** is a named column of a relation
- A **domain** is the set of allowable values for one or more attributes
- The **degree** of a relation is the number of attributes it contains
- The **cardinality** of relation is the number of tuples it contains.

Note: throughout this textbook the terms 'relation' and 'table' will be used synonymously as will 'tuple' and 'row'. These terms are further explained using the example which follows.

Figure 2.1: Sample relation

Film

attributes

filmNo	title	director	country	year	genre
005	Reservoir Dogs	Tarantino	US	1992	Crime
006	Pulp Fiction	Tarantino	US	1994	Crime
008	Trainspotting	Boyle	UK	1996	
109	Infernal Affairs	Wai-Keung	China	2002	Crime
111	Snakes on a Plane	Ellis	US	2006	Disaster

tuple

relation

In figure 2.1, the **relation** (or table) is given the name 'Film'; a **tuple** is a row and represents a **instance** of a Film; an **attribute** is a named column such as filmNo and title; the **domain** for the attribute 'year' might be the range of years when films have been made; the domain for 'title' is the set of all permissible values of film title; the **degree** of the relation is 6; the **cardinality** 5.

It is often required to be able to identify uniquely each of the different instances which a relation contains. In order to do this we use a '**primary key**', discussed in section 2.3.

Properties of relations

- Relation names are unique – there is only one relation in the database with Film as the title
- Attribute names are unique within a relation
- A cell of a relation contains atomic values – this is explained below
- Attribute values in a column are all from the same domain or pool of values
- Each tuple is unique – there are no duplicate rows
- The order of attributes is not significant
- The order of tuples is not significant.

Atomic values in cells

It is worth explaining in more detail the third item in the above list of properties of relations: 'a cell of a relation contains atomic values'. This means that every cell contains only one value. For example, in the Film relation above, the cell in the second data row, fifth column contains only a single data value '1994'. It only contains one year value (the year the film 'Reservoir Dogs' was made) and cannot contain more than one. This is to be expected as each tuple represents an instance of a film so we would expect only one year for a given film.

The requirement for atomic values applies to all the cells in the relation. So, for example, the director attribute cell can only contain one attribute value. The design of the relation above will not work if we allow for the possibility that a film can be directed by more than one director. The important concept to understand at this stage is that all the cells must contain atomic or single values. (We will see later how to redesign the model so that we incorporate the more realistic situation that a film can be directed by more than one director.)

Null values

It was stated above that every cell cannot contain more than one value. A possibility is that a cell will contain nothing at all – for example if the data value at the time of entry was not known, as in the Film relation above where the genre (category) for the film 'Trainspotting' is unknown.

A special value called the **null value** may be created (i.e. implemented by the database management system) when there is no value for an attribute. This is not the same as a data value being a zero or a space.

A null value can be used for one of two reasons: either an entry is not applicable or it is not known.

- For example, the attribute 'flatNumber' might be included in a table as part of an address. This attribute applies only to those people who live in flats and is 'not applicable' (and therefore contains null) for those people who live in houses
- An example where a null value is used where an attribute value is 'not known' is the attribute height, if a person's height were unknown.

Relational database structure

Before data is stored in a relation it must be defined using what is called a data definition language (DDL) – i.e. the names of each relation are declared and the attributes within each relation are specified and this information about the structure of the data is stored in the database. We examine this idea in more detail in section 2.4 on Database Languages and show how we can define a relation in SQL in Chapter 5.

2.3 Relational database integrity constraints

Besides the structural definition of a database described above, part of the specification of the relation is a set of **integrity constraints**. These are included to try to ensure that data entered into the database is as correct as possible – they are conditions that are specified which restrict the entry of any 'illegal' data.

Categories of integrity constraints

There are a number of categories of constraints which can be defined in a relational database which may apply to domains, types, attributes and databases. In this section we will examine the following:

- **Domain constraints**
- **Type constraints**
- **Key constraints.**

Domain constraints

We saw earlier that a domain is the set of allowable values for one or more attributes. Domain constraints are used to specify data values or a range of values when data is inserted into a column in a relation. For example, an email address attribute may be used in a number of relations, all with the same properties. The benefit is that a domain for email address is defined once and used in a number of relations rather than setting up each relation's constraints individually.

Not all DBMSs explicitly support domains definition creation. In Oracle's case, for example, you can implement each domain constraint as column constraints for every column in which the domain is used. So, for example in the Film relation example, we might include the column constraint that the 'year' attribute (the year the film was made) must lie between 1890 and the current year. We will see in Chapter 5, 'Introduction to SQL', how a constraint can be defined on a column using the 'Check' clause.

Type constraints

A type constraint specifies the legal values for a scalar data type (i.e. a data type that holds only one value at a time); in this sense, it is also a domain constraint. There are built-in types which relational database systems allow for attributes. Built-in types vary from one DBMS to the next, but common ones are integer, real, character, string and date. So a student name might be defined as a string type, a sum of money as a real number type and a date of birth as a date type. We will examine in Chapter 5 the allowable types when creating relations using the Oracle DBMS and also we will look at Oracle's user defined types in Chapter 8.

Key constraints

Consider the property mentioned above: 'each tuple is distinct – no duplicates are allowed'. This implies that in each tuple (row) there is an attribute (or group of attributes) that uniquely identifies each tuple in the relation. As we shall see these concepts are particularly important for the relational model.

- A primary key is a unique identifier for the relation – that is, an attribute (or combination of attributes) with the property that, at any given time, no two tuples contain the same values for that attribute (or combination of attributes)
- A foreign key is an attribute in a relation which is also the primary key in another relation.

In the above relation in figure 2.1 it is likely that we would choose the filmNo as our primary key as this attribute uniquely identifies each tuple. We now introduce the attribute director number (directorNo) in the Film relation and a second relation Director, which is used to hold director details. The primary keys of each relation are respectively filmNo and directorNo. The directorNo in the Film relation is an example of a foreign key – an attribute in relation Film which is also the primary key in another relation, Director.

Figure 2.2: Sample relations – FILM and DIRECTOR

filmNo	title	directorNo	country	year	genre		directorNo	dName
005	Reservoir Dogs	101	US	1992	Crime		101	Tarantino
006	Pulp Fiction	101	US	1994	Crime		322	Boyle
008	Trainspotting	322	UK	1996			166	Wai-Keung
109	Infernal Affairs	166	China	2002	Crime		753	Ellis
111	Snakes on a Plane	753	US	2006	Disaster			

Film — Director

The way the two relations are linked together using primary and foreign keys is an important characteristic of relational databases. We will examine more about relationships in the next chapter, 'Database design using entity-relationship modelling'.

A key (whether primary or foreign) with more than one attribute is known as a **composite key**. Such keys will be discussed in the next chapter. For the moment it is important to know that the primary and foreign keys are included when specifying the characteristics of a relation. This will help ensure the validity or integrity of the data. We will examine here two types of integrity: referential and entity.

Referential integrity

As we saw in figure 2.2, it is common for relations to be linked to one another using primary and foreign keys. A problem could arise if, in our example above, a Director tuple were deleted and the corresponding tuples in the Film relation were left unchanged. Let us assume that the first Director tuple '101 Tarantino' is deleted and the first 2 tuples (with directorNo 101) of the Film relation are left unchanged. We therefore have foreign keys in the Film relation which do not exist in the Director relation. This situation is a violation of what is known as referential integrity.

Figure 2.3: Relations illustrating a violation of referential integrity

Film

filmNo	Title	directorNo	Country	year	genre
005	Reservoir Dogs	101	US	1992	Crime
006	Pulp Fiction	101	US	1994	Crime
008	Trainspotting	322	UK	1996	
109	Infernal Affairs	166	China	2002	Crime
111	Snakes on a Plane	753	US	2006	Disaster

Director

directorNo	director Name
~~101~~	~~Tarantino~~
322	Boyle
166	Wai-Keung
753	Ellis

The referential integrity rule states that the database must not contain any unmatched foreign key values.

In other words, a foreign key (such as directorNo) in a relation (such as Film) which matches the primary key in another relation (Director), must either:

• be equal to the value of a primary key in one tuple of the second relation (Director) or
• be wholly null (i.e. empty).

Looking at the Film and Director relations above, it ought to be impossible to delete a director 101 in the Director relation and at the same time leave 101 undisturbed in the Film relation. If that Director tuple is deleted, it is important that all references to the tuple are deleted as well: otherwise an attempt to access the deleted tuple will result in an error. The referential integrity rule, besides applying to deletion also applies to update and insertion. For example, it ought to be impossible to update a Director tuple (e.g. 166 amended to 999) and at the same time leave the Film relation unchanged. If it is possible, then referential integrity is violated. Modern DBMSs have mechanisms to ensure referential integrity as we shall see in Chapter 5.

Entity integrity

When a table is created for a relational database, we will normally define all primary and foreign keys. When a new tuple or row is added to a relation, a check will be made by the DBMS to ensure that the new tuple has a unique primary key. So if a new film is added to the Film relation above, a check is made to ensure that a tuple with that film number does not already exist in the table. The primary key (the film number in this case) is used to identify a tuple and can also be used to connect that tuple to other tuples in other relations, using the primary key/foreign key link as described earlier. It is therefore important that the primary key has a value associated with it – i.e. it must not be allowed to have a null value.

The entity integrity rule states that the primary key (or attributes which forms part of it) of a relation must always have a known value and cannot be null.

2.4 Relational query languages

We saw in Chapter 1 that two functions of the database management system (DBMS) were to provide a language to create and change database structures (data definition language or DDL) and to insert, amend, change and query data in the database (data manipulation language or DML). Relational database systems provide special-purpose languages to achieve these functions, the most well known being SQL (Structured Query Language).

Relational calculus & relational algebra

Many high-level relational data manipulation languages (such as SQL) are based on either relational algebra or relational calculus. They are theoretical languages and were defined by E F Codd. Both these formal languages, relational calculus and relational algebra, have influenced commercial relational query languages in use today, for example SQL and visual query languages such as Query-By-Example (QBE). They illustrate the basic operations required by any such data manipulation language.

A query written in relational calculus describes the desired result without specifying how the result is achieved – languages based on relational calculus are called nonprocedural or **declarative.**. A query written in relational algebra, on the other hand, consists of a collection of step-by-step 'procedures' for computing the desired result and is said to be **procedural**. Relational algebra is examined more fully later in this section.

SQL

Structured Query Language (SQL), which is based on both relational algebra and relational calculus, was developed in the 1970s by IBM to support its relational products and has become the most important query language for relational databases. SQL was adopted by the American National Standards Institute (ANSI) and the International Standards Organisation (ISO) in 1986 and 1987 respectively. Since then it has continued to evolve. SQL is examined in detail in Chapters 5 and 6.

Relational algebra (RA)

Relational algebra refers to a collection of operations that act on relations and produce a single relation as a result. The reasons for studying RA include:

- Relational algebra is used as the basis for other, higher-level, data manipulation languages including SQL. We will use relational algebra to explain, in Chapters 5 and 6, how SQL queries are evaluated

- The algebra serves as a convenient basis for optimisation. An optimiser is an important component of a DBMS. When implementing a query, there is usually more than one way of performing the data access. It is up to the optimiser to decide which strategy to adopt. We will see in Chapter 7 that DBMSs often use the relational algebra as a high-level intermediate language into which SQL code is translated during the query optimisation process

- The algebra is also used as a measure to compare high-level relational languages such as SQL, and to test if the language is **relationally complete** – for example, to check if the query language is as powerful as the algebra.

There are a number of syntaxes available to illustrate the relational algebra operations. Here we use a fairly user-friendly syntax.

Relational algebra operators

Each RA operator takes one or more relations as its input and produces a new relation as output. Codd originally defined eight operators, in two classes:

The special relational operators:	RESTRICT	PROJECT
	JOIN	DIVIDE

Set operators:	UNION	INTERSECTION
	DIFFERENCE	Cartesian PRODUCT

The operators Restrict and Project act on single relations; Join, Divide, Union, Intersection, Difference, and Cartesian Product act on two relations at a time. The result of the each of the operations on the relation or relations is to produce one single relation. The relational algebra operators are described below.

RESTRICT (originally called SELECT)

This extracts tuples which satisfy a given condition from a single relation. For example, in the Film relation in figure 2.4, the condition would be 'all films directed by Tarantino'. The result is a new relation of the shaded area (2 tuples in this case).

Figure 2.4: Example of Restrict

Film

filmNo	title	director	country	year	genre
005	Reservoir Dogs	Tarantino	US	1992	Crime
006	Pulp Fiction	Tarantino	US	1994	Crime
008	Trainspotting	Boyle	UK	1996	
109	Infernal Affairs	Wai-Keung	China	2002	Crime
111	Snakes on a Plane	Ellis	US	2006	Disaster

Relational algebra operation:

Restrict from Film where director = 'Tarantino'

PROJECT

This extracts specified attributes from a specified relation. For example, in figure 2.5, we extract from the relation Film the attributes or columns 'title' and 'year'. The result is a new relation of the shaded area (2 columns in this case).

Figure 2.5: Example of Project

Film

filmNo	title	director	country	year	genre
005	Reservoir Dogs	Tarantino	US	1992	Crime
006	Pulp Fiction	Tarantino	US	1994	Crime
008	Trainspotting	Boyle	UK	1996	
109	Infernal Affairs	Wai-Keung	China	2002	Crime
111	Snakes on a Plane	Ellis	US	2006	Disaster

Relational algebra operation:

Project over Film [title, year]

JOIN

The Join operator is used when we require data from more than one table. The operation involves the linking of relations together by combining rows which are related in some way. Various forms exist, such as natural join, equi-join, theta-join and outer join. The natural join is a special case where the link is through some shared characteristic (attribute) usually a foreign key. In the example below, the Film relation has been altered to include a director number and a Director relation has been included. When we join the two tables together, we use the attribute directorNo as the common value.

Figure 2.6: Example of Join

Film

filmNo	title	directorNo	country	year	genre
005	Reservoir Dogs	101	US	1992	Crime
006	Pulp Fiction	101	US	1994	Crime
008	Trainspotting	322	UK	1996	
109	Infernal Affairs	166	China	2002	Crime
111	Snakes on a Plane	753	US	2006	Disaster

Director

directorNo	dName
101	Tarantino
322	Boyle
166	Wai-Keung
753	Ellis

The resulting relation is:

filmNo	title	directorNo	country	year	genre	dName
005	Reservoir Dogs	101	US	1992	Crime	Tarantino
006	Pulp Fiction	101	US	1994	Crime	Tarantino
008	Trainspotting	322	UK	1996		Boyle
109	Infernal Affairs	166	China	2002	Crime	Wai-Keung
111	Snakes on a Plane	753	US	2006	Disaster	Ellis

Relational algebra operation:

Film **Join** Director where Film directorNo = Director directorNo

The result of a Join operation is a new wider relation: each row is formed by joining two tuples (rows) in the original relations such that they have the same values in the common domain. In figure 2.6, the Film and Director relations are joined to produce a new relation. Note that when a natural join is performed the resulting relation only includes one copy of the 'join attributes' (in the example one copy of 'directorNo').

Other types of joins will be examined in Chapter 5.

Note that in the above example it is likely that filmNo would be chosen as the primary key of the Film relation; also directorNo for the Director relation. Note also that directorNo is a foreign key in the Film relation. **When joining relations together, they are usually (but not always) joined using a primary and foreign key 'link'.**

UNION

This builds a relation consisting of all tuples appearing in either or both of two specified relations. The two relations must be **union-compatible**, which means that they must have the same number of attributes and these attributes must come from the same domain, i.e. the corresponding attributes must be from the same pool of values and of the same type (e.g. numerical, character).

To demonstrate the Union operation the following two film relations will be used: one for English language films; the other for Canadian films.

Figure 2.7: Example relations which are union-compatible

EnglishLanguageFilm

filmNo	title	director	year
005	Reservoir Dogs	Tarantino	1992
006	Pulp Fiction	Tarantino	1994
008	Trainspotting	Boyle	1996
110	Videodrome	Cronenberg	1983
111	Snakes on a Plane	Ellis	2006
115	eXistenZ	Cronenberg	1999

CanadianFilm

filmNo	title	director	year
110	Videodrome	Cronenberg	1983
112	Mon Oncle Antoine	Jutra	1971
115	eXistenZ	Cronenberg	1999

The union of the two relations produces a relation of **either** English language films **or** Canadian films **or both**.

> **Relational algebra operation:**
>
> **Union** EnglishLanguageFilm **with** CanadianFilm

The resulting relation is shown in the next figure.

Figure 2.8: Example of a union

filmNo	title	director	year
005	Reservoir Dogs	Tarantino	1992
006	Pulp Fiction	Tarantino	1994
008	Trainspotting	Boyle	1996
110	Videodrome	Cronenberg	1983
111	Snakes on a Plane	Ellis	2006
112	Mon Oncle Antoine	Jutra	1971
115	eXistenZ	Cronenberg	1999

INTERSECTION

This builds a relation consisting of all tuples appearing in both of two specified relations. Again the two relations must be union-compatible. For example, if we have the two film relations as above, then the intersection of the two relations produces a relations of films which are English language **and (at the same time)** Canadian.

Relational algebra operation:

Intersection EnglishLanguageFilm **and** CanadianFilm

The resulting relation is shown in figure 2.9:

Figure 2.9: Example of Intersection

filmNo	title	director	year
110	Videodrome	Cronenberg	1983
115	eXistenZ	Cronenberg	1999

With the Intersection operation the order of the relations (or operands) can be reversed without affecting the result. In the example above the following operation would give the same result:

Intersection CanadianFilm and EnglishLanguageFilm

Note that the operators union, intersection and join all display this characteristic that their operands can be reversed and produce the same result – they are said to be **commutative**. Other operators involving two operands (difference and divide) are not commutative.

DIFFERENCE

This operation builds a relation consisting of all tuples appearing in the first but not the second of two specified relations. The two relations must be union-compatible. For example, if we have the two film relations as above, then the difference of the two relations is: 'all English language films, which are not Canadian'.

Relational algebra operation:

Difference EnglishLanguageFilm **and** CanadianFilm

The resulting relation is shown in figure 2.10:

Figure 2.10: Example of Difference

filmNo	title	director	year
005	Reservoir Dogs	Tarantino	1992
006	Pulp Fiction	Tarantino	1994
008	Trainspotting	Boyle	1996
111	Snakes on a Plane	Ellis	2006

The order of the relations can be reversed, giving a different result. In our example it is possible to use the difference operator to output the difference of the two relations where Canadian film is the first and English language film is the second to give 'all Canadian films, which are not English language'.

Relational algebra operation:

Difference CanadianFilm **and** EnglishLanguageFilm

The resulting relation is shown in figure 2.11.

Figure 2.11: Another example of Difference

filmNo	title	director	year
112	Mon Oncle Antoine	Jutra	1971

PRODUCT

This builds a relation from two relations, consisting of all possible pairs of tuples from the two relations. So given relations R and S, then R times (product) S gives us:

Figure 2.12: Product

R		S		R * S	
a		1		a	1
b	*	2	=	a	2
		3		a	3
				b	1
				b	2
				b	3

For example, given the Film and Director relation below:

Figure 2.13: Example of Product

Film

filmNo	title	directorNo	year
005	Reservoir Dogs	001	1992
008	Trainspotting	008	1996

Director

directorNo	dName
001	Tarantino
004	Spielberg
008	Boyle

.../cont

filmNo	title	directorNo	year	directorNo	dName
005	Reservoir Dogs	001	1992	001	Tarantino
005	Reservoir Dogs	001	1992	004	Spielberg
005	Reservoir Dogs	001	1992	008	Boyle
008	Trainspotting	008	1996	001	Tarantino
008	Trainspotting	008	1996	004	Spielberg
008	Trainspotting	008	1996	008	Boyle

Relational algebra operation:

Film **product** Director

Note that the two relations, Film and Director, have an attribute in common (directorNo) and this attribute appears twice in the resulting relation. The result of the Cartesian product gives a new relation showing every combination, where each tuple from one relation is associated with each tuple of the other relation – i.e. each film is associated with all the directors: this produces a relation with 6 tuples as there are 2 films and 3 directors and thus 2*3 combinations.

DIVIDE

This operator takes two relations, one **binary** (with 2 columns) and one **unary** (with a single column). It builds a relation consisting of all values of one attribute of the binary relation that match (in the other attribute) all values in the unary relation.

Figure 2.14: Examples of Divide

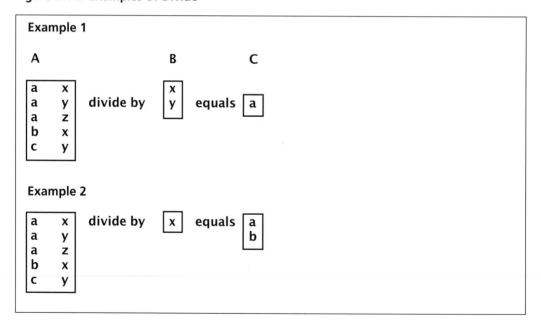

Further relational algebra examples

Consider the following relations for a group of cinemas:

Figure 2.15: Example relations for a group of cinemas

Film

filmNo	title	directorNo	year
109	Infernal Affairs	166	2002
111	Snakes on a Plane	753	2006
115	Last King of Scotland	277	2006
.	.	.	.
.	.	.	.

Director

directorNo	dName
166	Wai-Keung
277	MacDonald
753	Ellis
.	.
.	.

Cinema

cinemaNo	cinemaName	address
1001	Roxy Hendon	High Road
1002	Roxy T P	Upper Lane
1003	Roxy Enfield	Market Way
.	.	.

Screeening

cinemaNo	filmNo	showDate	takings (£k)
1001	109	01-02-07	41
1001	111	01-02-07	53
1001	115	01-02-07	38
1002	111	09-03-07	75
1002	115	09-03-07	19
.	.	.	.

Relational algebra statements to answer example queries

- List each film title and the year the film was made:

   F1= Project over Film [title, year]

As noted above the result of the relational algebra operations on the relation or relations is to produce one single relation. In our example the result is placed in the relation F1.

- List film titles and years for films made after 2004:

   F1= Restrict from Film where year>'2004'
   F2= Project over F1 [title, year]

In this case F1 is used as a temporary relation. The result (a single relation) is placed in F2. The resulting relation would be identical if the statements were reversed.

- List film titles and director names:

   F1= Film Join Director where Film directorNo = Director directorNo
   F2= Project over F1 [title, dName]

- List film titles and cinema names and the amount of takings for each screening of the films in the cinemas:

   F1= Film Join Screening where Film filmNo = Screening filmNo
   F2= Cinema Join F1 where F1 cinemaNo = Cinema cinemaNo
   F3= Project over F2 [title, cinemaName, takings]

To illustrate the set operators, union, intersection and difference we need to use two relations that are union compatible. We will use the two relations below for cinemas based in London and for cinemas with total takings of more than £100k:

CinemasBasedInLondon

cinemaNo	cinemaName	address	town	totalCapacity	totalTakings (£k)
1001	Roxy Hendon	High Road	London	2000	90
1002	Roxy T P	Upper Lane	London	4000	153
1003	Roxy Enfield	Market Way	London	1500	138
.	.	.	.		.

CinemaHighTakings

cinemaNo	cinemaName	address	town	totalCapacity	totalTakings (£k)
1002	Roxy T P	Upper Lane	London	4000	153
1003	Roxy Enfield	Market Way	London	2000	138
1006	Roxy Reading	New Street	Reading	1650	175
1017	Roxy Oxford	Old Lane	Oxford	2600	219
.	.	.	.		.

- List the cinema number and name of all cinemas which are either based in London or whose takings are greater than £100k or both:

  C1=Union CinemasBasedInLondon with CinemaHighTakings
  C2= Project over C1 [cinemaNo, cinemaName]

- List details of all cinemas based in London and whose takings are over £100k for cinemas with a capacity of less than 2000:

  C1= Intersection CinemasBasedInLondon and CinemaHighTakings
  C2= Restrict from C1 where totalCapacity<2000

- List details of all cinemas whose takings are greater than £100k but are not based in London:

  C1= Difference CinemaHighTakings and CinemasBasedInLondon

We will look at further examples of relational algebra operations (including those involving divide operations) in Chapter 5 and 6, when we study SQL.

2.5 Strengths and weaknesses of relational DBMSs

Relational database systems are by far the most important type of database around today. There has been a widespread acceptance of this model for the traditional business applications, including payroll, order processing and airline reservations systems. There has also been a widespread acceptance for applications which access databases over the Internet. Well-designed relational databases can provide appropriate data storage and retrieval facilities over a long timescale for a variety of applications.

Because of the dominance of relational databases, this book is largely concerned with the relational model, although the object-oriented and object-relational models are discussed in Chapter 8. In this section we look at a number of advantages of relational database systems over other methods (including file-based systems and other types of DBMSs) and also several weaknesses that are cited by the proponents of object-oriented database systems.

Strengths

- Relational databases support a **simple data structure**, namely tables or relations
- Relational databases **limit redundancy** or replication of data. As all the data pertaining to a particular object is stored together, and then linked to related objects, there is no need to store data about the original object in more than one place. In practice, not all redundancy is eliminated – as we shall see (in Chapter 4), the process of normalisation will lead to some controlled redundancy
- Data **inconsistencies** are **avoided**. By storing the data relating to an object in one place, it only needs to be kept up to date in that one place. This saves time at the data entry stage and reduces the likelihood of inconsistencies arising
- To a large extent, relational databases provide **physical data independence**. Database users do not have to be aware of the underlying structure of the objects in the database. The specification of the structure (the relations, attributes and relationships), the constraints, the access methods, etc. are stored separately and are independent of the application programs that use the data. This makes programming and program maintenance easier
- Relational databases offer **logical database independence**, in that data can be viewed in different ways by different users and these user views are shielded from changes to the conceptual schema (the global view of the data). With relational databases this is achieved with the definition of an appropriate SQL view
- **Expandability** is relatively easy to achieve – by adding new views of the data as they are required
- Relational databases support **ad hoc queries** (one-off or tailor-made) using SQL or another appropriate query language.

Weaknesses

- Relational databases are purported to be a **poor representation of 'real world'** entities and their relationships. When relational databases are designed, entities are fragmented into smaller relations through the process of normalisation. This **fragmentation** leads to the creation of relations which do not correspond to entities in the real world. Such a design is inefficient, as many joins may be required in order to access data about an entity
- The model is said to suffer from **semantic overloading** in that one construct (the relation) is used to represent two different things (entities and relationships): there is no means for differentiating between entities and relationships. The normalised component, the relation, is not sufficient to represent both the data and the relationships. With relational databases, as an entity is broken up into several relations, then querying becomes cumbersome since project, select, and join operations have to be used frequently to reconstruct the entities
- Also it is **difficult to represent hierarchies** of data. For example, both students and lecturers may share some of the same data (name, address, etc). In a relational database we would have to define three relations: one for the 'super class' person as well as for student and lecturer, and to retrieve the information may well require a join

- In a relational database, any of the data values in a relation, i.e. the intersection of a row and column, must be of an atomic data type (single valued). Therefore there is a **difficulty in representing complex data types**. As a simple example, consider an attribute 'address'. In a relational database, either we define an address attribute as one atomic value of type string or it could be defined as a number of attributes (one each for street, city, country and postcode). In the latter case, writing queries would be more complicated, as each field would have to be mentioned. A better solution is to allow structured data types – such as the type address with subparts street, city, country and postcode. With this solution an instance of type address can either be viewed as a whole or as individual subparts

- Relational database tables assume a **horizontal and vertical homogeneity** in data: horizontally, each tuple of a relation is made up of the same attributes; and vertically, the values in a column of a relation come from the same domain. This can be a disadvantage in that it is not possible to store closely related objects in the same category if they differ slightly in the attributes they possess. For example, there may be adult and child aeroplane tickets, with children having the additional attribute 'guardian'. We will see in Chapter 8 that relational database systems are not naturally suited to support certain complex applications such as 'advanced database applications' including computer-aided design (CAD). A clear illustration of the drawbacks of a homogeneous data structure is the so-called 'parts explosion'. Here, some object (such as a motor car) is composed of parts and subparts; these latter items in turn are composed of other parts and subparts, and so on. Data types exhibiting this arrangement can only be stored in relational databases with great difficulty

- Relational database implementations support a small, **fixed collection of data types** and do not permit users to define new types. In many applications the attributes' domains require far more complex data types. Many relational DBMSs allow the storage of binary large objects (BLOBs). A BLOB is a data value that contains binary information representing images, digitised videos or audios, or any large and unstructured object. In a relational database, it is held as an attribute which references to a file. Storing the data in external files is not a good way of manipulating this data: the DBMS has no knowledge of the structure of this data and cannot perform queries or operations on it. In addition, BLOBs cannot contain other BLOBs. As an example, a picture can be stored as a BLOB by a relational database management system (RDBMS). The complete picture can be displayed but not part of it, and the internal structure is not known to the RDBMS

- There is also a difficulty in implementing **recursive queries**. As an example we might have a relational database application for a library which included the relation BookTitle which holds information on all the book titles stored in the library and includes attributes isbn (International Standard Book Number), title and value. An example of a recursive query on this relation would be: 'find books which have the same book title as a book entitled Gardening for Beginners'. This query involves searching the same relation twice. We shall see in Chapter 6 that recursive queries can be quite difficult to specify and implement

- SQL is **not computationally complete**: it supports only a limited number of operations and does not allow new operations to be defined. It does not, for example, support branching, looping and subroutines. Because of this, the SQL standard provides embedded SQL to help develop more complex database applications. Embedded SQL statements are written within application programming languages such as Java or C++ . We will see in Chapter 6 how Oracle has developed the language PL/SQL which has SQL embedded within it

- The use of embedded SQL leads to the so-called **impedance mismatch** problem. The main difference between a query language such as SQL from traditional, high-level languages of procedural or functional programming is that the latter can handle a single data record at a time, whereas SQL handles a table at a time.

This mismatch between the two forms of processing results in increased programming effort and use of resources. Furthermore, SQL and high-level programming languages represent data in different ways. Especially when attributes of date and time are concerned, SQL has the corresponding date types that automatically 'translate' the value to a meaningful format. High-level programming languages need to convert integer values to the date and time formats. Such type conversion again leads to increases in programming effort and use of resources

- There is **no support for domain-specific organisational constraints** in the relational model. Organisational constraints are additional rules specified by the owners of a database that the database must satisfy. For example we might want to have a limit on the number of borrowers who could become members of a library and disallow new additions to a borrower table when this limit is reached. This type of business rule cannot be implemented in SQL and thus they have to be programmed into the applications using the database – leading to duplication of effort and inconsistent data.

2.6 Summary

This chapter has described the structure of the relational model and explained the basic concepts, including relation, attribute, null value, primary key and foreign key. Readers were introduced to data integrity issues including referential integrity and entity integrity. Data manipulation and the eight relational algebra operators as a means of querying a relational database were described. Finally the strengths and weaknesses of the relational approach were discussed.

2.7 Review questions

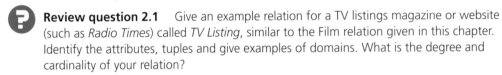

Review question 2.1   Give an example relation for a TV listings magazine or website (such as *Radio Times*) called *TV Listing*, similar to the Film relation given in this chapter. Identify the attributes, tuples and give examples of domains. What is the degree and cardinality of your relation?

Review question 2.2   Explain, giving an example, how relations are linked together in the relational model.

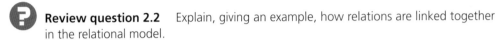

Review question 2.3   Examine the following two relations in a university library and state the primary keys.

BookTitle

isbn	title	publisherNo	value
0-88-123456	Great Expectations	1001	15.00
0-33-543216	Little Dorrit	1001	9.99
0-10-876543	Martin Chuzzlewit	4302	12.50
0-07-123678	Dombey and Son	2772	7.99
0-66-974145	Oliver Twist	1001	15.00

BookCopy

isbn	bookCopyId	dateAcquired
0-88-123456	1	12-12-06
0-88-123456	2	12-12-06
0-88-123456	3	05-05-07
0-33-543216	1	12-01-06
0-10-876543	1	01-07-06
0-07-123678	1	06-06-06
0-07-123678	2	06-06-06

Review question 2.4   Examine the 'Properties of relations' in section 2.2. Suggest an example relation Loan for a university library database and show how your relation adheres to these properties. Identify a primary key for your relation.

Review question 2.5 Examine the two relations Film and Director. Discuss any violations to referential and entity integrity constraints

Film

filmNo	title	directorNo	country	year	genre
005	Reservoir Dogs	101	US	1992	Crime
006	Pulp Fiction		US	1994	Crime
	Trainspotting	322	UK	1996	
109	Infernal Affairs	166	China	2002	Crime
111	Snakes on a Plane	753	US	2006	Disaster

Director

directorNo	dName
322	Boyle
166	Wai-Keung
753	Ellis
874	Mamet

 Review question 2.6 A library keeps information on books held, borrowers who use the library and the loans made for these books by the borrowers.

Given the four relations 'BookTitle', 'BooksCopy', 'Borrower' and 'Loan', write the relational algebra statements required to answer the queries below. What is the result of your query?

BookTitle

isbn	title	publisherNo	value
0-88-123456	Great Expectations	1001	15.00
0-33-543216	Little Dorrit	1001	9.99
0-10-876543	Martin Chuzzlewit	4302	12.50
0-07-123678	Dombey and Son	2772	7.99
0-66-974145	Oliver Twist	1001	15.00

BookCopy

isbn	copyId	date Acquired
0-88-123456	1	12-12-06
0-88-123456	2	12-12-06
0-88-123456	3	05-05-07
0-33-543216	1	12-01-06
0-10-876543	1	01-07-06
0-07-123678	1	06-06-06
0-07-123678	2	06-06-06

Borrower

borrowerNo	name
1001	Jo
1003	Jay
1005	Jamil
1006	Jenny

Loan

isbn	copyId	borrowerNo	dateOut	dateBack
0-88-123456	1	1001	03-06-07	03-07-07
0-88-123456	3	1003	11-07-07	11-08-07
0-10-876543	1	1001	03-06-07	03-07-07
0-07-123678	2	1001	03-06-07	03-07-07
0-88-123456	1	1005	11-07-07	
0-07-123678	2	1005	11-07-07	
0-88-123456	3	1006	12-07-07	

a) List each book title and value.

b) List all book title details for books valued over £10.

c) List isbns, book titles, copy ids and dates acquired for books in the library

d) List book titles, copy ids, dates acquired, borrower name and the dates the books were borrowed and returned (dateOut, dateBack) for each loan made by borrower 1001

Review question 2.7 Given the two tables 'Books by Dickens' and 'Books published after 1850', write the relational algebra statement required to answer the queries below. What is the result of your query?

BooksByDickens

isbn	title	author	publisherNo	yearOfPublication	value
0-88-123456	Great Expectations	Charles Dickens	1001	1861	15.00
0-33-543216	Little Dorrit	Charles Dickens	1001	1857	9.99
0-07-123678	Dombey and Son	Charles Dickens	2772	1848	7.99
0-10-876543	Martin Chuzzlewit	Charles Dickens	4302	1844	12.50
0-66-974145	Oliver Twist	Charles Dickens	1001	1839	15.00

BooksPublishedAfter1850

isbn	title	author	publisherNo	yearOfPublication	value
0-22-876543	The Europeans	Henry James	1006	1877	11.00
0-32-765435	The Moonstone	Wilkie Collins	1002	1868	12.50
0-33-768646	Armadale	Wilkie Collins	1006	1866	12.50
0-88-123456	Great Expectations	Charles Dickens	1001	1861	15.00
0-33-543216	Little Dorrit	Charles Dickens	1001	1857	9.99

a) List title, author and year of all books which are either written by Dickens or published after 1850 or both

b) List details of all books written by Dickens and (at the same time) published after 1850 for books valued at greater than £12

c) List the isbn, title and year of publication of all books published after 1850 but not written by Dickens.

CHAPTER 3

Database design using entity-relationship modelling

OVERVIEW

This chapter provides a starting point in learning how to develop a database application. The objective is to introduce students to the process of developing a **conceptual model** of the real world which is of interest and is relevant to an application. A number of different methods have been developed to arrive at the conceptual model. We focus on a well-known, graphical technique of representing the data in an organisation, namely **entity-relationship modelling** which was mentioned in Chapter 1.

Entity-relationship modelling has been around for some time and it is used extensively in the design of databases although no widely accepted standards prevail. It involves the identification of the **entities**, the **attributes** and **relationships** between the entities and any **constraints** on these. This top-down method is known as entity-relationship modelling and was developed by Chen in 1976.

Entity-relationship modelling can easily be applied to a relational database where data is viewed as a set of relations or tables (but it is not limited to this model). We examine how to map the entities into tables suitable for relational database implementation. Other models discussed in this book map more easily to object-oriented and object-relational databases which we discuss later in this book in Chapter 8. In that chapter we will show how entity-relationship modelling can be adapted for object-oriented database design.

Learning outcomes	On completion of this chapter, you should be able to:

- Identify the elements in a specific application area that need to be included in the design of a database solution. This includes the entities, the relationships between them, and the data items (attributes) contained in those entities

- Construct an entity-relationship diagram using UML notation

- Understand how an initial entity-relationship model is checked and validated, and how any problems are resolved

- Explain and apply the mapping of the entities into tables suitable for relational database implementation.

3.1 The data modelling process

Data modelling as part of the development process

We saw in Chapter 1 that the main tasks facing the database designer, at the analysis and design stage of the database system life cycle, are as follows:

- Requirements analysis
- Database design which includes:
  - conceptual data modelling
  - logical data modelling
  - physical data modelling
- Process modelling
- User interface design (menu, form, report and web page design)
- Prototyping
- Implementation and testing
- Monitoring, tuning and maintenance.

The design of a database system consists of two parallel activities, data modelling and process modelling. Data modelling is concerned with the design of the data content and structure of the database. On the other hand, process modelling is concerned with the design of the data processing and software applications. The two activities of data and process modelling are closely related.

The database design activities are further described thus:

- **Conceptual data modelling:** a concise description of the data requirements of an application. It involves identifying the entities, attributes, relationships and constraints in an application. It is a high-level model which is not concerned with implementation considerations (such as whether or not a relational DBMS is to be used) or physical considerations (such as concerns about physical storage requirements)
- **Logical data modelling:** this stage involves mapping the conceptual model to one suitable for implementation using a particular type of DBMS. This model therefore takes into account the architecture model (whether the target database is relational, object-oriented, etc). It is not concerned with the actual DBMS software to be used (e.g. Microsft Access or Oracle), nor is it concerned with the physical design of the database
- **Physical data modelling:** the physical model is derived from the logical model: the target data model is refined to a more detailed level and takes into account both the facilities and constraints of the target DBMS (such as Oracle, MySQL or Microsoft SQL Server). The degree of changes made from the logical model to the physical model will depend largely on the type of system that is being built. The physical design may also differ from the logical model to improve performance or simplify query complexity. A complete physical data model will include details of file organisations and index construction, physical storage objects such as tablespaces (used by some DBMSs as physical portions of the database for allocating tables, indexes and other database objects), constraint definitions, user views and security mechanisms.

This rest of this chapter is concerned with conceptual and logical modelling, which incorporates a set of techniques which can be used at a number of different points within the development process.

3.2 The conceptual model

Conceptual data modelling

Conceptual data modelling is concerned with the design of the data content and structure of the database. It gives us a formal model of an organisation which is achieved through the consolidation of the user requirements specification. This model is derived from a perceived reality – it is an **abstraction** of a complex view which will try to meet the requirements which have earlier been identified.

The information gathered from fact-finding, for example by interviewing users, is appraised and the basic data and relationships are established. The result of the data analysis is a representation of the users' view of the data. It is a model which is independent of the target DBMS software, and hides details of how the data will be stored and accessed within a computer.

Typically the design of a database application is complex, involving dozens of entities and hundreds of attributes. The resulting model documents the structure of and interrelationships between the data and constraints. It is presented as a combination of simple diagrams and written definitions. This graphical summary can be used to validate the correctness of the model, it can be presented to users in an easily understood form and is used throughout the design and implementation process by all designers, programmers and others involved.

The first step in developing a conceptual data model involves determining the major elements of data to be stored. These are referred to as **entities**. Returning to the university library system discussed in Chapter 1, a database for such an application will typically contain entities relating to students, books, loans and reservations. Each of the entities identified will contain a number of properties, or **attributes**. For example, the entity 'book' will contain attributes such as title, author and ISBN; the entity 'student' will possess attributes such as name, address and student number. When we have decided which entities are to be stored in a database, we need to consider how they are related to one another. Examples of such **relationships** for the university library system might be that a borrower can borrow a number of books, and that a librarian can make a number of book purchases.

The process of developing a conceptual model involves the identification of the following:

- The **entities** and **attributes** to be stored
- The **relationships** between the entities
- The **constraints** which try to ensure the accuracy and consistency of the data.

3.3 Entities, attributes and relationships

Entities

An entity is anything relevant to the organisation about which information is or could be kept. It can be defined as a group of logically associated data items identified by a unique key. The term 'entity type' is used to describe all the entities relevant to the organisation which fit a given definition.

Figure 3.1: Entity examples

Entity type	Entity occurrence
Student	Lewis Hamilton, Andy Murray
Building	Buckingham Palace, College Building
Car	X123 LSO, S234 TJH

Identifying entities

Identifying entities can be a difficult task. The analyst must gain a thorough understanding of the system environment. The entities could come to light, for example, from the dataflow diagrams produced during systems investigation. Another method is to find the things in the environment which need to be individually identified and referred to. Notional keys can be used to identify a range of other data – for example, a customer number identifies customer name and address, class, credit limit, etc, which leads us to identify the customer entity. Examples of notional keys for a university could include:

- Student number
- Course code
- Module code
- Employee number.

Attributes

An attribute is a property or characteristic of an entity about which there is a need to record data. An attribute type is the collection of all values of a defined property associated with a given entity type.

Figure 3.2: Attribute examples

Entity type	Attribute type	Attribute occurrence
Student	name date of birth sex	Jawad Bhatti 28.07.1980 male
Building	address annual rent	6 High Road £90 per sq. metre

Note: an attribute type in one context can be an entity type in another.   For example, to a car manufacturer *colour* is an attribute of the entity type *car*; to a paint manufacturer *colour* may well be an entity type.

Types of attributes

Several types of attributes can be identified: simple and composite; single-valued and multi-valued; stored and derived; and null-valued. The latter was examined in the previous chapter.

- **Composite attributes** can be divided into smaller subparts. For example a date attribute (as in date of birth) can be subdivided into day, month and year. An attribute is designated as composite if a user refers to both the composite and also the subparts; otherwise it is designated as simple. An example of a **simple attribute** is annual rent in the building entity above

- **Single-valued attributes** have a single value for a particular entity occurrence. In the student entity above the student's sex has a single value: either male or female

- **Multi-valued attributes** have a set of attributes for the same entity occurrence. An example of multi-valued attributes is 'courses' as an attribute of student – i.e. a student may be registered on more than one course. We will see that relational database systems do not support relations which include multi-valued attributes. Thus changes will have to be made to our model when mapping from an entity-relationship model to a one suitable for implementation using a relational DBMS. We will also see in Chapter 8 that object-oriented database systems support multi-valued attributes

- **Derived attributes** are attributes which can be calculated from one or more related attributes or entities. For example, the attribute age can be derived from the current date and the **stored attribute** 'date of birth'. The attribute 'Number of Database Students' can be derived by counting the number of students in a student entity where the course attribute value is 'Database'.

Relationships

A relationship is an association between entities that is operationally significant to the organisation.

Figure 3.3: Relationship examples

	Entity	**Relationship**	Entity
At Middlesex University	Student	**takes**	Courses
	School	**employs**	Lecturers
At Jaguar Motor Manufacturer	Assembly	**has**	Parts
	Employee	**works on**	Contracts

The entity-relationship diagram (ERD)

Entities and relationships can be used to produce a pictorial representation of what an organisation is interested in. This picture is called an entity-relationship diagram or ERD. Figure 3.4 shows an ERD for the following scenario:

A university library keeps information on books held, students who borrow these books and the loans which the students make. In addition, information is held about the authors and publishers of these books. A database designer has established the entities and attributes needed to carry out typical library functions and produced the entity-relationship diagram shown in figure 3.4.

Figure 3.4: Example of an entity-relationship diagram

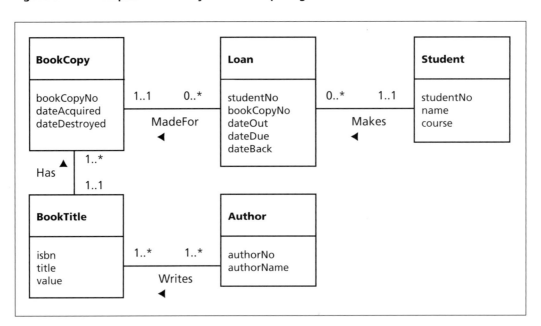

The BookCopy entity holds information on the physical books stored in the library, whereas the BookTitle entity holds information on a particular publication of a book (identified by the ISBN or international standards book number). For example, there are two copies of 'Pride and Prejudice', with book copy numbers of 101 and 102. A book may have a number of authors. Also, a book still out on loan will have a blank (null) date back field in the Loan entity. As copies of books become old, damaged and dirty the books are removed from the library and destroyed. Destroyed book copies have a date indicating when they were destroyed; otherwise the date is null.

- Note that, traditionally, entity names in the ERD are in the singular form
- Rectangles are used to denote entity types (named normally as a noun) and lines represent relationship types
- The lines are labelled with the names of the relationship (normally as a verb)
- The arrow symbol indicates the correct direction for the name of the relationship to make sense. For example, a student makes many loans.

Figure 3.4 is in the **unified modelling language** (UML) notation, which will be used for all entity-relationship diagrams throughout this text. A UML diagram shows the maximum and minimum times that an entity occurrence can exist in a relationship. For example, a student can borrow zero or more books. This is called an optional relationship: occurrences of an entity (student) can exist independently of the loan entity; otherwise the relationship is mandatory: every occurrence of an entity participates in the relationship. For example, in the book-title/authorship relationship, a title cannot exist without at least one author. The notation used will be explained more fully below.

An ERD is drawn because:

- By analysing the entities and relationships of an organisation, hundreds of entities may be identified. The diagram provides a concise summary of the results of the analysis

- The diagram provides a model for communication to designers, programmers and end users which is fairly non-technical and easy to understand
- The ERD will be used as the basis of database design. The structure of the model will be mapped onto the logical structure of the database.

UML class diagrams

There are a number of different notations in use to represent the entities and relationships between them. The UML includes a number of techniques which are useful for database applications. Examples include:

- **Use case diagrams** for defining the interactions between external users and the system under consideration to achieve business goals
- **State diagrams** for depicting the various states that an object may be in and the transitions between these states.

In this chapter we use a modified version of the UML **class diagram** (Booch et al 1999) to assist in representing our model. We will also use the traditional entity-relationship modelling terminology (e.g. entity, attribute and relationship) along with the UML notation. UML notation is particularly relevant for object-oriented design and applications as we shall see in Chapter 8.

The cardinality of a relationship

The cardinality of a relationship concerns the number of instances involved in the relationship (whereas the cardinality of a relation is the number of tuples in that relation – as defined in Chapter 2). There are several relationship types:

- **One-to-one relationship**
- **One-to-many relationship**
- **Many-to-many relationship**
- **Recursive relationship.**

One-to-one relationship

Here, an occurrence of the first entity type is related to exactly one occurrence of the second entity type, and each occurrence of the second type to exactly one of the first.

Figure 3.5: One-to-one relationship example

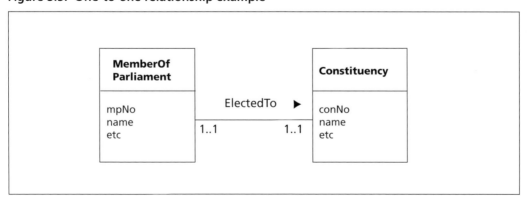

It helps the understanding of ERDs, when stating the relationships between the two entities, to 'read' the diagrams in the following way:

Examine the relationships firstly from left to right and then from right to left. To describe the relationship in figure 3.5, use two sentences, each sentence starting with the word 'one':

- **One Member of Parliament is elected to one constituency; one constituency has one Member of Parliament elected to it.**

(Note that it does not matter if, when 'reading the relationship', we start from left to right or right to left. Alternatively it may be necessary to 'read' the relationship from top to bottom and then from bottom to top if the two entitles have been drawn above and below one another.)

One-to-many relationship

Here an occurrence of the first entity type may be related to several occurrences of the second, but each occurrence of the second is related to a maximum of one occurrence of the first.

Figure 3.6: One-to-many relationship example

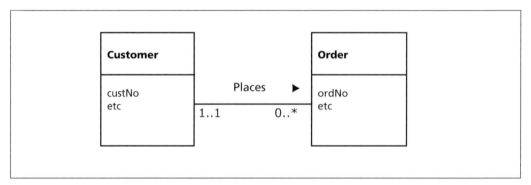

So, in figure 3.6, stated as the two sentences starting with the word 'one':

- **One customer places zero or more orders; one order is placed by one customer.**

Many-to-many relationship

Here an occurrence of the first entity type may be related to several occurrences of the second and vice versa.

Figure 3.7: Many-to-many relationship example

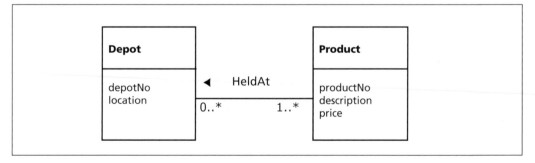

Again, stated as the two sentences starting with the word 'one':

- **One product is held at zero or more depots; one depot holds one or more products.**

Recursive relationship

It is possible for an entity to have a relationship with itself, i.e. entity occurrences relate to other occurrences of the same entity.

Figure 3.8: Recursive relationship example

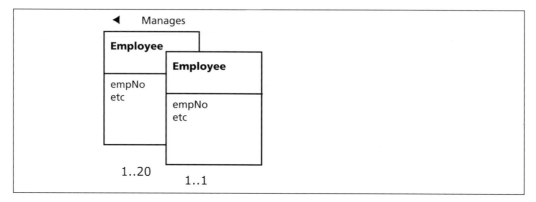

In this example:

- **One employee (a manager) manages one to twenty employees; one employee is managed by one employee (manager).**

The degree of a relationship

The number of participating entities in a relationship is called the degree of a relationship. A relationship of one degree is called a **unary** relationship – this is the same as the recursive relationship described above, an example of which is 'Manages'.

A relationship of degree 2 is called **binary** and this is the most common. An example of this type is the relationship 'Places', as seen previously, and repeated below:

Figure 3.9: Binary relationship example

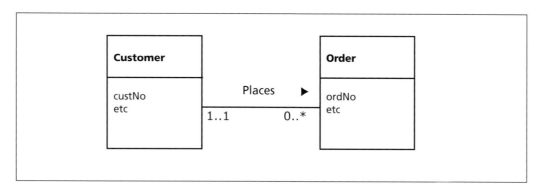

A relationship of degree 3 is called **ternary**. An example of this type of relationship is:

Figure 3.10: Ternary relationship example

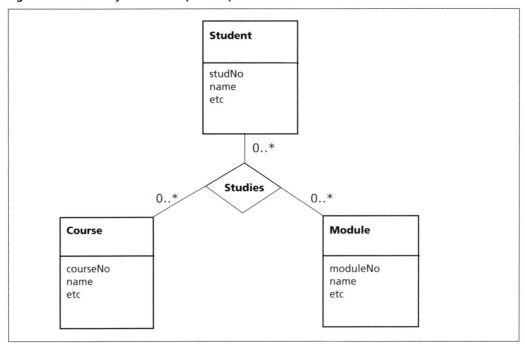

Here a student can study many courses with many (shared) modules. Note the **diamond shape** for relationships which involve more than two entities. There is no limit to the number of entities participating in a relationship although relationships with degree greater than 4 (**quaternary**) are not common. In this text all further examples will involve binary and occasionally unary relationships.

Sets of entities involving more than one relationship

There may be more than one relationship between two entities. An example of this is:

Figure 3.11: Double relationship example

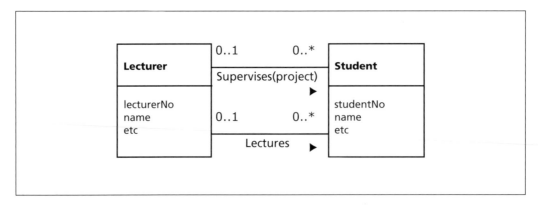

In this example one lecturer supervises zero or more students in their final year project. Also one lecturer gives lectures to zero or more students.

Occurrence diagrams

These diagrams are used to show the relationship occurrences between sample entity occurrences and are often drawn to assist in the understanding of the model.

Figure 3.12: Example occurrence diagram for a one-to-one relationship

Member of Parliament	ElectedTo	Constituency
Jo		Brent
Jean		Haringey
Amir		Bethnal Green

Figure 3.13: Example occurrence diagram for a one-to-many relationship

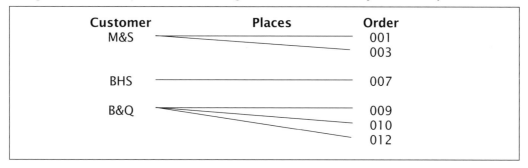

Figure 3.14: Example occurrence diagram for a many-to-many relationship

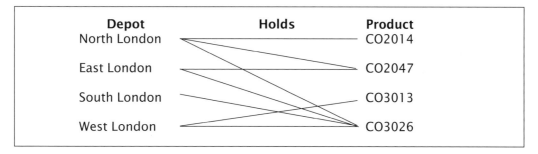

Membership class: mandatory and optional relationships

There are two possible ways that an entity type can exist in a relationship. In some cases every occurrence of an entity participates in the relationship; in other cases it may be ruled that occurrences of an entity can exist independently. We have already discussed that the terms mandatory and optional are used to distinguish between these two situations. The membership class of a relationship defines whether it is mandatory or optional for an entity to participate in a relationship.

With the UML notation, which we have used to draw our entity-relationship diagrams, optional and mandatory relationships are easily represented in our diagram using the minimum and maximum values.

For example, assume we have the rules:

- 'A trade union has one or many employees; one employee belongs to zero or one trade union'

Figure 3.15: Optional/mandatory example

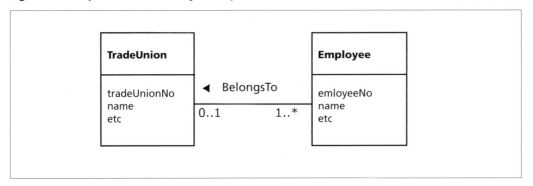

So for an optional relationship, where it is ruled that occurrences of an entity can exist independently (an employee occurrence can exist without belonging to a trade union), the minimum value of zero is used. Another example involving optionality is given next.

Figure 3.16: Further example of an optional relationship

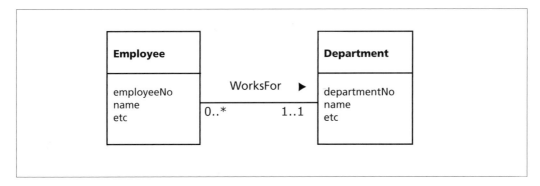

In this example one employee works for exactly one department; one department has zero or more employees, i.e. a department can exist in the database independent of any employees. This might be the situation when a department has just been set up and employees have not as yet been assigned to it. In this situation every occurrence of employee participates in the relationship 'WorksFor' and is thus a mandatory relationship. An occurrence of department can exist independently.

Key attributes

We defined various types of keys in Chapter 2 when considering relational databases. In our entity-relational model it is usual to specify one or more of the attributes of an entity as a 'key' of the entity.

Three types of keys are considered here:

- **A candidate key** is an attribute (or set of attributes) which is a unique and irreducible identifier for the entity. The *uniqueness* property means that, at any given time, no two entity occurrences contain the same values for that attribute (or combination of attributes). *Irreducibility* means that an attribute or set of attributes cannot be removed from the key, because it will no longer uniquely identify all tuples. So for example in a customer entity, the key made up of the attributes customerNo and address may be unique in each of the tuples of the entity, but is reducible to the attribute customerNo. In this example this single attribute key is irreducible. Note that in other cases a candidate key may be made up of more that one attribute

- **A primary key (Pk)** is also a unique identifier for the entity. There may be several candidate keys for a relation. One candidate key is chosen as the primary key

- **A composite key** is a key that consists of more than one attribute. For example in figure 3.17 in the Loan entity copied below, the primary composite key might be identified as studentNo, bookCopyNo. This assumes that in the database a tuple with a particular studentNo, bookCopyNo combination will be unique. If a student borrows the same book more than once, the key should also include the dateOut (and possibly 'time' to ensure uniqueness). So the primary key might be identified as studentNo, bookCopyNo, dateOut.

Figure 3.17: Entity loan with composite primary key

Loan
studNo (Pk) bookCopyNo (Pk) dateOut (Pk) dateDue dateBack

Note that the primary key is denoted using (Pk) in the UML diagram.

3.4 Producing the entity-relationship model: the top-down approach

The main phases involved in producing the conceptual data model are:

- Define the entities

- Define the relationships

- Establish the key attributes for each entity

- Identify the initial structure of the model, by drawing a first attempt at an ERD

- Complete each entity with all its attributes

- Validate the model by checking that the model can support the processing requirements. At the same time functional requirements of the system are established using another technique called process modelling (e.g. using data flow diagrams). We discuss this phase in the next section

- Refine the model as necessary. This technique is an iterative one: initial discussion with the user will yield a list of possible entities and an initial ERD can be drawn; this is used as a basis for further discussion with the users. Successive versions of the model will be more detailed, until all concerned are satisfied with the model.

The technique described above is a **top-down approach** to conceptual data modelling, where we start off by selecting the entities and work down to the attributes. Another data modelling method, a **bottom-up approach** known as **normalisation** (examined in Chapter 4), starts with the identification of the attributes of interest and then builds the entities. This is a formal method, consisting of a number of stages, arriving at data in various states or 'normal forms'. With each stage of normalisation, undesirable properties of the data are eliminated. Normalisation is used to validate the initial results or to improve the quality of the E-R model. It may be carried out after or in tandem with the top-down E-R method.

3.5 Validating the data model

As stated earlier, this chapter emphasises the data modelling (conceptual and logical) part of database system life cycle. At the same time the functional requirements of the system are established using another technique called process modelling (e.g. using dataflow diagrams, etc.).

Having arrived at an initial data structure, the data model is validated (sixth bullet point above). Validation involves four separate tasks:

- **Check the model can support the processing requirements**
- **Check for redundant relationships**
- **Check for connection traps**
- **Check model is acceptable to the users.**

The last task, 'Check the model is acceptable to users', involves discussions to make sure what has been interpreted by the designer reflects reality and that no entities or relationships have been left out. We shall now consider the first three tasks listed above.

Check the model can support the processing requirements

Relationships denote access from one entity occurrence to another. An access path is the pathway in the ERD which must be followed for a functional requirement to be realised. An example of an access path is shown in figure 3.18.

Returning again to the university library example (figure 3.4), suppose there is a functional requirement to list the book copy numbers and date acquired of all book copies loaned to student Erica Baker where the date that the book was loaned out was 7th March 2008. The access path is shown by the dotted line in the figure.

Figure 3.18: Access path example

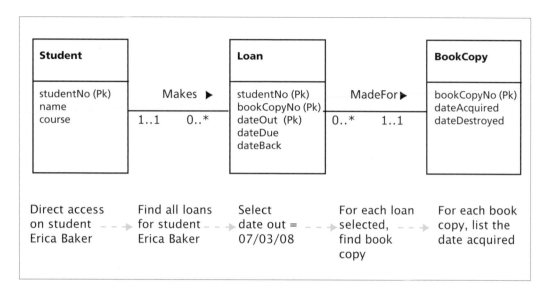

For each process (established at the process modelling stage) the data model should be checked to ensure that access paths can provide the necessary data requirements.

Check for redundant relationships

This involves removing unnecessary or duplicated access paths between entities.

For example, consider the ERD below. A customer places many orders and each order contains a number of order lines depending on the number of products ordered. (The Product entity has not been included for simplicity.) There are two paths between entities Customer and OrderLine: one direct; the other through the entity Order.

There are two ways, therefore, of satisfying the requirement to find all occurrences of OrderLine associated with a particular occurrence of a Customer: either access path Customer-OrderLine or access path Customer-Order-OrderLine.

Figure 3.19: Redundant relationships example

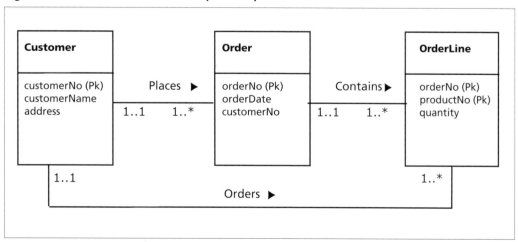

It should be noted that data models are not concerned with simplicity or speed of access, but ensuring that all necessary relationships are included in the model to meet the requirements. Since access path Customer-Order-OrderLine can satisfy the requirement, the relationship between Customer and OrderLine is redundant and can be removed (assuming the latter relationship is not required by some other processing).

Check for connection traps

The term 'connection trap' is used to describe a problem which arises in data modelling due to the misinterpretation of the meaning of relationships. The particular cases of **fan trap** and **chasm trap** identified by Howe in 1981 are described here.

Fan traps

Fan traps are associated with structures of the form many:1/1:many, where the relationships fan out from the same entity. For example:

Figure 3.20: Fan trap example

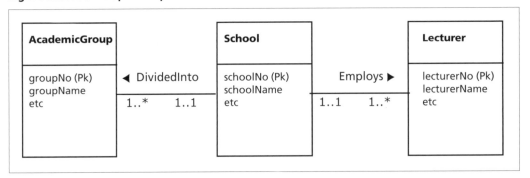

A university has a number of schools (for example the School of Computing). Each school is divided into a number of academic groups (for example, Information Systems and Computing Science). From the model it might be thought that the existence of a connection from Academic Group to Lecturer via School means that it would be possible to deduce which lecturer belongs to which academic group. The occurrence diagram below demonstrates that this is not so: there is no way of knowing which of lecturers Jialiang, Jane, Jim belong to group 1 and which to 2, etc.

Figure 3.21: Occurrence diagram for the fan trap example

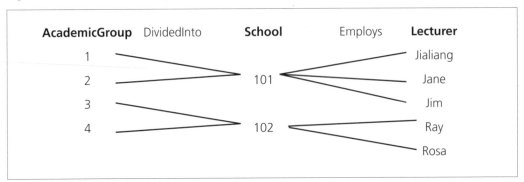

A revised entity-relationship structure is shown in figure 3.22.

Figure 3.22: Revised ERD with the fan trap removed

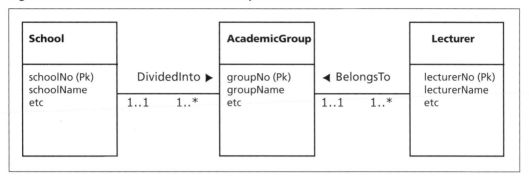

A potential connection trap does not always matter, because the enterprise might not be interested in a particular relationship. Usually they can be eliminated when necessary by rearranging relationships or by defining a complex relationship.

Chasm traps

In this case the model suggests that there is a relationship between entity types but the access pathway does not exist between certain entity occurrences. We will illustrate this with the following example:

Figure 3.23: Chasm trap example

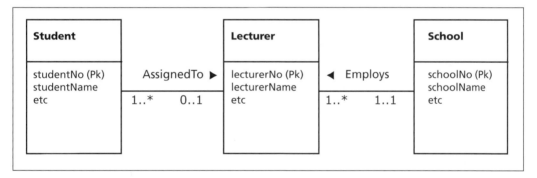

A designer has modelled the fact that a school has many lecturers who are responsible for looking after students in the role of personal tutor. A student is assigned to one tutor only. Note that it is possible for a student, perhaps one who is new to a school, not to have been assigned to a personal tutor. A problem might arise when we want to know which students are allocated to each school. The occurrence diagram below illustrates the problem.

Figure 3.24: Occurrence diagram for the chasm trap example

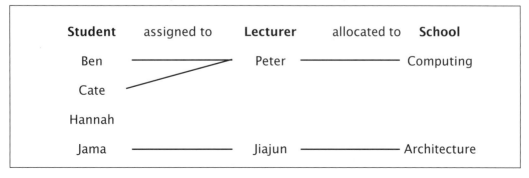

It is obvious from the diagram that we cannot answer the question 'To which school does Hannah belong?' We cannot answer this question, because this pupil has not yet been assigned to a personal tutor. The inability to answer such questions results in loss of information and is the result of what is known as a chasm trap. To solve this problem it is necessary in introduce another relationship, this time between Student and School.

Figure 3.24: Redesigned example, with chasm trap removed

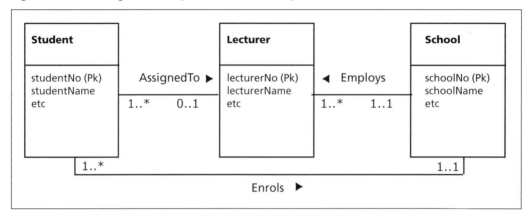

An occurrence diagram could be constructed thus:

Figure 3.26: Occurrence diagram, with chasm trap removed

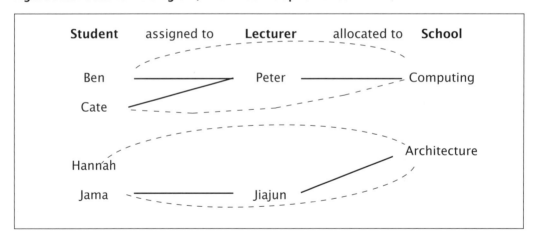

It is now possible to answer the question 'To which school does Hannah belong?'.

The enhanced entity-relationship model

The entity-relationship model was proposed in 1976 by Peter Chen. Since then his basic approach has been extended to include additional semantic concepts. In Chapter 8 we look at the enhanced entity-relationship model, which includes two abstraction mechanisms: generalisation and specialisation, which enable more complex applications to be represented in data models.

3.6 The logical model: mapping to a relational database

In this section we consider how the conceptual model is converted to a model suitable for a RDBMS. It is likely that a relational database system will be implemented but there are other possibilities such as an object-oriented database. We will examine the process of mapping to an object-oriented database in Chapter 8.

In order to design a relational database using an entity-relationship model, we need to be able to convert our design from a diagrammatic format into a set of relations that will contain the values of the actual data items. The form of the relationships identified between entities will affect the relations that we construct: the cardinality, the degree and membership class will all have an effect on the structure of the database.

Producing the logical data model: main phases

The main phases involved in producing the logical data model are:

• Derive the relations from the conceptual data model

• Check the relations to ensure they are normalised

• As with the initial E-R model, validate the relational model – that is:

    - check the model can support processing requirements

    - check for redundant relationships

    - check for connection traps

    - check the model is acceptable to the users.

The first phase is discussed in the following sections. Normalisation is discussed in Chapter 4. The validation process is similar to that discussed for E-R modelling. A further example of a connection trap is given for this phase.

Deriving relations from the conceptual data model

The main task in mapping the conceptual data model to a relational one is to derive the relations from the entities and relationships. Generally when converting to the relational model, entities established for the conceptual model will map to one or more relations. Here we use the relation diagram (based on UML) to represent the relations and links between them, the attributes, the primary and foreign keys.

We saw in Chapter 2 that in the relational model the relationship between two relations is represented by placing a copy of the primary key of one relation into another relation. This new attribute is called a foreign key, an attribute in a relation which is also the primary key in another relation.

We can transform entity-relationship diagrams into a relational one by following simple rules which will specify the number of relations needed, depending on the cardinality (one-to-one, one-to-many or many-to-many) and the membership class (mandatory or optional) of the entities participating in the relationship. For simplicity we will assume that all relationships in the E-R model are binary.

We now look in more detail at how the mapping is achieved for different cardinalities, using an example which we met earlier, the university library database. We also expand the model to include a one-to-one relationship between Student and a new entity Library Card. One Student is allocated one Library Card and one Card is allocated to precisely one Student.

Figure 3.27: Entity-relationship diagram for a university library

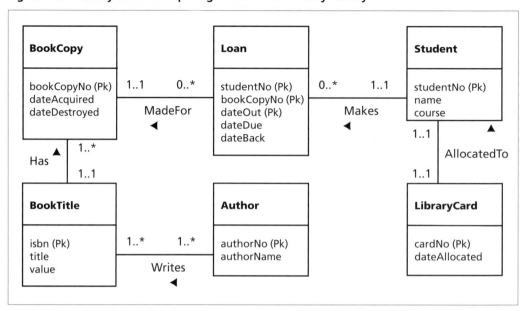

Mapping one-to-one relationships into relations

In the case of one-to-one relationships a decision is made whether to combine the two entities to produce one relation or whether to map to two relations. In all cases either one or two relations will be created from the original two entities. As a guide there are rules to help in the decision depending on whether the membership class is mandatory or optional. We will see that the rules are used as a guide only and in many cases commonsense will show that keeping the two relations or combining into one is more convenient even if 'it flouts the rules'.

We will look at the following situations:

- **Mandatory for both entities**
- **Mandatory for one entity, optional for the other entity**
- **Optional for both entities.**

Mandatory for both entities

For the situation when there is mandatory participation on both ends of the one-to-one relationship, a single relation will be able to represent the information represented by each entity and the relationship that exists between them. Look at the one-to-one relationship in our example.

Figure 3.28: Part of ERD: mandatory for both entities

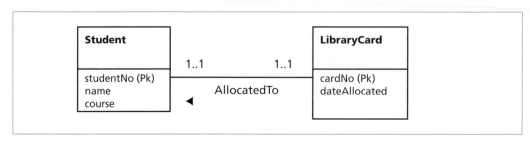

In this case a student is allocated precisely one library card and a card is allocated to precisely one student. The two entities are now converted into one single relation.

This new relation holds information about all the students and their library cards. The cards do not need to be held in a separate relation as each student has one card, and each card relates only to one student.

Figure 3.29: Student relation as part of the relation diagram

Mandatory for one entity, optional for the other entity

In this case, two relations will be needed, one for each entity. To illustrate this we have adapted our original ERD thus:

Figure 3.30: Part of ERD: mandatory for one entity, optional for the other

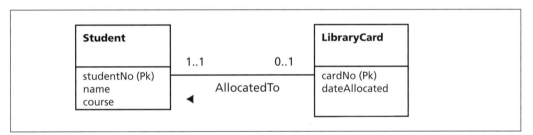

Optionality has now been introduced into the model. Here a student is allocated zero or one library card, i.e. some students may exist in the database but have for some reason not been allocated library cards. A particular card occurrence will always relate to precisely one student.

Figure 3.31: Part of relation diagram for Student & LibraryCard

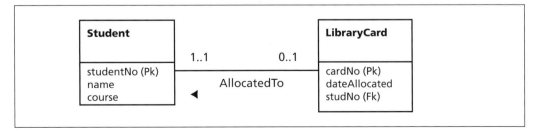

In the relational model the two entities are converted into two relations and the foreign key is placed on the side which includes a zero in the minimum..maximum pair, i.e. 0..1. This means that a foreign key value, in this case, will never be a null value.

The student identifier is stored in the LibraryCard relation in order to show the connection between Students and Library Cards. If, alternatively, we had placed the foreign key, cardNo, in the Student relation, then those students who had not been allocated a card would have a null value for this data item. The reason for including such a rule in the conversion is for efficiency of data storage. If only a few students had been allocated a card it is more efficient to place the foreign key in the Library Card relation. Nowadays, with secondary storage not at a premium, the storage saved may often be trivial.

Optional for both entities

When both entities are optional, we have to make the decision where to place the foreign key. The decision may be based on the expected statistics – i.e. on how likely an instance in one entity will be linked to another instance in the other entity.

In the next example, optionality has been introduced into both sides of the relationship.

Figure 3.32: Part of ERD: optional for both entities

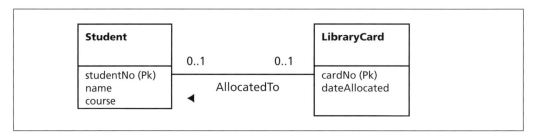

Here a particular Student instance is allocated zero or one Library Card; a Card instance is allocated to zero or one Student. The latter situation might happen if cards are created and card details are held in the database before they are allocated. We now have to decide where to place the foreign key in order to link the two relations. We may arbitrarily place the foreign key in one of the relations or, given that when library cards are created they do not have a corresponding student, then we might decide to place the foreign key in the Student relation thus:

Figure 3.33: Part of a relational diagram for Student & Library Card

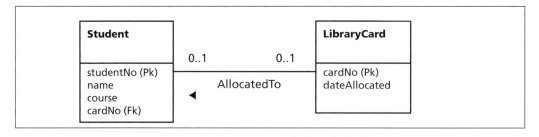

For students who have not been allocated a library card, a null value is placed in the corresponding cardNo attribute (i.e. the foreign key value).

Generally, for one-to-one relationships, the decision as to how to convert to the relational model will be based on the particular circumstances, and the guidelines above will not always be followed. For example, it may be convenient to convert to one relation even when the 'rules' would indicate that two relations are needed. This might happen if only a very small number of tuples are likely to be optional in a relation – then the creation of a new table might be deemed unnecessary.

Another example would be cases where the two entities are conceptually separate, for example in the case in figure 3.5, earlier, where we have the two entities Member of Parliament and Constituency and we may wish to hold details of each in two separate tables.

Mapping one-to-many relationships into relations

Converting a one-to-many relationship between two entities in the E-R model to one in the relational model involves the placement of a copy of the primary key of one relation into another relation.

A one-to-many relationship in our example above involves the two entities BookCopy and BookTitle. This represents the fact that there may be a number of copies of a particular book in the library. Put another way: one BookTitle has many BookCopies and one BookCopy relates to one BookTitle:

Figure 3.34: E-R diagram for BookCopy and BookTitle

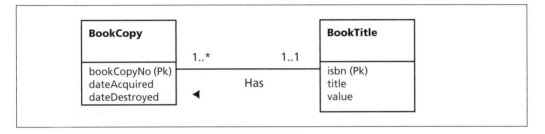

Converting the E-R model to a relational one, we have the following relation diagram:

Figure 3.35: Relation diagram for BookCopy and BookTitle

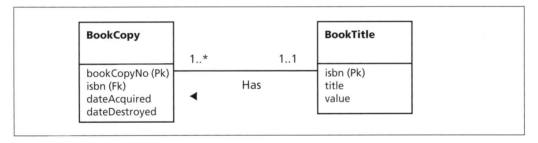

Notice that the BookCopy entity is linked to the BookTitle entity via the *primary* key isbn (International Standard Book Number) in BookTitle and *foreign* key isbn in BookCopy.

Note also that students often make errors when placing the foreign key in a one-to-many relationship and also confuse the positions of the one (1..1) and the many (1..*) pair.

'Reading' the relationship using the two sentences each starting with the word 'one' is useful for understanding where to place the 'one' and where to place the 'many'. In this example: one book title has many copies; one copy represents one title.

There is a simple rule about the placement of the foreign key which, if used, should avoid such errors:

• Always place the foreign key on the 'many side' of a one-to-many relationship.

Thus in our example the foreign key isbn is placed in the BookCopy entity, on the 'many side' of the relationship.

Mapping many-to-many relationships into relations

Many-to-many relationships need to be eliminated because relational DBMSs do not support many-to-many relationships directly. Remember that, with a many-to-many relationship, an occurrence of the first entity type may be related to several occurrences of the second and vice versa. When converting to a relational model, many-to-many relationships are decomposed into two one-to-many relationships. A copy of the primary key of each entity (relation) is placed in a new relation. In many cases both of these foreign keys will form the primary key of this new relation. Sometimes in addition to the composite primary key we find that there are one or more non-key attributes for this new relation.

In our ERD for the university library above, we have a many-to-many relationship between BookTitle and Author: a book can be written by a number of co-authors and an author may have written a number of books. Thus an instance of the BookTitle is related to several instances of the entity Author and an instance of the Author entity is related to several instances of the BookTitle entity.

Figure 3.36: Many-to-many relationship for BookTitle and Author

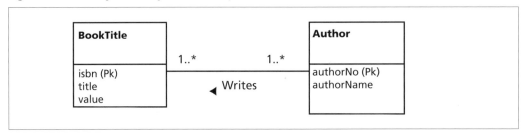

When converting to the relational model, the many-to-many relationship is decomposed to produce three relations: one relation to represent each of the original entities and a new relation, the **link relation** is also introduced – in this case the Authorship relation. After decomposition we have the following relation diagram:

Figure 3.37: Relation diagram including link relation Authorship

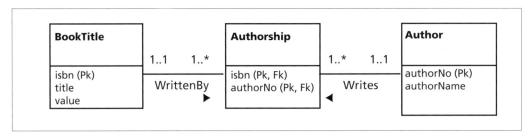

 In the example above the resulting link relation Authorship contains a primary, composite key (isbn, authorNo). These attributes are also foreign keys, as they are primary keys in the relations BookTitle and Author respectively. In the relational model these 'foreign keys' link the entities together.

Thus an instance of the BookTitle entity is related to several instances of the link entity Authorship and an instance of the Author entity is related to several instances of the Authorship entity.

Note that when decomposing a many-to many relationship the results will usually (but not always) follow the same pattern in that the result will be two one-to-many relationships with the 'many side' of each relationship attached to the link relation, which is placed between the two original entities.

In this example the resulting link relation contains a primary, composite key (isbn, authorNo) only – it does not contain any non-key attributes. In this case the creation of the link relation is to represent the many-to-many relationship between the original two entities. In some cases it may be that when the new link relation is established it is found that, besides the composite primary key, there are other non-key attributes which also need to be included.

To illustrate this situation we examine the many-to-many relationship between the entities BookCopy and Student:

Figure 3.38: Many-to-many relationship for BookCopy and Student

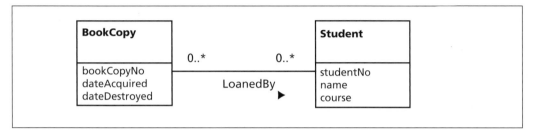

To decompose the many-to-many relationship a third **link** entity is introduced - in this case the Loan entity. The figure below shows the complete entity-relationship diagram (see Figure 3.4) for the university library now mapped to a relational database - i.e. the relation diagram.

Figure 3.39: Relation diagram for the university library

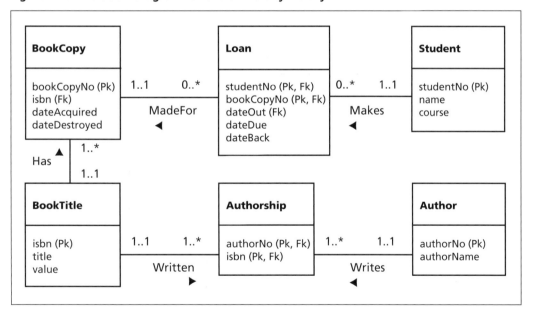

In Figure 3.39, the resulting link relation Loan contains a primary, composite key (studentNo, bookCopyNo). These attributes are also foreign keys as they are primary keys in the relations Student and BookCopy respectively. In the relational model these 'foreign keys' link the entities together.

We have also introduced the non-key attributes dateOut, dateDue and dateBack. Such entities with their attributes may well come to light at the conceptual data modelling stage, as was the case in this example (see figure 3.4 which includes the Loan entity). It is, however, good practice to examine all link relations to see if there are any non-key attributes which had previously been undetected.

Validate the relational model: checking for connection traps

We consider here an example of a fan trap. You may remember that fan traps are associated with structures of the form many:1/1:many, where the relationships fan out from the same entity. A more complex example than that discussed earlier in this chapter is the situation where three entities are connected with many-to-many relationships in a triangular form. For example, suppose we want to hold information for race horse stables. We want to know about jockeys, the horses that they ride and the races that they take part in. Assume a jockey competes in many races; a jockey rides many horses; a horse is ridden by many jockeys; a horse rides in many races; a race has many jockeys; a race will have many horses.

A database designer might create the following relation diagram after decomposing the many-to-many relationships:

Figure 3.40: Relation diagram with fan traps

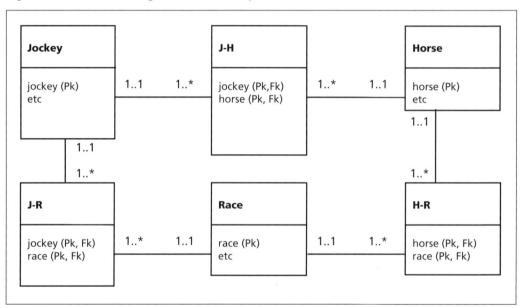

From the above structure we can tell which jockey rode a particular horse and we can tell which jockey rode a particular race. We can also get the information connecting horse to race. However, we cannot tell, for example, which jockey rode a particular horse in a particular race. The reason for this is that there are three fan traps in the above structure. This is illustrated using the following sample link relations (relations Race, Jockey and Horse tables have been omitted for simplicity):

Figure 3.41: Jockey example sample relations

J-H			H-R			J-R	
jockey	**horse**		**horse**	**race**		**jockey**	**race**
Sunil	Best Mate		Best Mate	Gold Cup		Sunil	Gold Cup
Sunil	Desert Orchid		Desert Orchid	Grand National		Sunil	Grand National
Susan	Best Mate		Best Mate	Grand National		Helen	Grand National
Helen	Laughing Boy		Laughing Boy	Gold Cup		Helen	Gold Cup
•	•		•	•		•	•

From the relations we can tell, for example, that Sunil rode Best Mate and that he also rode Desert Orchid. We can tell that Sunil rode in the Gold Cup and the Grand National. We can also tell that Best Mate rode in the Gold Cup and the Grand National. But we cannot tell that Sunil rode Best Mate in the Gold Cup. Instead of the structure above we might redesign our model to include a relation called Run which represents an outing for a jockey riding a horse in a particular race. Sample data is given below:

Figure 3.42: Relation Run

jockey	horse	race
Sunil	Best Mate	Gold Cup
Sunil	Desert Orchid	Grand National
Helen	Best Mate	Grand National
Helen	Laughing Boy	Gold Cup
•	•	• •

We have decided to include such an entity in our design as we need the combination of the three attributes to know what is valid data or otherwise. For example, we can now tell that Sunil rode Best Mate in the Gold Cup.

3.7 Summary

In this chapter we were concerned with the modelling of the 'real world' view of data – i.e. the conceptual data model. In particular, you were introduced to the process known as entity-relationship modelling and shown how to map the E-R model to one suitable for implementation using a relational database.

3.8 Review questions

 Review question 3.1 Define the following terms connected to entity-relationship modelling, giving examples of each for an application of your choice:

Entity	Attribute
Relationship	Candidate key
Primary key	Foreign key
Composite key	

 Review question 3.2 For the ERD below, decompose the many-to-many relationship. State the two new relationships as two sentences, each starting with the word 'one'.

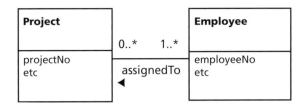

 Review question 3.3 A cinema complex has a number of screens where films are shown. A designer has documented the following entities and attributes. Complete the entity-relationship diagram by indicating primary keys, drawing lines to indicate relationships, showing cardinality and relationship names and direction:

Cinema
cinemaNo
cName
cAddress

Screen
screenNo
capacity

Screening
date
time
takings

Film
filmNo
title
director

Now convert your entity-relationship diagram to a relation diagram: i.e. mapping any one-to-one relationships as in rules in section 3.6; include foreign keys and decompose any many-to-many relationships.

Review question 3.4   Middlesex Transport is responsible for running a fleet of buses throughout North London. The buses are housed in one of three depots: Holloway, Hornsey and Islington. Each depot is identified by its depot number; in addition the depot name and address are recorded.

Each bus is identified by its registration number. Details of the buses' models are also held, for example 'Routemaster' and 'Spirit of London'. The buses run on various routes which are described by their starting and finishing point, for example 'Camden Town/ Hendon'. Each route is identified by its route number. Only buses from particular depots will travel on a particular route, so, for example, only buses from the Islington depot will travel on the Camden Town/Hendon route. Buses are classified by various types such as 'double-decker', 'bendy bus', etc. There are restrictions on some bus types for some of the routes; for example, routes with low bridges may exclude double-decker buses, and bendy buses may be unable to operate around some corners. For this reason, buses are designated to particular routes.

The bus company employs bus drivers to operate the buses and cleaners who help maintain them. Both the bus drivers and cleaners work at one particular depot. Drivers and cleaners have an employee number, name, and salary. In addition the company holds information on the date that the driver passed his/her PCV (passenger carrying vehicle) driving test.

For cleaning purposes the depots are organised with cleaners being responsible for a number of buses; each bus has one cleaner who is particularly responsible for that bus. In the case of bus drivers, they can only drive buses where they have completed training for the type of bus; the date when training is completed is recorded. In addition, bus drivers can only drive buses where they have had practice on particular routes.

Study these requirements and then draw an entity-relationship diagram using UML notation. Indicate the primary keys. Now convert to a relation diagram mapping any one-to-one relationships as in the rules in section 3.6; include foreign keys and decompose any many-to-many relationships. Make any assumptions that you need to make about optional/mandatory relationships.

Review question 3.5   Consider a hospital information system with the following characteristics:

- A patient can either be a resident patient who is admitted to the hospital or an outpatient who comes to the hospital for an outpatient clinic

- For both types of patient we will need to hold the patient's name, telephone number, address, date of birth and the patient's family doctor (GP)

- For a resident patient we will need to hold the ward name where the patient is currently residing, the admission date of the patient, and also information about any operations that the patient has had

- The operation information will include the date and time of the operation, the doctor (assume one) who carried out the operation plus the theatre where the operation took place

- For both GPs and hospital doctors we will hold the doctor's name and telephone number; in addition we will hold the GP's address and the hospital doctor's specialism code (for example, he or she may specialise in ENT, problems relating to ear, nose and throat) – assume one per hospital doctor

- For outpatients we will need to hold information about the outpatients' appointments: the appointment date and time and the hospital doctor who attended to the patient.

Study the case above and then draw an ERD using UML notation. Indicate the primary keys. Now convert to a relation diagram mapping any one-to-one relationships as in the rules in section 3.6; include foreign keys and decompose any many-to-many relationships. Make any assumptions that you need to make about optional/mandatory relationships.

 Review question 3.6   What is an access path? Specify the access path for the following query relating to the data model in review question 3.5.

Find the names of hospital doctors who have operated on patients who have the same GP as patient John Smith

CHAPTER 4

Database design using normalisation

OVERVIEW

Following on from Chapter 3 and the discussion of entity-relationship modelling, this chapter focuses on another method of developing a conceptual model, namely **normalisation**. This method is often used in addition to entity-relationship modelling to support relational database design.

We start this chapter by examining a 'poor' database design and the problems or **anomalies** that might exist in such a design. We next introduce the reader to an important concept of data design, that of **functional dependency**. We then show how anomalies can to a great extent be eliminated with the formal technique of normalisation using a set of rules or guidelines called normal forms. In particular we examine first, second and third normal forms. In addition the higher normal forms of Boyce-Codd, fourth and fifth normal forms will be introduced.

We also introduce a case study (the bus depots' database) which will be used in a number of chapters in this book.

Learning outcomes	On completion of this chapter, you should be able to:

- Describe the problems associated with un-normalised data

- Explain and apply the concepts of functional dependency

- Apply the normal forms of first normal form (1NF), second normal form (2NF) and third normal form (3NF) to relations

- Apply the higher normal forms of Boyce-Codd normal form (BCNF), fourth normal form (4NF) and fifth normal form (5NF).

4.1 Introduction

We have seen in the previous chapter how relationships between entities can be identified, described and represented in a graphical technique known as entity-relationship modelling. This is a top-down method since we use as a starting point the main entities and design a model with its full set of entities, attributes and relationships. We now look at a bottom-up method of database design called normalisation.

Normalisation is a formal method for analysing data into its constituent entities and attributes – it starts with the identification of the attributes of interest and builds the entities from these attributes. It consists of a number of stages, arriving at data in various states or 'normal forms'. It involves the identification of functional dependencies, where we look for attributes that enable the identification of other attributes. With each stage of normalisation, undesirable properties of the data are eliminated. Normalisation is therefore used to improve the quality of the database design and may be carried out in parallel with or after the top-down entity-relationship modelling process, to validate or cross-check the emerging model.

E F Codd, a British computer scientist working for IBM in the 1970s, originally defined first normal form (1NF), second normal form (2NF) and third normal form (3NF) in 1972 in his paper 'Further Normalisation of the Data Base Relational Model'.

There are other normal forms, but we shall initially consider Codd's original three. Designing your tables to conform to third normal form is usually sufficient to ensure good design. However, there are situations where anomalies can occur for data that has been normalised to 3NF. The higher normal forms address these anomalies - we examine Boyce-Codd normal form, fourth normal form and fifth normal form later in this chapter.

4.2 The bus depots' database

The examples and exercises in this chapter are based on the bus depots' database case which was first introduced in review question 3.4. This case study will also be used in other chapters in this book, particularly the SQL and PLSQL examples in the following chapters. Details of the case and the relation model are given below:

Middlesex Transport is responsible for running a fleet of buses throughout North London. The buses are housed in one of three depots: Holloway, Hornsey and Islington. Each depot is identified by its depot number; in addition the depot name and address are recorded.

Each bus is identified by its registration number. Details of the buses' models are also held, for example 'Routemaster' and 'Spirit of London'. The buses run on various routes which are described by their starting and finishing point, for example 'Camden Town/Hendon'. Each route is identified by its route number. Only buses from particular depots will travel on a particular route, so, for example, only buses from the Islington depot will travel on the Camden Town/Hendon route. Buses are classified by various types such as 'double-decker', 'bendy bus', etc. There are restrictions on some bus types for some of the routes; for example, those with low bridges may exclude double-decker buses and bendy buses may be unable to operate around some corners. For this reason buses are designated to particular routes.

The bus company employs bus drivers to operate the buses and cleaners who help maintain them. Both the bus drivers and cleaners work at one particular depot. Drivers and cleaners have an employee number, name, and salary. In addition the company holds information on the date that the driver passed his/her PCV (Passenger Carrying Vehicle) driving test.

For cleaning purposes the depots are organised with cleaners being responsible for a number of buses; each bus has one cleaner who is particularly responsible for that bus. In the case of bus drivers, they can drive buses only where they have completed training for the type of bus and the date when training is completed is recorded. In addition, bus drivers can drive buses only on routes where they have had practice on that route.

Figure 4.1: The relation diagram for the bus depots' database:

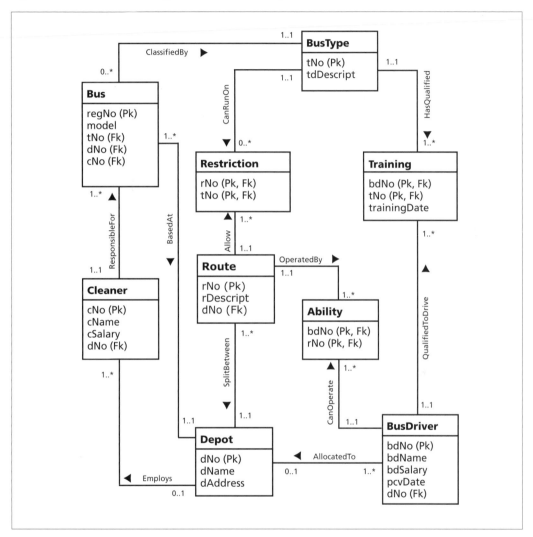

Note that the above model is (arguably) in normalised form. For the purposes of illustration in this chapter on normalisation, some new entities and attributes will be introduced to exemplify data in un-normalised form.

4.3 Un-normalised data

Well-normalised databases have a design that reflects the true dependencies between entities, allowing the data to be updated quickly with little risk of introducing inconsistencies. Before discussing how to design a well-normalised database using Codd's normalisation techniques, we first consider a 'poor' database design.

Consider for example a relation 'Bus' which includes bus registration number, model, type number, type description, depot name (note that names have changed slightly from the above case study for the purposes of this example):

Figure 4.2: Bus relation

registration number	model	type number	type description	depot name
A123ABC	Routemaster	1	double-decker	Holloway
D678FGH	Volvo 8700	2	metrobus	Holloway
H259IJK	Daf SB220	3	midibus	Hornsey
P200IJK	Mercedes 709D	2	metrobus	Hornsey
P300RTY	Mercedes Citaro	4	bendy bus	Hornsey
R678FDS	Daf SB220	1	double-decker	
W653TJH	Routemaster	1	double-decker	

There are several problems with this relation:

- **Redundancy:** the 'type description' is repeated for each 'type number' in the relation. For example, all occurrences of type '1' have a description 'double-decker'. The 'model' is also repeated for a particular 'type description'; for example, a Routemaster is always a double-decker bus

- **Update anomalies:** as a consequence of the redundancy, inconsistencies may occur after update. For example, we could update the 'type description' in one tuple, while leaving it fixed in another

- **Deletion anomalies:** if we should delete all the buses of a particular type, we might lose all the information about that type. So for example if we delete bus with registration 'H259IJK' above, then information about bus type number '4' is lost

- **Insertion anomalies:** the converse to deletion anomalies is that we cannot record a new bus type in our table unless there exists a bus of that type. So, for example, if there is the type 'open top' we cannot store this in our database. We might consider getting round this by storing null values in the registration number attribute. This is, however, not a good option as it would violate the entity integrity rule, that the primary key of a relation (in this case 'registration number') should not contain a null value.

4.4 Functional dependencies

Determinants

A formal definition for the term 'functional dependence' is:

- Given a relation which has attributes (x, y, …), we say that an attribute y is functionally dependent on another attribute x, if and only if, each x-value has associated with it precisely one y-value (at any one time).

Contrary to first appearances, this is actually a fairly simple concept and easily explained with an example.

Examine the Cleaner relation in figure 4.3. It includes the attributes' names as given in the ERD above and also shows, in brackets, fuller names to aid the following explanation:

Figure 4.3: Cleaner relation

cNo (Cleaner no.)	cName (Cleaner name)	cSalary (Cleaner salary)	dNo (Depot no.)
110	John	2550	101
111	Jean	2500	101
112	Betty	2400	102
113	Vince	2800	102
114	Jay	3000	102

Here attributes cName, cSalary and dNo are each functionally dependent on attribute cNo. That is, given a particular cleaner number value, there exists precisely one corresponding value for the cleaner name, cleaner salary and depot number. So cleaner 110 has precisely one name, salary and depot number.

In general, the same x-values may appear in many different tuples of the relation (in cases where the x-value is not a primary key); if y is functionally dependent on x then every one of these tuples must contain the same y-value.

Going back to the Cleaner example, we can represent these functional dependencies diagrammatically as:

Figure 4.4: Cleaner determinacy diagram

This is an example of a **determinacy diagram**. The arrow line can be read as 'determines' (reading from left to right). So we say, for example 'cNo determines cName'. We can also 'read' the diagram from right to left. This time the arrowed line is read as 'functionally dependent on'. So we say, for example 'cName is functionally dependent on cNo'.

The attribute or group of attributes on the left-hand side is called the **determinant**. When the value of one attribute allows us to identify the value of another attribute in the same relation, the first attribute is called a determinant. The determinant of a value is not necessarily the primary key. In the example, cNo is a determinant of cName, because knowing the cleaner's number we can determine the cleaner's name.

Recognising these functional dependencies is an important part in understanding the meaning or semantics of the data. The fact that cName, cSalary and dNo are functionally dependent on cNo, means that each cleaner has one name, has one salary and works at precisely one depot.

Composite attributes

The notion of functional dependence can be extended to cover the case where the determinant (particularly the primary key) is composite – i.e. it consists of more that one attribute. For example, given the Training relation which relates to bus drivers and the types of buses that each driver is trained to drive:

Figure 4.5: Training relation

bdNo (Driver no.)	tNo (Type no.)	trainingDate (Training date)
001	1	09-jan-2006
001	2	09-jan-2006
006	2	09-feb-2006
007	1	09-feb-2006
•	•	•
•	•	•

Remember that bdNo and tNo in the above relation are the bus driver's number and type number of bus for which he/she is trained to drive. Together, the bdNo and tNo provide the Training relation's primary key – a composite key. In this relation the attribute trainingDate is functionally dependent on the composite key (bdNo, tNo): given a particular combination of bdNo and tNo values, there exists precisely one corresponding trainingDate value. This functional dependency can be represented diagrammatically as shown in figure 4.6

Figure 4.6: Function dependency with composite determinant

Full functional dependence

We say that attribute y is fully functionally dependent on attribute x if it is functionally dependent on x and is not functionally dependent on any subset of x where x is a composite attribute.

For example, in the Training relation above, trainingDate is functionally dependent on the composite attribute (bdNo, tNo) but it is not functionally dependent on the bdNo or the tNo alone. A bus driver number can have more than one training date; a type number can also have a number of training dates; however, a bus driver number and type number together has precisely one training date. In this case, therefore, training date is fully functionally dependent on the primary key.

Partial dependence

A different form of dependence is partial dependence. Where we have a data value that depends on only a part of a composite primary key, then we have a partial dependency. So, for example, we might include the attribute tDescript (type description, such as double-decker or bendy bus) as a column in the Training relation above. In this case, tDescript is functionally dependent on the partial key tNo (type number). The attribute tDescript is therefore not fully functionally dependent on the primary key. We will see that where we have such attributes, we must put them in separate relations.

Figure 4.7: Partial function dependency

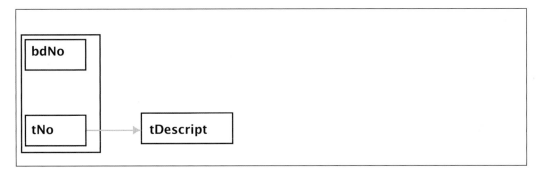

Transitive dependencies

We now examine another type of dependency known as transitive dependency.

This occurs when the value of an attribute is not determined directly from the primary key, but through the value of another attribute and this attribute in turn is determined by the primary key.

Consider a relation with three attributes: attribute 1, attribute 2 and attribute 3 and where attribute 1 is the primary key.

If

attribute 1 determines attribute 2

and

attribute 2 determines attribute 3

... then

attribute 1 must determine attribute 3 – i.e. a transitive dependency.

In this situation, to avoid a transitive dependency attribute 3 is removed from the original relation, leaving behind attribute 1 and attribute 2 and a new relation is created with attribute 2 and attribute 3.

To illustrate transitive dependencies we will add two further columns to the original Training relation concerning the people who trained the bus drivers – i.e. trainer number (trainerNo) and trainer name (trainerName).

Figure 4.8: Extended Training relation

bdNo (Driver no.)	tNo (Type no.)	trainingDate (Training date)	trainerNo (Training no.)	trainerName (Training name)
001	1	09-Jan-2006	A123	Tony
001	2	09-Jan-2006	G533	Pat
006	2	11-Feb-2006	J972	Nawaz
007	1	11-Feb-2006	A123	Tony
•	•	•	•	•
•	•	•	•	•

Figure 4.9: Transitive dependency

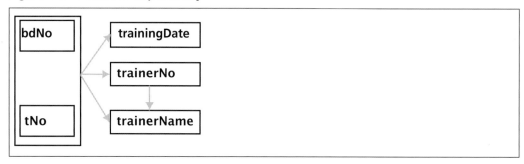

The transitive dependencies are denoted by the vertical arrow in the diagram; the composite key (bdNo, tNo) determines trainingDate as before and also determines trainerNo and trainerName. Additionally we have trainerNo determines trainerName, which is a transitive dependency. The occurrence of trainerName in this relation creates unnecessary redundancy. To avoid a transitive dependency, trainerName is removed from the original relation, leaving behind primary key attributes (bdNo, tNo) plus trainerNo and trainingDate. A new relation is created with trainerNo and trainerName.

4.5 Normalisation

The normal forms

Simply put, normalisation is the process of breaking up larger relations into many small ones using a set of rules. The process involves identifying functional dependencies. If attributes are found that are not directly dependent on the primary key, these are extracted to form new relations. The process is carried out until all the data in each relation is clearly and uniquely associated with other data in the same table. This reduces redundancy (although it does not eliminate it) and makes the data easier to maintain.

A number of normal forms have been proposed, but the first five normal forms have been widely accepted. Initially we shall consider the first three. The normal forms progress from first normal form, to second, and so on. Data in 2NF implies that it is also in 1NF – i.e. each level of normalisation implies that the previous level has been met.

Other normal forms such as Boyce-Codd (BCNF – an extension of 3NF), 4NF and 5NF also exist and these are examined later in the chapter. The following figure shows the correspondence between the various normal forms:

Figure 4.10: Correspondence between the normal forms

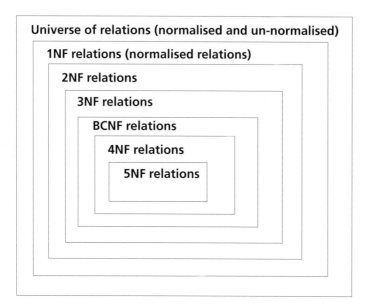

Note on how the normalisation process is carried out

There are a number of different ways of illustrating the normalisation technique. In this book we use determinacy diagrams to show the outcome of the process at each stage. So that the reader can fully understand how the data is transformed we also use sample data: initially relations in un-normalised form, then in first, second and third normal form. Once the reader understands how the process works, the determinacy diagrams can be used alone.

An example of normalisation to 3NF

Consider the following example: paper records are kept about the cleaners at the Middlesex Garage and the buses they look after. Note that two extra attributes, roster number and roster date have been added to the original bus depots' case study, and it is assumed that cleaners are not allocated to any particular garage or bus. A cleaner ticks against the appropriate job after he/she has completed the cleaning of a particular bus.

Figure 4.11: Sample rosters

Cleaner Roster

Roster number   105   Roster date   6th March 2008

Cleaner Roster

Roster number	104	Roster date	6th March 2008
Depot number	101	Depot name	Holloway
Cleaner no	135		
Cleaner name	Jo Brown		

Registration number	Model	Bus type number	Type description	Job completed
A123ABC	Routemaster	1	double-decker	√
D678FGH	Volvo 8700	2	metro bus	√
D345GGI	Volvo 8500	1	double-decker	
G233HGF	Mercedes 709D	2	metro bus	
B683KLH	Daf SB22	3	midi bus	
B409NCS	Routemaster	1	double-decker	

If Roster were identified as a relation, it might look like:

Figure 4.12: The un-normalised relation

roster No	roster Date	cNo	cName	dNo	dName	regNo	model	tNo	tDescript	status
104	6-3-08	135	Jo Brown	101	Holloway	A123ABC	Routemaster	1	double-decker	c
						D678FGH	Volvo 8700	2	metrobus	c
						D345GGI	Volvo 8500	1	double-decker	
						G233HGF	Mercedes 709D	2	metro bus	
						B683KLH	Daf SB22	3	midi bus	
						B409NCS	Routemaster	1	double-decker	
105	6-3-08	166	Lee Zua	102	Hornsey	R123HFD	Mercedes 405G	5	bendy bus	c
						C189RTB	Mercedes 709D	2	metro bus	
•	•	•	•	•	•	•	•	•		•
•	•	•	•	•	•	•	•	•		•

First normal form (1NF)

The next step in the normalisation process is to remove the repeating groups from the un-normalised relation. A relation is in 1NF if, and only if, all domains contain only atomic or single values – i.e. all repeating groups of data are removed. A repeating group is a group of attributes that occurs a number of times for each record (tuple) in the relation. So, for example, in the Roster relation each roster record has a group of buses (roster record 104 has 6 buses).

Selecting a suitable key for the table

In order to convert an un-normalised relation into 1NF, we must identify the key attribute(s) involved. From the un-normalised relation we can see that each roster has a rosterNo, each cleaner a cNo, each depot a dNo, each bus a regNo and each type a tNo. In order to convert an un-normalised relation into normal form, we also have to identify a key for the whole relation.

You may remember from Chapter 2 that a primary key is a unique identifier for an entity, that is, an attribute (or combination of attributes) with the property that, at any given time, no two entity occurrences contain the same values for that attribute (or combination of attributes). Bearing this definition in mind, on examination the primary key of the relation is rosterNo, regNo. We now draw the determinacy diagram for the Roster relation:

Figure 4.13: Determinacy diagram for 1NF

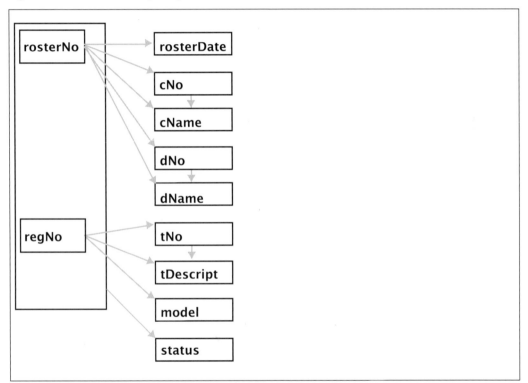

Note that the arrows coming directly from rosterNo indicate that rosterDate, cNo, cName, dNo and dName are functionally dependent on the key attribute rosterNo and not on the composite key; similarly the arrows coming directly from regNo indicate tNo, tDescript and model are functionally dependent on regNo. Notice that only 'status' is functionally dependent on the whole of the composite primary key.

To convert an un-normalised table of data into 1NF we need to remove repeating values, so that there is a single value at the intersection of each row and column. The original table of data is converted into a relation in 1NF as shown in figure 4.14. The relation has the same structure as the determinacy diagram, both being in 1NF.

Figure 4.14: Relation in first normal form

roster No	roster Date	cNo	cName	dNo	dName	regNo	model	tNo	tDescript	status
104	6-3-08	135	Jo Brown	101	Holloway	A123ABC	Routemaster	1	double-decker	c
104	6-3-08	135	Jo Brown	101	Holloway	D678FGH	Volvo 8700	2	metrobus	c
104	6-3-08	135	Jo Brown	101	Holloway	D345GGI	Volvo 8500	1	double-decker	
104	6-3-08	135	Jo Brown	101	Holloway	G233HGF	Mercedes 709D	2	metro bus	
104	6-3-08	135	Jo Brown	101	Holloway	B683KLH	Daf SB22	3	midi bus	
104	6-3-08	135	Jo Brown	101	Holloway	B409NCS	Routemaster	1	double-decker	
105	6-3-08	166	Lee Zua	102	Hornsey	R123HFD	Mercedes 405G	5	bendy bus	c
105	6-3-08	166	Lee Zua	102	Hornsey	C189RTB	Mercedes 709D	2	metro bus	
•	•	•	•	•	•	•	•	•		•
•	•	•	•	•	•	•	•	•		•

The problems with 1NF are as follows:

- **Redundancy:** e.g. roster date, cleaner name, etc. are repeated
- **Insertion anomaly:** a cleaner cannot be inserted into the database unless he/she has a bus to clean
- **Deletion anomaly:** deleting a tuple might lose information from the database. For example, if there is only one cleaner cleaning a particular bus and he/she leaves the company, then we lose information about the buses he/she cleaned
- **Update anomaly:** e.g. a change to the cleaner name means it must change in all tuples that include that cleaner name.

Second normal form (2NF)

We now describe the second step in the normalisation process using the relation above which is in first normal form:

Firstly we determine the functional dependencies on the identifying attributes (i.e. the primary key (rosterNo, regNo) and its composite parts.

If the key is composite, in order for a relation to be in 2NF, the other attributes must be functionally dependent on the whole of the key. In other words we are looking for partial functional dependencies. You will recall from Figure 4.13 that the roster date is functionally dependent on the partial key rosterNo – there is only one rosterDate for a particular rosterNo. Also cNo, cName, dNo, dName are all functionally dependent on the partial key rosterNo . In addition, the attributes tNo, tDescript and model are functionally dependent on the partial key regNo. The attribute 'status' is, however, the only attribute fully functionally dependent on the whole of the primary key.

The next stage in the second normal form process is to rewrite the entities so that all the non-key attributes are fully functionally dependent on the primary key, as is reflected in the determinacy diagrams below. Note that this step does not arise for relations that have a single attribute primary key – we need only consider relations with composite keys as in our example.

Figure 4.15: Determinacy diagrams for 2NF

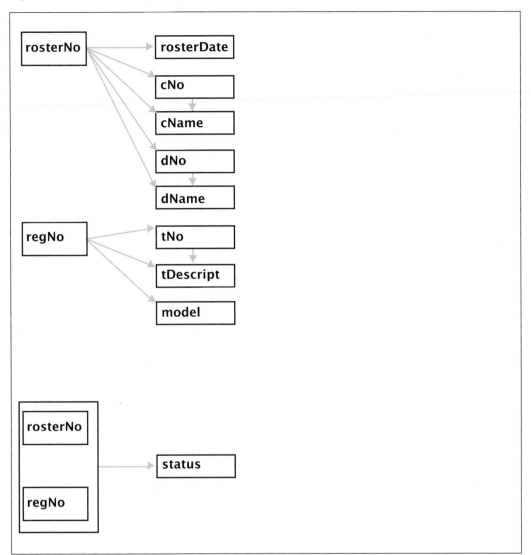

We thus have three new relations, as shown in figure 4.16.

Figure 4.16: Relations in 2NF

Roster

rosterNo	rosterDate	cNo	cName	dNo	dName
104	6-03-08	135	Jo Brown	101	Holloway
105	6-03-08	166	Lee Zua	102	Hornsey
•	•	•	•	•	•

Bus

regNo	model	tNo	tDescript
A123ABC	Routemaster	1	double-decker
D678FGH	Volvo 8700	2	metrobus
D345GGI	Volvo 8500	1	double-decker
G233HGF	Mercedes 709D	2	metro bus
B683KLH	Daf SB22	3	midi bus
B409NCS	Routemaster	1	double-decker
R123HFD	Mercedes 405G	5	bendy bus
C189RTB	Mercedes 709D	2	metro bus
•	•	•	•

BusCleaning

rosterNo	regNo	status
104	A123ABC	c
104	D678FGH	c
104	D345GGI	
104	G233HGF	
104	B683KLH	
104	B409NCS	
105	R123HFD	c
105	C189RTB	
•	•	•

The three relations Roster, Bus and BusCleaning have primary keys rosterNo, regNo and (rosterNo, regNo) respectively.

2NF has less redundancy than 1NF – in the example we have removed the duplication of bus and roster information. However there are still a number of problems:

- **Redundancy:** for example, in the Roster relation, cleaner name is repeated for each cleaner number
- **Insertion anomaly:** a new bus type cannot be inserted into the database unless a bus is inserted with that type
- **Deletion anomaly:** deleting a tuple might lose information from the database. For example, if we delete a bus we might lose information about the bus type
- **Update anomaly:** e.g. a change to the cleaner name means it must change in all tuples which include that cleaner name.

Third normal form (3NF)

A 3NF relation is in 2NF but also it must satisfy the non-transitive dependency rule, which states that every non-key attribute must be non-transitively dependent on the primary key. Another way of saying this is that a relation is in 3NF if all its non-key attributes are directly dependent on the primary key. Transitive dependencies are resolved by creating new relations for each entity.

There are three transitive dependencies in the Roster and Bus relations above as is illustrated by vertical lines in figure 4.15. There are no transitive dependencies in the BusCleaning relation. So, for example, in the Roster relation: cNo is functionally dependent on rosterNo; cName is functionally dependent on rosterNo; additionally cName is functionally dependent on cNo.

We therefore have the transitive dependency:

> If rosterNo determines cNo and cNo determines cName
>
> then ...
>
> rosterNo determines cName.

The determinacy diagrams for third normal form are given below:

Figure 4.17: Determinacy diagrams for 3NF

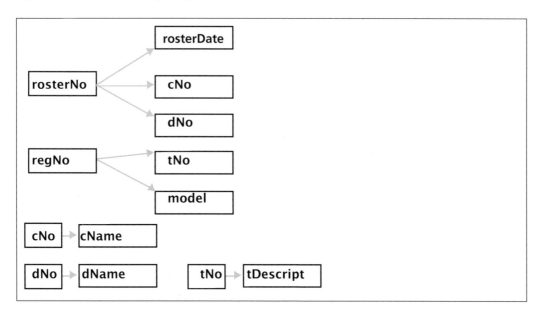

The normalisation of 2NF to 3NF involves the removal of transitive dependencies. This is done by placing the attributes in new relations. The new relations must also include copies of the determinant (as the primary keys). The determinants' attributes (cNo, dNo and tNo) act as foreign keys in the original relations.

The complete 3NF model includes the new relations and in addition the relation BusCleaning which had been created at 2NF, as shown in figure 4.18.

Figure 4.18: Relations in 3NF

Bus

regNo	model	tNo
A123ABC	Routemaster	1
D678FGH	Volvo 8700	2
D345GGI	Volvo 8500	1
G233HGF	Mercedes 709D	2
B683KLH	Daf SB22	3
B409NCS	Routemaster	1
R123HFD	Mercedes 405G	5
C189RTB	Mercedes 709D	2
•	•	•

Cleaner

cNo	cName
135	Jo Brown
166	Lee Zua
•	•

Depot

dNo	dName
101	Holloway
102	Hornsey
•	•

BusType

tNo	tDescript
1	double-decker
2	metrobus
3	midi bus
5	Bendy bus
•	•

Roster

rosterNo	rosterDate	cNo	dNo
104	20-03-06	135	101
105	20-03-06	166	102
•	•	•	•

BusCleaning

rosterNo	regNo	status
104	A123ABC	c
104	D678FGH	c
104	D345GGI	
104	G233HGF	
104	B683KLH	
104	B409NCS	
105	R123HFD	c
105	C189RTB	
•	•	•

By creating the new entities we have removed the transitive dependency from the Bus relation. These entities above are now in 3NF.

4.6 Higher normal forms

So far we have discussed the three most common normal forms. Designing tables to comply with 3NF (and hence 2NF and 1NF) is sufficient in most cases to ensure good design and the removal of anomalies. However, some undesirable dependencies may still exist after 3NF which result in redundancy still remaining. The higher normal forms address less common problems associated, in particular, with large and complex databases.

Boyce-Codd normal form (BCNF)

Boyce-Codd normal form is an extension of 3NF and was introduced to cover situations that 3NF did not address. It is a stronger form of 3NF and applies to situations where there are overlapping candidate keys. If a table has no non-key fields (such as the Restriction table in figure 4.1), it is automatically in BCNF.

- **A relation is in BCNF if all the determinants are candidate keys.**

To demonstrate the BCNF process we will firstly consider the following relations based on the bus depots' database with the addition of the attributes bus driver's address, a pay code and an hourly wage in the BusDriver relation:

> Depot (dNo, dName, dAddress)
> BusDriver (bdNo, bdName, bdAddress, dNo, payCode, hourlyWage)

A bus driver belongs to a depot. A bus driver will have a pay code, and his or her hourly wage will depend on this pay code. On examination you should be able to work out that both relations are in 2NF as they are in 1NF (no repeating groups) and all non-key attributes are fully functionally dependent on the primary keys (dNo and bdNo respectively). For the purposes of explaining BCNF we will call these relations the '2NF relations'. Looking for transitive dependencies, you will notice that hourlyWage is transitively dependent on bdNo via payCode.

The relations in 3NF are therefore:

> Depot (dNo, dName, dAddress)
> BusDriver (bdNo, bdName, bdAddress, dNo, payCode)
> PayRate (payCode, hourlyWage)

For the purposes of explaining BCNF we will call these relations the '3NF relations'. To understand BCNF you may need to be reminded of **candidate keys** and **determinants**:

- A candidate key is an attribute (or set of attributes) which is a unique and irreducible identifier for the entity. The uniqueness property means that, at any given time, no two entity occurrences contain the same values for that attribute (or combination of attributes). *Irreducibility* means that an attribute or set of attributes cannot be removed from the key, because it will no longer uniquely identify all tuples. For example, in the BusDriver relation, bdNo and the composite attributes (bdName, bdAddress) are candidate keys. One candidate key is chosen as the primary key; of the two candidate keys, it is probable that bdNo would be chosen.

- When the value of one attribute allows us to identify the value of another attribute in the same relation, this first attribute is called a determinant. The determinant of a value is not necessarily the primary key.

In our example, dNo is a determinant of dName and dAddress: knowing the depot number we can determine the depot name and address. Also in the 2NF BusDriver relation, the combination of (bdName, bdAddress), as a candidate key, is a determinant of dNo, payCode and hourlyWage.

In this relation (2NF BusDriver) payCode is a determinant of hourlyWage, but payCode is not a candidate key. This contravenes the BCNF rule that all the determinants are candidate keys. The 2NF relation, as well as not being in 3NF is also, in this example, not in BCNF.

The determinacy diagram for the BusDriver 2NF relation above, including (bdName, bdAddress) as a candidate key, is shown in figure 4.19

Figure 4.19: Determinacy diagram for the 2NF BusDriver relation

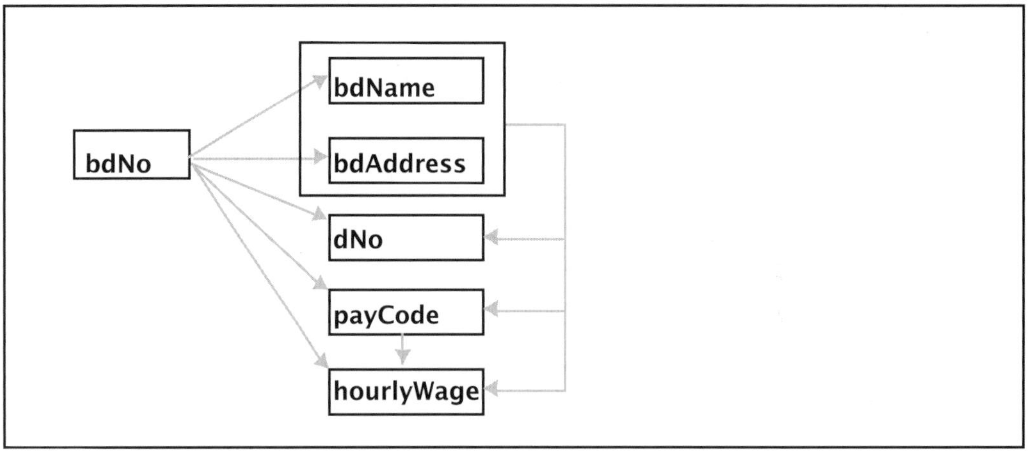

The determinacy diagram for the BusDriver 3NF relation above, including (bdName, bdAddress) as a candidate key, is given in figure 4.20:

Figure 4.20: Determinacy diagram for the 3NF BusDriver relation

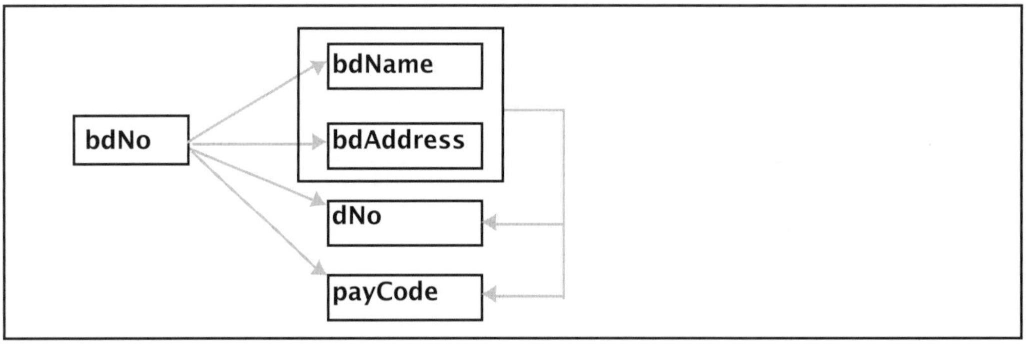

On examination, the 3NF BusDriver relation is in BCNF, as all the determinants are candidate keys. A relation in BCNF is also in third-normal form. In this example there was no difference between the resulting relations after either process was performed.

We will now look at another example where a relation is in 3NF but violates BCNF. Again we will use relations based on the bus depots' database but adapted to illustrate BCNF. We now allow bus drivers to be based at more than one depot. At each depot there are a number of managers to whom the bus drivers report – i.e. the bus driver will report to one manager at each of his or her depots. A manager works at one depot only. A schema in 3NF is:

BusDriver (bdNo, bdName, bdSalary)

BusDriverDepotManager (bdNo, dNo, manager)

Notice that the original foreign key, depot number (dNo), has now been removed from the BusDriver relation as we have a new business rule that a driver can be based at more than one depot. Thus we have to create a new relation (BusDriverDepotManager) which relates the bus driver to each of the depots where he or she is based, and to the manager for that depot. The two relations above are in 3NF as they are in 2NF and there are no transitive dependencies.

A sample relation for BusDriverDepotManager is given in figure 4.21.

Figure 4.21: Example BusDriverDepotManager relation

BusDriverDepotManager

bdNo	dNo	manager
001	101	Lily Allen
001	102	Amy Winehouse
001	103	Jose Gonzales
006	102	Kanye West
007	101	Lily Allen
007	103	Shakira
008	102	Amy Winehouse
•	•	•

As with relations which are not in first, second or third normal forms, there are problems of insertion, deletion and update anomalies with the relation above. For example we cannot insert a new manager unless there is at least one bus driver who is managed by that person. On examination of the relation the candidate keys are (bdNo, dNo) and also (bdNo, manager) which overlap as they both share the attribute bdNo.

The determinacy diagram for the BusDriverDepotManager is shown in figure 4.22.

Figure 4.22: Determinacy diagram for the BusDriverDepotManager relation

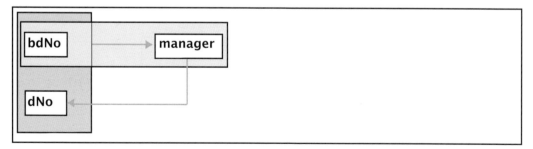

Notice that in the diagram there are overlapping candidate keys (bdNo, dNo) and (bdNo, manager). If we examine the determinants, we find that the candidate key (bdNo, dNo) is a determinant of manager and the manager is a determinant of dNo (a manager works at one depot only). The latter determinancy contravenes the BCNF rule which states that all the determinants must be candidate keys.

Problems of BCNF are resolved by converting the original BusDriverDepotManager into two relations, BusDriverManager and ManagerDepot, as shown in figure 4.23.

Figure 4.23: Relations in BCNF

BusDriverManager

bdNo	manager
001	Lily Allen
001	Amy Winehouse
001	Jose Gonzales
006	Kanye West
007	Lily Allen
007	Shakira
008	Amy Winehouse
•	•

ManagerDepot

manager	dNo
Lily Allen	101
Amy Winehouse	102
Kanye West	102
Shakira	103
Jose Gonzales	103
•	•

Notice that the insertion anomaly identified earlier has now been resolved. We can now insert a new manager (into the ManagerDepot relation), without the earlier restriction that at least one bus driver is managed by the new manager. Consider whether an alternative solution would resolve the BCNF problem – by creating a ManagerDepot relation as above and a second relation BusDriverDepot which links the bus driver to the depot (dNo).

Fourth normal form (4NF)

The 4NF rule is concerned with dependencies within a composite key (consisting of at least 3 attributes). A relation is in 4NF if there are no multi-valued dependencies between the attributes – i.e. it forbids independent one-to-many relationships between attributes.

Assume that at our first attempt to design the BusDriver's relation we include the bus type that each driver can drive and the type of licence that each driver holds such as full driving licence, large goods vehicles (LGV) and passenger-carrying vehicles (PCV). There is in fact no real relationship between bus type and licence – they are only included together in the relation by virtue of the association with the bus driver. A sample relation might look like figure 4.24.

Figure 4.24: BusDriver relation 1 including multi-valued dependencies

BusDriver

bdNo	bdName	bdSalary	busType	licence
001	Jane Brown	1800	double-decker	
001	Jane Brown	1800	bendy bus	
001	Jane Brown	1800	metrobus	
001	Jane Brown	1800		Full
001	Jane Brown	1800		PCV
006	Sally Smith	1750	double-decker	
006	Sally Smith	1750		Full
006	Sally Smith	1750		PCV
006	Sally Smith	1750		LGV
007	James Bond	1500	bendy bus	
007	James Bond	1500	metrobus	
007	James Bond	1500		Full
008	Maggie May	2200	bendy bus	
008	Maggie May	2200		Provisional
•	•	•	•	•

So, for example, Jane Brown can drive three types of buses and has a full and a PCV licence. Notice that we might identify the primary key of this relation as the composite (bdNo, busType, licence). However, as some fields include null values this violates the entity integrity rule which states that all primary keys cannot contain null values. The relation as it stands is therefore not satisfactory as it does not contain a primary key.

There are two multi-valued dependencies in the above scheme, i.e. independent many-to-many relationships: one between attributes bdNo and busType and another between bdNo and licence. The approach taken above gives rise to repetition of data (the bus driver's name 'bdName') and null values throughout the table. Such a structure will cause insertion, deletion and update anomalies – for example if we update a bus driver's name, can we be sure that the name is updated in every row where it appears?

Another approach which reduces the size of the table and the number of null values would be to enter a busType against a licence (even although there is no relationship between the two) as in the following relation:

Figure 4.25: BusDriver version 2 including multi-valued dependencies

BusDriver

bdNo	bdName	bdSalary	busType	licence
001	Jane Brown	1800	double-decker	Full
001	Jane Brown	1800	bendy bus	PCV
001	Jane Brown	1800	metrobus	
006	Sally Smith	1750	double-decker	Full
006	Sally Smith	1750		PCV
006	Sally Smith	1750		LGV
007	James Bond	1500	bendy bus	Full
007	James Bond	1500	metrobus	
008	Maggie May	2200	bendy bus	Provisional
•	•	•	•	•

Again we have redundancy and insertion, deletion and update anomalies – for example if we delete row one because Jane Brown can no longer drive a double-decker we lose the information that she has a full licence. The solution is to divide the single relation into three – the basic bus driver details, the bus drivers' bus types and the bus drivers' licences, thus:

Figure 4.26: Relations in 4NF

BusDriver

bdNo	bdName	bdSalary
001	Jane Brown	1800
006	Sally Smith	1750
007	James Bond	1500
008	Maggie May	2200
•	•	•

BusDriverBustype

bdNo	busType
001	double-decker
001	bendy bus
001	metrobus
006	double-decker
007	bendy bus
007	metrobus
008	bendy bus
•	•

BusDriverLicence

bdNo	licence
001	Full
001	PCV
006	Full
006	PCV
006	LGV
007	Full
008	Provisional
•	•

Fifth normal form (5NF)

5NF takes the process further by removing additional redundancy by splitting relations up into ever smaller ones. A relation is in 5NF when its information cannot be reconstructed from other smaller relations.

To illustrate 5NF we examine firstly a different example which we originally looked at in our discussion of connection traps in Chapter 3. Suppose we want to hold information for race-horse stables. We might want to know about the jockeys, the horses that they ride and the races that they take part in. We might design a relation called Run which represents an outing for a jockey riding a horse in a particular race. Sample data is given below:

Figure 4.27: Relation in 5NF

Run

jockey	horse	race
Sunil	Best Mate	Gold Cup
Sunil	Desert Orchid	Grand National
Helen	Best Mate	Grand National
Helen	Laughing Boy	Gold Cup
•	•	•

We have decided to design the relation as above as we need the three attributes to know what are valid combinations of data. For example, Helen riding Best Mate in the Grand National does not imply that she rides Best Mate in the Gold Cup, which has in fact been raced by Sunil. The relation is in 5NF as we cannot decompose this relation further without losing information concerning valid combinations.

We might decide that this form is also suitable for the bus depots' database where we include the relation relating bus drivers to bus types and routes thus:

Figure 4.28: Relation not in 5NF

busDriver	busType	route
Jane Brown	double-decker	Finchley/Tottenham
Jane Brown	bendy bus	Hendon/Crouch End
James Bond	bendy bus	Finchley/Tottenham
•	•	•

Here a bus driver can drive a certain type of bus; a bus type can run on certain routes and a route can be operated by certain bus drivers. This form would be necessary if we had the rule that Jane Brown can drive double-deckers on route Finchley/Tottenham and bendy buses on route Hendon/Crouch End but cannot drive bendy buses on Finchley/Tottenham and double-deckers on Hendon/Crouch End. This rule was not part of our original scenario.

Suppose instead we had the rule: if a bus driver can operate a route, and he or she is trained to drive that bus type which can run on that route, then he or she operates that route with that bus type. In order for this data to be in 5NF we would need to reconstruct our relation into three separate smaller ones, as shown in figure 4.29. These relations are Ability, Training and Restriction, which are included in the original bus depots' scenario.

Figure 4.29: Relations decomposed into 5NF

busDriver	route
Jane Brown	Finchley/Tottenham
Jane Brown	Hendon/Crouch End
James Bond	Finchley/Tottenham
•	•

busDriver	busType
Jane Brown	double-decker
Jane Brown	bendy bus
James Bond	bendy bus
•	•

busType	route
double-decker	Finchley/Tottenham
double-decker	Hendon/Crouch End
bendy bus	Finchley/Tottenham
bendy bus	Hendon/Crouch End
•	•

With this scheme it is recorded that Jane Brown can drive both double-decker and bendy buses and can operate on routes Finchley/Tottenham and Hendon/Crouch End and there are no restrictions on combinations of these. The three relations are now in fifth normal form.

Fifth normal form deals with cases where the information content can be reconstructed from smaller relations. The term **non-loss decomposition** is used to describe such a situation, i.e. decomposition from which the original relation can be reconstructed from the resulting relations. Problems associated with fifth normal form are quite rare and when the process is carried out it aims to remove redundancy even further by splitting relations up into ever smaller ones consisting of little more than the primary keys. However, the key has to be repeated in all the related tables, thus causing additional joins for queries and redundancy of keys. In deciding whether to produce a data model in 5NF we would have to weigh up reducing data redundancy against the requirement for extra joins and redundant keys.

4.7 Review of normal forms

Details of the normal forms are given in figure 4.30.

Figure 4.30: Review of normal forms

Normal form	What it is	What process does	How it is achieved
1NF	Relation in 1NF if: • it contains scalar values only, i.e. only one value at a time	• Removes repeating groups	• Make a separate relation for each group of related attributes • Give each new relation a primary key
2NF	Relation in 2NF if: • in 1NF • all non-key attributes are dependent on the whole of the primary key and not on part of it	• Removes redundant data	• If an attribute determines only part of a multi-valued key, remove it to a separate relation
3NF	Relation in 3NF if: • in 2NF • non-key attributes are dependent on primary key and independent of each other. (This means that non-key attribute must be non-transitively dependent on the primary key; if a non-key attribute is changed, that change should not affect the others)	• Further reduces redundancy	• Make a separate relation for attributes transitively dependent on the primary key • Give each new relation a primary key • Original relation will include a foreign key to link to new relation
BCNF	Relation in BCNF if • there are non-trivial dependencies between candidate key attributes	• Further reduces redundancy	• Where there is a determinant which is not a candidate key separate it out into a distinct relation
4NF	Relation in 4NF if • in 3NF and no relation contains two or more 1:m or m:n relationships that are not directly related	• Further reduces redundancy	• Isolate independent multiple relationships making a separate relation for each multi-valued dependency • Give each new relation a foreign key which links to the original (reduced) relation
5NF	Relation in 5NF if • in 4NF and if it cannot be non-loss decomposed into smaller relations	• Further reduces redundancy but produces many small tables which may lead to extra joins and redundant keys	• Isolate semantically-related multiple relationships

There are trade-offs which database designers have to make – they have to consider the extent to which a design is normalised and the performance of the implemented system. In some designs it may be felt that the normalisation process has created too many small relations. In this case it may be necessary to **denormalise** the relations which have already been established, i.e. data in two or more normalised tables are put back into one denormalised relation. The reason for doing this is because fully normalised relations tend to perform less well when subjected to large volumes of transactions. By denormalising the data, the performance is improved as there are less joins when performing queries. Also too many small relations use more storage space. Properly normalised relations can always be put back together with no loss or gain of information.

4.8 Summary

This chapter introduced readers to normalisation as a bottom-up tool for designing data for a database system. Normalisation has the advantage over top-down modelling in being a formal technique – at each stage in the process a particular type of undesirable property or anomaly is eliminated. Three normalisation processes were described – first, second and third normal forms and also the higher normal forms of BCNF, fourth normal form and fifth normal form. By performing the normalisation process, a more flexible design is achieved and the problems of redundancy, update, deletion, and insertion anomalies are removed to a large extent.

4.9 Review questions

Review question 4.1   What is normalisation and what is its purpose?

Review question 4.2   'Help At Home' is an agency which provides various services such as baby-sitting and dog walking. Details of all bookings and a record of the service carried out are kept as in the examples shown below. Assume only one person (an employee) is involved in carrying out each particular service. An hourly rate is charged depending on the type of service required. Note that customers will be able to make only one booking for a particular service per day.

Booking record example 1

Customer name: John Smith   **Customer no:** 111
○ **Tel:**   0208 980 2223
Date of booking: 11.08.08
Type of service required: 01
Service required: Baby-sitting
Date service is required: 16.08.08
Person carrying out job: Issa Ahmed
○ **Charge per hour:**   £7
Hours: 5

Booking record example 2

Customer name: John Smith   **Customer no:** 111
○ **Tel:**   0208 980 2223
Date of booking: 18.09.08
Type of service required: 02
Service required: Dog walking
Date service is required: 30.09.08
Person carrying out job: Ben Brown
○ **Charge per hour:**   £10
Hours: 1

Discuss the problems associated with this representation above.

Review question 4.3   Extract the appropriate information from the details in review question 4.2 and write it in the form of a universal relation (un-normalised form).

Review question 4.4   Identify a primary key for the whole relation in review question 4.3.

Review question 4.5   What is the first normal form rule? Provide a determinacy diagram for the relation in the previous question.

Review question 4.6   Convert the un-normalised table in review question 4.3 into relations in first normal form.

Review question 4.7   What is the second normal form rule? From your solution to review question 4.6, produce a second normal form determinacy diagram.

Review question 4.8   Re-write the relations in review question 4.6 so that all the non-key attributes are fully functionally dependent on the primary key.

Review question 4.9   What is the third normal form rule?   From your solution to review question 4.8, produce a third normal form dependency diagram.

Review question 4.10 Re-write the relations in review question 4.8 so that all transitive dependencies are removed.

Review question 4.11 How does BCNF differ from 3NF?

Review question 4.12 Are there are disadvantages in normalising data to 5NF?

Introduction to SQL

OVERVIEW

In this chapter, the reader is introduced to the query language SQL, the standard relational database language. The reader is presented with some of the data definition features of SQL, namely the ability to create table definitions. He/she is also introduced to SQL data manipulation. The statements available to load data into tables and to change that data are discussed: insert, update and delete. We look at how the relational algebra operators project, restrict, product and join are implemented in SQL using the select statement.

Note that the example queries later in this chapter have been executed in Oracle 10g using the Bus Depots' database, which was introduced in section 4.2 of Chapter 4. Details of the sample data used can be found in the Appendix. The reader should refer to the entity-relationship diagram and the Appendix to assist in the understanding of each query execution code. In this chapter and the next, all SQL and PL/SQL code is executed using SQL*Plus, an Oracle command line utility.

Learning outcomes On completion of this chapter, you should be able to:

- Understand the data definition feature of SQL: create table

- Understand how to insert data into tables and amend and delete that data

- Understand some further basic data manipulation features of SQL – including simple select, arithmetic expressions, natural join, aggregate functions, sorting and grouping

- Understand how the relational algebra operators of project, restrict, product and join are implemented in SQL.

5.1 The SQL language

SQL standards

SQL or Structured Query Language is the standard query language for relational databases.

It allows users to create database objects and manipulate and view data. The language was originally introduced in the 1970s when IBM developed an experimental database language to support its relational database products. It soon became very successful and was taken up by commercial enterprises, including Oracle, who released the first commercial relational database management system in 1979.

SQL was adopted by the American National Standards Institute (ANSI) in 1986, and the following year the International Standards Agency (ISO, 1987) published its SQL standard.

Since then there have been further releases. The first major revision led to SQL-92, with new features such as extra types, operators, integrity constraints and scalar functions. More features were added with the next major release of the standard (SQL-99, also known as SQL3) and included facilities associated with object-oriented databases. With the SQL-2003 standard, XML-related specifications (SQL/XML) were introduced, along with OLAP (Online Analytical Processing) features, and further improvements to the previous standard such as new data types and generated columns.

At the present time a large number of database vendors are marketing numerous products based on SQL. On the whole, implementations do not conform fully to the ISO standard and manufacturers provide additional features. In the case of Oracle, it supports numerous extensions that go beyond the ISO SQL standard. In the examples in this book we will be using Oracle SQL, a partial implementation of the SQL3 standard. The latest standard, SQL:2006, further defines ways in which SQL could be used with XML (e.g. storing and querying XML data in a relational database).

In our introduction to relational database systems in Chapter 2 the formal relational terminology originally defined by Codd (such as relation, attribute and tuple) was introduced. In this chapter the ISO terminology will be mostly used (i.e. table, column and row).

Components of SQL

There are two categories of commands in SQL:

1. Data definition language (DDL) which is used to create database objects and to control access to the database.
2. Data manipulation language (DML) which is used to insert, update, delete and query data in the database.

In this chapter and the following we will be examining these in detail.

5.2 Data definition

Creating tables in SQL

The CREATE statement in SQL is used for creating a range of database objects, including tables, views and indexes. The CREATE TABLE statement has a variety of options. We will start with a simple example for creating a table called BusDriver. Note that in this example, and those which follow, we have only emboldened those reserved words which relate to the topic being discussed.

```
create table BusDriver
    (bdNo        varchar2(5),
    bdName       varchar2(20),
    bdSalary     number(6,2),
    pcvDate      date,
    dNo          varchar2(5));
```

To create a table, you specify the name of the table followed by a list of column names with their data type. Some data types available in Oracle are illustrated in the table below:

Datatype	Description	Max size (Oracle10g)
VARCHAR2(length)	Variable length character string. You must specify size	4000 bytes
NUMBER(p,s)	This is used to store general numbers. These have precision (the maximum number of digits to be stored) and scale (optional – the number of digits to the right of the decimal point)	p can range from 1 to 38; s can range from –84 to 127.
DATE	Valid date range. Used to store day, month and year fields, e.g. 19-jan-2006	from January 1, 4712 BC to December 31, 9999 AD.

Oracle provides a number of other data types including CHAR, used for fixed length strings, BLOB (binary large object) and LONG, used to store large amounts of text.

Integrity constraints

We now expand our CREATE TABLE definition to include specifications of the primary and foreign keys thus:

```
create table BusDriver
    (bdNo        varchar2(5)      Not Null,
    bdName       varchar2(20),
    bdSalary     number(6,2),
    pcvDate      date,
    dNo          varchar2(5),
    constraint pkbdNo primary key(bdNo),
    constraint fkdNo foreign key(dNo) references Depot(dNo) );
```

These additional clauses are known as **integrity constraints**. Other constraints are possible including domain constraints.

The first constraint, 'constraint pkbdNo primary key(bdNo)', which specifies the primary key, is used to ensure **entity integrity**. The entity integrity rule states that no attribute which forms part of the primary key of a relation can accept null values. This is achieved in SQL by stating the primary key in the clause and by defining the key attribute 'bdNo' as NOT NULL. Any attempt to insert a row with a null value for a primary key, or a duplicate value for a primary key within a table, will result in rejection.

The second constraint, 'constraint fkdNo foreign key(dNo) references Depot(dNo)', is used to ensure **referential integrity**. This rule states that the database must not contain any unmatched foreign key values. Put another way, a foreign key in a table such as the depot number (dNo) above, must match the primary key in another table (Depot) or be of null values. That is, if there is an attempt to insert a bus driver with a depot which does not exist in the related table Depot, then the insert will be rejected.

Defining a composite key

To define a primary key constraint where the key is made up of more than one attribute is simply done by listing all the attributes. For example the CREATE statement for the Ability table, which consists of a composite primary key (bdNo, rNo) is:

```
create table Ability
    (bdNo      varchar2(5) not null,
    rNo        varchar2(5) not null,
    constraint pkdrRoute primary key(bdNo, rNo),
    constraint fkbdNo foreign key(bdNo) references BusDriver(bdNo),
    constraint fkrNo foreign key(rNo) references Route(rNo));
```

The Check clause

The CHECK clause is a column-based constraint which allows us to specify the permitted values of a column, either the specific values or the range of values allowed. For example, if we wish to specify that a bus driver's salary must lie within a given range (more than 1500 and less than 5000):

```
create table BusDriver
    (bdNo       varchar2(5) not null,
    bdName      varchar2(20),
    bdSalary    number(6,2),
    pcvDate     date,
    dNo         varchar2(5),
    constraint pkbdNo primary key(bdNo),
    constraint fkdNo foreign key(dNo) references Depot(dNo),
    constraint bdSal check( bdSalary>1500 and bdSalary <5000));
```

The Default clause

We can make sure that the DBMS automatically inserts a default value for an attribute. This value will be used whenever a row is inserted and there is a null value for that particular attribute. For example, if we wish the bus driver's depot to default to depot 101:

```
create table BusDriver
    (bdNo       varchar2(5),
    bdName     varchar2(20),
    bdSalary   number(6,2),
    pcvDate    date,
    dNo        varchar2(5) default '101',
    constraint pkbdNo primary key(bdNo),
    constraint fkdNo foreign key(dNo) references Depot(dNo));
```

Note that this constraint is placed in the column declaration.

Modifying a table definition

The ALTER statement can be used when there is a requirement to modify the structure of an existing table. For example, if we wish to add a new column 'telephone number' to the depot table:

alter table Depot
add telephoneNumber varchar2(10);

To change the name of this column

alter table Depot
rename column telephoneNumber to telNo;

To delete this column

alter table Depot
drop column telNo;

Dropping tables

To remove a table from the database, the Drop Table statement is used. For example:

drop table BusDriver;

The drop table statement as shown here will not drop a table if it is linked to another through a foreign key. To avoid this problem we use:

drop table <tablename> **cascade constraints**;

5.3 Data manipulation: loading the tables

We now look at some data manipulation statements: INSERT, UPDATE and DELETE. The data manipulation statement SELECT will be introduced in the next section.

Adding new rows to a table: Insert

The INSERT statement is used to add rows to an existing table. The following example inserts a single row into the bus drivers' table:

insert into BusDriver
values ('101','Paresh Patel',1900,'09-feb-2006','101');

Note that attributes which have been defined as type varchar are surrounded by single quotes.

Changing data in a table: Update

The UPDATE statement is used to change the values of existing data in a table. For example the following query increases James Bond's salary by 10%:

```
update BusDriver
set bdSalary = bdSalary*1.1
where bdName = 'James Bond';
```

Note that the WHERE clause is optional. It is also possible to include a SELECT statement that can be used to return values to which the updated columns will be set. In the following example, James Bond's row is updated, setting his depot number to the one for Islington.

```
update BusDriver
set dNo =
   (select dNo
   from Depot
   where dName = 'Islington')
where bdName = 'James Bond';
```

Removing data in a table: Delete

The DELETE is used to remove rows from a table. For example, to delete James Bond's record:

```
delete from BusDriver
where bdName = 'James Bond';
```

We can also remove a number of rows at a time. For example, to delete all bus drivers who work at the Islington depot:

```
delete from BusDriver
where dNo in
   (select dNo
   from Depot
   where dName = 'Islington');
```

Again this example includes a SELECT statement. It returns the dNo for the Islington depot. We will see in the next section how powerful this statement is.

5.4 Data manipulation: the select statement

SQL data manipulation and relational algebra (RA)

We have seen in Chapter 2 that the manipulative part of the relational model consists of a set of operators known collectively as relational algebra. The eight relational algebra operators originally defined by Codd are listed below. If you have forgotten the details, go over the relational algebra operations in Chapter 2.

Set operators:	UNION	INTERSECTION
	DIFFERENCE	Cartesian PRODUCT
The special relational operators:	RESTRICT	PROJECT
	JOIN	DIVIDE

Implementing RA operations in SQL

As we have seen in Chapter 2, relational algebra (RA) is used as the basis for other, higher-level data manipulation languages including SQL. RA is also used as a measure to compare high-level relational languages (such as SQL), to test if the language is relationally complete – i.e. to check if the query language is as powerful as the algebra.

We now look (in this chapter and the following chapter) at how these operations have been implemented in SQL. The RA operations all take one or more relations and generate a new relation from this. In SQL this is achieved with different forms of the SELECT statement.

The SELECT statement

The SELECT statement is used to query data in the database. A simplified general form of the SELECT statement is given below:

```
SELECT [DISTINCT | ALL] <*| output columns >
   FROM <input tables>
[WHERE <search condition> ]
[GROUP BY <grouping columns>  [HAVING condition] ]
[{UNION | UNION ALL | INTERSECT | MINUS} SELECT command ]
[ORDER BY <ordering columns>  [ASC | DESC]
```

where standard symbols are used: [ ] means optional; | indicates choice of alternatives and < > indicates one or more.

The following table describes the purpose of a number of the clauses in the SELECT statement.

SELECT clause	Purpose
SELECT [DISTINCT] <output columns >	specifies columns in output
FROM <input tables>	specifies tables used in query
WHERE <search condition>	eliminates unwanted rows
GROUP BY <grouping columns>	groups rows
HAVING <condition>	eliminates unwanted groups
ORDER BY <ordering columns>	sorts rows

Some simple examples of SELECT statements are given below:

1. **select** bdName
   from BusDriver;

2. **select** *
   from BusDriver
   where bdName = 'Peter Piper';

Note: the semi-colon (;) at the end of the above examples (and, indeed, all SQL statements, including data definition and data manipulation statements) acts as a separator between statements. The semi-colon is not strictly required when executing only one statement.

All SELECT statement will have the two clauses: SELECT and FROM. The FROM clause specifies the table or tables to be used (BusDriver in both previous examples). The SELECT clause specifies the columns, which will appear in the output – bdName in the first example.

In the second example an asterisk (*) is used in place of a column name or names. This causes all columns or attributes of the specified table to be output.

Implementing RA restriction

Restriction generates the output from those rows that satisfy a condition, e.g. list details of bus drivers who have passed their PCV driving test after 09-jan-2000.

BDNO	BDNAME	BDSALARY	PCVDATE	DNO
001	Jane Brown	1800	09-FEB-85	101
006	Sally Smith	1750	09-MAR-96	
007	James Bond	1500	09-JAN-99	102
008	Maggie May	2200	09-JAN-00	102
009	Jack Jones	1400	09-AUG-01	101
010	Peter Piper	3500	09-JUN-04	104
011	John Peel	2000	09-FEB-05	102

In SQL a **search condition** is included in the WHERE clause to restrict the output.

```
select *
from BusDriver
where pcvDate > '09-jan-2000';
```

Implementing RA projection

Projection outputs a subset of the attributes of all rows, e.g. list registration numbers with models.

REGNO	MODEL	TNO	DNO	CNO
A123ABC	Routemaster	1	101	110
D678FGH	Volvo 8700	2	101	110
D345GGG	Volvo 8500	1	101	112
H259IJK	Daf SB220	3	102	114
P200IJK	Mercedes 709D	2	102	113
P300RTY	Mercedes Citaro	4	102	113
R678FDS	Daf SB220	1		110

In SQL the desired attributes are listed in the SELECT clause.

  select regNo,model
  from Bus;

The following example illustrates the two relational algebra operations of restriction and projection, i.e. it lists the number and salary of bus driver Peter Piper.

  select bdNo, bdSalary
  from BusDriver
  where bdName = 'Peter Piper';

Calculated values

Arithmetic expressions can be used in both the SELECT clause and the WHERE clauses. So, for example, if we wanted to display the annual salary of the cleaners based at depot 101:

  select cName, cSalary *12
  from Cleaner
  where dNo = '101';

This gives the following output based on our sample data (see Appendix):

CNAME	CSALARY*12
John	30600
Jean	30000

Note that the output data is displayed as above but the data in the database remains unchanged.

Naming query columns

Notice that the column heading in the above example is the arithmetic expression itself. We are able to change the heading for any attribute to make it more readable:

  select cName, cSalary *12 "annual salary"
  from Cleaner
  where dNo = '101';

giving a result this time of:

CNAME	annual salary
John	30600
Jean	30000

DISTINCT and ALL

The keyword DISTINCT is used in the SELECT clause to suppress unwanted duplicate rows. So, for example, to list the bus drivers' numbers of those who have done training since 09-feb-2006:

select distinct bdNo
from Training
where trainingDate >'09-feb-2006' ;

This gives the following output from our sample data. Note that if DISTINCT is omitted the default is ALL and in this case all 11 rows would be output with a number of duplicated rows.

BDNO
008
011
007
009

Retrieving from a list of values using IN

If we wish to search for values in a given list, we can use the IN predicate. The example below is to list the names of bus drivers who belong to depots who have the depot numbers 101 or 102. Note that NOT IN is also allowed.

select bdName
from BusDriver
where dNo **in** ('101','102');

Querying over a range of values

When we wish to test whether a value falls within a certain range, we use the keyword BETWEEN. For example, to find names of bus drivers who earn >=2000 and <=3000:

select bdName, bdSalary
from BusDriver
where bdSalary **between** 2000 **and** 3000;

BDNAME	BDSALARY
Maggie May	2200
John Peel	2000

Searching for partial matches

The LIKE keyword is used for pattern matching, that is, it allows us to search for items when we only know part of a character string value. LIKE is used along with the symbol '%' and '_':

- % means zero or more characters
- _ (underscore) means exactly one character.

The following two queries are used to find bus details of type Mercedes and cleaners' names with exactly four characters beginning with 'J' and ending in 'n'. (This will output John and Jean.)

> **select** *
> **from** Bus
> **where** model **like** 'Mercedes%';
>
> **select** cName
> **from** Cleaner
> **where** cName **like** 'J__n';

Testing for null values in a table

IS NULL and IS NOT NULL are used to test for the presence or absence of a null value in a field. From Chapter 2 you may recall that null values are used either when the value of a field is unknown at the time when the record was entered, or was not applicable to that field for that particular record. So, for example, we might want to find all bus drivers who have not been assigned to a depot. In this case we could assume the information was not known when the row was inserted.

> **select** bdName
> **from** BusDriver
> **where** dNo **is null;**

BDNAME
Sally Smith

Extending the WHERE clause using AND, OR

The general form of the select clause which we saw above can now be given in more detail:

> SELECT [DISTINCT | ALL] <*| output columns >
> FROM <input tables>
> [WHERE < search condition> < AND/OR search condition>]

SQL provides a number of operators and keywords for use in the search condition. We have already seen examples of the normal comparison operators =, <, > and so on. We have also seen IN, BETWEEN, LIKE and IS NULL. Each of these can be combined with NOT. We can also combine search conditions by using the logical operators AND and OR.

For example, to find bus drivers who earn less than 1750 *and* have a PCV date later than 09-jan-1999:

> **select** *
> **from** BusDriver
> **where** bdSalary < 1750
> **and** pcvdate >'09-jan-1999';

BDNO	BDNAME	BDSALARY	PCVDATE	DNO
009	Jack Jones	1400	09-AUG-01	101

Alternatively, to find bus drivers who earn less than 1750 *or* have a PCV date later than 09-jan-1999:

> **select** *
> **from** BusDriver
> **where** bdSalary < 1750
> **or** pcvdate >'09-jan-1999';

BDNO	BDNAME	BDSALARY	PCVDATE	DNO
007	James Bond	1500	09-JAN-99	102
008	Maggie May	2200	09-JAN-00	102
009	Jack Jones	1400	09-AUG-01	101
010	Peter Piper	3500	09-JUN-04	104
011	John Peel	2000	09-FEB-05	102

Aggregate functions

SQL provides a wide range of predefined functions to perform manipulation of data. There are four types of functions: arithmetic, date, character and aggregate. Examples of **arithmetic** are *sqrt* (square root), *round* (used for rounding numbers) and *least* (for returning the smallest value in a list). Examples of **date** functions are *sysdate* (current date) and *months_between* (returns the number of months between two dates). **Character** functions include *length* (returns the length of a string) and *lower* (converts a string to all lower-case characters).

We shall examine **aggregate functions** here. This type of function is applied to sets of rows in a table and returns a summary value – always one. For example, in the bus driver's table we might want to find the minimum and maximum salary, the average salary, the total salary bill and the number of bus drivers.

For this type of query, SQL has provided the following aggregate functions:

Function	Meaning	Example
min(expression)	Returns the lowest value of a specified column	min(bdSalary)
max(expression)	Returns the highest value of a specified column	max(bdSalary)
avg(expression)	Returns the average of the values of a specified column. It will ignore null values	avg(bdSalary)
sum(expression)	Returns the sum of the values of a specified column	sum(bdSalary)
count(expression) or count(*)	Returns the number of rows in the specified table (i.e. only the number of rows in which the expression is not null). count(*) counts all rows	Examples: count (*) count (bdNo)

The following example is to find the oldest and latest training dates for bus driver 007.

```
select min(trainingDate), max(trainingDate)
from Training
where bdNo = '007';
```

min(trainingDate)	max(trainingDate)
09-FEB-06	09-MAR-06

Implementing RA Cartesian product

In SQL, if you specify more that one table in a SELECT clause with no 'WHERE condition', then you automatically get the product of the tables. For example:

```
select *
from Bus, Depot;
```

This query will give every combination of bus and depot in the database, whether the bus is connected to that depot or not. Note that it is unusual for a query to require the use of product: all further examples and exercises will not involve a product of this type. There are cases, however, where a product is required, and Oracle has implemented the CROSS JOIN syntax to explicitly perform a product. The real importance of the product operator is that it is the basis of all join operators. A join is the projection and restriction of the product of tables. Note that a common SQL error is to perform a product where a join was intended.

Implementing RA join

A join involves linking two tables together by combining rows that are related to each other in some way. A join of two relations is equivalent to a restriction of a product of the two relations. More than two tables can be specified but they have to be joined two at a time. There are a number of categories of joins including natural joins, equi and non-equi, inner and outer joins.

An **equi-join** joins tables together on columns which have some shared characteristic. The column (or columns) from each of the two participating relations must be linked in some way – very often (but not exclusively) the primary key in one table is linked to the foreign key in the other. In an equi-join both of these linked columns will be displayed. For example we want to list buses plus information about the depot where the bus is based. We need therefore to join the Bus relation to the Depot relation. To do this we must specify the **join condition** for the columns to be paired:

select *
from Bus, Depot
where Bus.dNo = Depot.dNo;

giving:

REGNO	MODEL	TNO	DNO	CNO	DNO	DNAME	DADDRESS
A123ABC	Routemaster	1	101	110	101	Holloway	Camden Road
D678FGH	Volvo 8700	2	101	110	101	Holloway	Camden Road
D345GGG	Volvo 8500	1	101	112	101	Holloway	Camden Road
H259IJK	Daf SB220	3	102	114	102	Hornsey	High Road
P200IJK	Mercedes 709D	2	102	113	102	Hornsey	High Road
P300RTY	Mercedes Citaro	4	102	113	102	Hornsey	High Road

Oracle uses the equi-join as the default display (i.e. both columns are output). To avoid this we can project only those columns that we require or specify a natural join. The **natural join** is a special case of an equi-join but the join column (or columns) is displayed once only. To get the natural join of Bus and Depot:

select *
from Bus
natural join Depot;

DNO	REGNO	MODEL	TNO	CNO	DNAME	DADDRESS
101	A123ABC	Routemaster	1	110	Holloway	Camden Road
101	D678FGH	Volvo 8700	2	110	Holloway	Camden Road
101	D345GGG	Volvo 8500	1	112	Holloway	Camden Road
102	H259IJK	Daf SB220	3	114	Hornsey	High Road
102	P200IJK	Mercedes 709D	2	113	Hornsey	High Road
102	P300RTY	Mercedes Citaro	4	113	Hornsey	High Road

Using the natural join as above can produce some unexpected results. For example notice what happens when you produce an equi-join of Bus and Cleaner and then a natural join of Bus and Cleaner.

select *
from Bus, Cleaner
where Bus.cNo = Cleaner.cNo;

select *
from Bus
natural join Cleaner;

The equi-join, using the primary/foreign key join condition in this example, gives the expected result of the cleaners and their buses. However the natural join will base the join on other columns where there are common attributes – in this example the depot number (dNo) as well as the cleaner number (cNo), to give some odd results. In the rest of this book, where there are SQL examples involving join, the join condition will normally be used.

Using an alias in a multi-table join

The above query (the equi-join) can also be done using aliases. An alias is an abbreviation for a table name, such as 'b' for the Bus table. In this case, 'b' is used anywhere in the query to replace the table name 'Bus', apart from the table named in the FROM clause.

select *
from Bus b, Cleaner c
where b.cNo = c.cNo;

For all subsequent examples involving multi-table joins, aliases will be used. We shall see later that aliases are required for naming tables when there is the possibility of ambiguity.

Inner joins

The previous example, besides being a natural join is also an example of an **inner join**. An inner join retrieves data only from those rows where the join condition is met. The example below shows that rows that do not have a match are not included in the output.

Given the two tables Cleaner and Depot:

select * **from** Cleaner;

CNO	CNAME	CSALARY	DNO
110	John	2550	101
111	Jean	2500	101
112	Betty	2400	102
113	Vince	2800	102
114	Jay	3000	102
115	Doug	2000	102
116	Geeta	4000	

select * **from** Depot;

DNO	DNAME	DADDRESS
101	Holloway	Camden Road
102	Hornsey	High Road
104	Islington	Upper Street

The inner join of these tables gives the cleaners and the depots at which each cleaner is based, but only for those cleaners who are actually based at a depot. Cleaners who have not been assigned to a depot are not output.

> **select** *
> **from** Cleaner c, Depot d
> **where** c.dNo = d.dNo;

gives a result of 6 rows of output rather than 7, which might have been expected:

CNO	CNAME	CSALARY	DNO	DNO	DNAME	DADDRESS
110	John	2550	101	101	Holloway	Camden Road
111	Jean	2500	101	101	Holloway	Camden Road
112	Betty	2400	102	102	Hornsey	High Road
113	Vince	2800	102	102	Hornsey	High Road
114	Jay	3000	102	102	Hornsey	High Road
115	Doug	2000	102	102	Hornsey	High Road

Cleaner '116 Geeta', who is not based at a depot, is not output. Note that we have used aliases in our example 'Cleaner c, Depot d'.

We can also explicitly state that we require an inner join with the same results as before:

> select *
> from Cleaner c
> **inner join** Depot d
> **on** c.dNo = d.dNo;

Outer joins

Unmatched rows can be included in the output using an outer join. An outer join therefore shows the joined rows plus the rows which did not match in the first-named table (**left outer join**) or the second-named table (**right outer join**) or both tables (**full outer join**).

So we implement a left outer join to find the cleaners and the depots at which they are based, and also include those cleaners who have not been assigned to a depot:

> **select** *
> **from** Cleaner c
> **left** join Depot d
> **on** c.dNo = d.dNo;

CNO	CNAME	CSALARY	DNO	DNO	DNAME	DADDRESS
111	Jean	2500	101	101	Holloway	Camden Road
110	John	2550	101	101	Holloway	Camden Road
115	Doug	2000	102	102	Hornsey	High Road
114	Jay	3000	102	102	Hornsey	High Road
113	Vince	2800	102	102	Hornsey	High Road
112	Betty	2400	102	102	Hornsey	High Road
116	Geeta	4000				

Note that 7 rows are output including Geeta's information. To find the cleaners and the depots at which they are based, and also include those depots where no cleaners are assigned:

> **select** *
> **from** Cleaner c
> **right join** Depot d
> **on** c.dNo = d.dNo;

CNO	CNAME	CSALARY	DNO	DNO	DNAME	DADDRESS
110	John	2550	101	101	Holloway	Camden Road
111	Jean	2500	101	101	Holloway	Camden Road
112	Betty	2400	102	102	Hornsey	High Road
113	Vince	2800	102	102	Hornsey	High Road
114	Jay	3000	102	102	Hornsey	High Road
115	Doug	2000	102	102	Hornsey	High Road
				104	Islington	Upper Street

A **full outer join** combines the results of both left and right outer joins. The joined table will contain all records from both tables and, as before, will fill in nulls for missing data. So, to find the cleaners and the depots at which they are based, and also include those cleaners who have not been assigned to a depot and those depots where no cleaners are assigned:

> **select** *
> **from** Cleaner c
> **full outer join** Depot d
> **on** c.dNo = d.dNo;

Group by

Rows of data can be grouped in a table using the GROUP BY clause. This is particularly useful for when you wish to get the aggregate properties of values in the group. For example, to count the number of bus drivers who are based at each depot:

> **select** dNo, count(bdNo)
> **from** BusDriver
> **group by** dNo;

DNO	COUNT(BDNO)
101	2
	1
102	3
104	1

Notice that bus drivers who are not assigned to a depot are also included in the output. In the next example, multiple tables are specified (BusType, Bus and Depot) and the GROUP BY clause includes more than one column. The query is to list, for each depot, the types of buses based at the depot and a count of models of that type.

> **select** d.dName, tDescript, count(model)
> **from** Bustype bt, Bus b, Depot d
> **where** bt.tNo = b.tNo
> **and** d.dNo = b.dNo
> **group** by d.dName, tDescript;

DNAME	TDESCRIPT	COUNT(MODEL)
Holloway	doubledecker	2
Hornsey	midibus	1
Hornsey	bendy bus	1
Holloway	metrobus	1
Hornsey	metrobus	1

In the above example we have created a new relation when we joined the three tables together – i.e. the depots with their buses and the bus types of each bus. Within the table we have grouped the depots together (using depot name) and within each depot we have grouped the models together (by description) and counted these models.

The example above assumes that depot names and bus type descriptions are unique. Often this is not the case with names. For example, if we wanted to group the bus drivers by driver name, then the names may well not be unique. If there is a possibility that data items in columns are not unique, then the primary key of the table should be included in the GROUP BY clause, for example:

> **Group by** bdNo, bdName

Note that a common error when using the GROUP BY clause is:

> ORA-00979: not a GROUP BY expression

This is when you are trying to output values in the attribute list (columns) which are not single-valued in the group. For example:

> **select** dNo, bdSalary, count(bdNo)
> **from** BusDriver
> **group by** dNo;

The above query would produce an error message. This is because there are a number of bus driver salaries for each depot, and therefore bdSalary is not single-valued for the group.

Group by having

The HAVING clause can be included with GROUP BY and is used to eliminate unwanted groups. So, for example, to count the number of buses looked after by cleaners, excluding cleaners who look after less than 2 buses:

> **select** cName, count(regNo) "buses"
> **from** Bus b, Cleaner c
> **where** b.cNo = c.cNo
> **group by** c.cNo,cName
> **having** count(regNo) >1;

CNAME	buses
John	3
Vince	2

Sorting data

To sort data in a table (or joined tables) we use the ORDER BY clause. You can specify one or more columns as the sort key. For example, to sort the data in the Bustype table, ordered by type description:

> **select** *
> **from** BusType
> **order by** tDescript;

TNO	TDESCRIPT
4	bendy bus
1	doubledecker
2	metrobus
3	midibus
5	open top

By default, ORDER BY sorts in ascending order. To sort in descending order, the reserved word DESC is provided:

order by tDescript **desc;**

SQL also allows a sort within a sort. For example, list details of buses ordered by registration number within depot where the buses are based:

select dNo, regNo, model
from Bus
order by dNo, regNo;

DNO	REGNO	MODEL
101	A123ABC	Routemaster
101	D345GGG	Volvo 8500
101	D678FGH	Volvo 8700
102	H259IJK	Daf SB220
102	P200IJK	Mercedes 709D
102	P300RTY	Mercedes Citaro
	R678FDS	Daf SB220

It sorts the bus table using the first attribute in the ORDER BY list (dNo) and then uses the second attribute (regNo) to sort the registration numbers within each depot grouping.

5.5 Summary

This chapter introduced the reader to the query language SQL. The reader gained knowledge of the SQL data definition CREATE statement and the data manipulation statements of INSERT, UPDATE, DELETE and SELECT. For the SELECT statement we focused on understanding how the relational algebra operators (restrict, project, Cartesian product and join) are implemented in SQL using this statement.

5.6 Review questions

Review question 5.1   Explain the purpose of the integrity constraint, in the SQL *CREATE table* statement, relating to primary keys.

Review question 5.2   Explain the purpose of the integrity constraint, in the SQL *CREATE table* statement, relating to foreign keys.

Review question 5.3   How can we test if SQL is relationally complete?

Review question 5.4   How are the relational algebra commands 'restriction' and 'projection' implemented in SQL? Give examples of SQL queries to illustrate these.

Review question 5.5   A programmer wrote the following code. Give the English meaning of the code (from a user point of view). Now rewrite this code using aliases for table names.

```
select BusDriver.bdNo, bdName, dName
from BusDriver, Depot
where BusDriver.dNo = Depot.dNo
and bdName = 'James Bond';
```

Review question 5.6   A programmer wrote the following code to list the buses for which cleaner Vince is responsible. Comment on the code.

```
select regNo, model
from Bus, Cleaner
where cName = 'Vince';
```

Review question 5.7   What are aggregate functions? Describe the aggregate functions that SQL has provided.

Review question 5.8   What is the difference between an inner and outer join? How is the outer join implemented in Oracle's SQL?

Review question 5.9   Explain how the GROUP BY clause works. What restrictions exist on the contents of a select-list (i.e. first line of the SELECT statement) which appear in the same query as a GROUP BY clause?

Review question 5.10   What is the difference between the WHERE and the HAVING clauses?

Review question 5.11   The following is part of a larger relation diagram for a hospital. This subsystem concerns data about doctors who work at the hospital and the diagnoses that they make. It is assumed that the Patient entity exists with primary key patientNo, but it is not shown here. Each time a diagnosis (such as 'Broken Limb' or 'Multiple Sclerosis') is made on a patient, this is recorded showing the date and the doctor who carried out the procedure. The diagnosis is expressed as a code number called an SDC number (standard diagnostic category). The hospital keeps lists of diagnoses, together with estimates of the cost of treating a patient with this condition and the number of days of hospitalisation required:

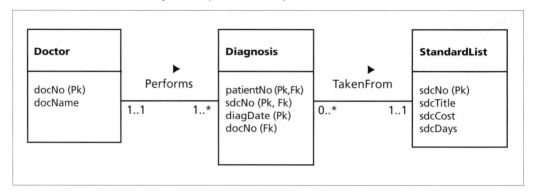

Give the English meaning of the following SQL command:

```
select  d.docName, sdc.sdcTitle, count(*),
    sum(sdc.sdcCost), sum(sdc.sdcDays)
from Doctor d, Diagnosis dg, StandardList sdc
where d.docNo = dg.docNo
and   dg.sdcNo = sdc.sdcNo
group by d.docNo, d.docName, sdc.sdcNo, sdc.sdcTitle
having sum(sdc.sdcCost) > 1000;
```

Review question 5.12   What is the difference between the GROUP BY and the ORDER BY clauses?

Review question 5.13   In SQL can I just ask for the first three rows in a table?

Further SQL & PL/SQL

OVERVIEW

In this chapter we again focus on **SQL**, introducing some additional features. We have already looked at the relational algebra operations project, restrict, product and join, and their implementation in SQL: we now examine the implementation of the other relational algebra operators, namely **union**, **intersection**, **difference** and **divide**. For the latter, the EXISTS and NOT EXISTS constructs are introduced. We also look further at joins: **self-joined tables** and **non-equi joins**, where we join tables on the basis of an operation other than equality. SQL often has more than one alternative for performing a query and sometimes **subqueries** can be used instead of joins. Subqueries are important in their own right and we will look at the two types: **noncorrelated** and **correlated subqueries**. Other features of SQL will be explained and investigated including **views** and running SQL **queries interactively**.

This chapter also introduces you to **PL/SQL**, Oracle's procedural language. The syntax and constructs will be looked at; in particular, **stored procedures** and **database triggers** will be examined. These features have been made available in a number of DBMSs including Oracle and are used for storing and applying logic at the database level rather than at application level. They provide those DBMSs with greater flexibility and power in dealing with complexities of many demanding business applications.

Learning outcomes   On completion of this chapter, you should be able to:

- Understand how the relational algebra operators – union, intersection, difference and divide – are implemented in SQL

- Understand features of SQL including self-joins, non-equi joins, subqueries, correlated subqueries, set comparison operators, existential qualification and views

- Understand how SQL has been extended procedurally into PL/SQL

- Explain how stored procedures and database triggers can be used to implement processing logic at the database level

---

Note that the example queries later in this chapter have been executed in Oracle 10g using the Bus Depots' database which was given in section 4.2. You will find details of the sample data used in the Appendix. You should refer to the entity-relationship diagram and the Appendix to assist in your understanding of each query execution code.

6.1 **Recursive relationships and self-joins**

In Chapter 3 we looked at recursive relationships, where an entity occurrence can relate to other occurrences of the same entity. The Bus Depots' database does not contain any obvious recursive relationships; however, by way of example, we could identify the following:

Figure 6.1: Recursive relationship examples

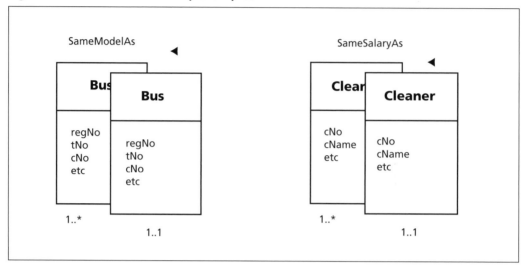

SQL allows you to join the same table together by using aliases. As we saw in the previous chapter, an alias is an alternative name for a table.

So for the query 'Find any buses which are the same model as bus H259IJK' then the SQL is:

> **select** b2.*
> **from** Bus b1, Bus b2
> **where** b1.regNo = 'H259IJK'
> **and** b1.model = b2.model;

which outputs:

REGNO	MODEL	TNO	DNO	CNO
H259IJK	Daf SB220	3	102	114
R678FDS	Daf SB220	1		110

You can think of the tables b1 and b2 as being two copies of the same Bus table, each with one alias name. Table b1 is used to search for 'H259IJK's record. Table b2 is used to find those records with the same model as b1 (i.e. 'H259IJK'). The tables have been joined in the usual way with a join condition. Notice that in the SELECT clause (the first line of the statement) you need to specify which table the output should come from – in this case b2. Note that to omit H259IJK from the final output we add the line:

> **and** b2.regNo <> 'H259IJK';

Another example illustrating a self-join

Suppose we want to list the names of cleaners who are responsible for any bus types that cleaner Betty is responsible for. This uses the Bus and Cleaner tables thus:

Figure 6.2: ResponsibleFor example

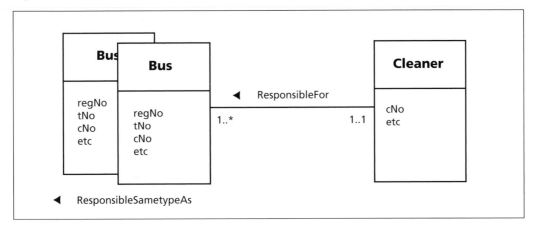

The **ResponsibleFor** relationship shows which rows are related to Betty's – i.e. Betty's buses; the **ResponsibleSameTypeAs** relationship finds all rows linked to those bus types. The ResponsibleFor relationship is used again to find who is linked to these bus types.

In SQL:

```
1  select distinct c2.cName
2  from    Bus b1, Bus b2,
3          Cleaner c1, Cleaner c2
4  where c1.cName = 'Betty'
5  and c1.cNo = b1.cNo
6  and b1.tNo = b2.tNo
7  and b2.cNo = c2.cNo
8  and c2.cName <> 'Betty';
```

CNAME
John

The code above is explained using the line numbers:

- Line 4: The copy of the Cleaner table (c1) is used to identify Betty's record(s) in the Cleaner table
- Line 5: The rows identified at 4 are joined to the copy of the Bus table (b1) to find the bus types for which Betty is responsible
- Line 6: The rows identified at 5 are joined, using the recursive relationship ResponsibleSameTypeAs, to find all rows for the same bus types in Bus (alias b2)
- Line 7: The rows identified at 6 are joined to a second copy of Cleaner (c2) to get all cleaner information for cleaners responsible for the same bus types as Betty
- Line 8: Lastly, Betty is eliminated from the output.

6.2 Subqueries

Subqueries using IN

In addition to joining tables together using a join condition, SQL provides an additional way of handling queries involving multiple tables – i.e. using subqueries. In a subquery, a SELECT statement (the inner SELECT) can be embedded inside the WHERE clause of a main SELECT query (the outer SELECT). To understand how a subquery is evaluated, consider the following example, to find cleaners who have been allocated to a bus:

```
select cName
from Cleaner
where cNo in
    (select cNo
     from  Bus);
```

CNAME
John
Betty
Vince
Jay

In a subquery the inner SELECT executes first and the result is passed to the outer SELECT. So in the example, 'select cNo from Bus' is evaluated and the result, i.e. all the cleaner numbers in the Bus table, is passed to the outer SELECT, so that the cleaner names for these cleaners can be output.

Note that the operator IN is used where the subquery returns a set of items in a column (zero or more). Other subquery operators are ANY, ALL and EXISTS. These are discussed later in the chapter. In the examples we have considered above, the subquery is embedded in the WHERE clause. Note that it is also possible to include subqueries in the SELECT and FROM clauses.

Subqueries using NOT IN

The keyword NOT can be used with the IN operator – this specifies that all rows are retrieved (from the table(s) in the outer SELECT) except for those rows that are returned by the inner SELECT. The following example finds those cleaners who have not been allocated to a bus:

```
select cName
from Cleaner
where cNo not in
    (select cNo
     from  Bus);
```

CNAME
Jean
Doug
Geeta

Subqueries using ANY and ALL

So far we have looked at subqueries which return zero or more values and have used the keywords IN or NOT IN. SQL also allows for the subquery to be preceded by a comparison operator and the keyword ANY or ALL.

If a subquery is executed which includes a comparison operator and ANY, this means that the condition will be true if it is satisfied by one or more values (i.e. any values) which the subquery returns. So, assuming the comparison operator is 'greater than'(>) then, >ANY means greater than at least one value, i.e. greater than the smallest value.

As an example we could find all those bus drivers whose salary is greater than the smallest salary in the Cleaner table.

```
select bdName
from BusDriver
where bdSalary > any
    (select cSalary
    from Cleaner);
```

BDNAME
Peter Piper
Maggie May

If a subquery is executed which includes a comparison operator and ALL, this means that the condition will be true if it is satisfied by all the values which the subquery returns. So, assuming the comparison operator is 'greater than', then >ALL means greater than every value, which amounts to greater than the greatest value.

As an example we could find all those cleaners whose salary is greater than the largest salary in the BusDriver table.

```
select cName
from Cleaner
where cSalary > all
    (select bdSalary
    from BusDriver);
```

CNAME
Geeta

Subqueries that return a single value

Where the inner SELECT returns a single value, the comparison operator '=' can be used. For example, to find any cleaners by name, whose earnings are exactly equal to the average cleaner's salary:

> **select** cName
> **from** Cleaner
> **where** cSalary =
>   (**select** avg(cSalary)
>   **from** Cleaner);

This example query will produce no rows. Note that other operators such as > or >= can also be used in subqueries instead of =.

Nested subqueries

Subqueries can be created to multiple levels. However, subqueries take longer to execute than joins, so deep levels of subqueries are not recommended. An example of a nested subquery is given, to find names of bus drivers who are trained to drive bendy buses.

> **select** bdName
> **from** BusDriver
> **where** bdNo **in**
>   (**select** bdNo
>   **from** Training
>   **where** tNo **in**
>   (**select** tNo
>   **from** BusType
>   **where** tDescript = 'bendy bus'));

BDNAME
Maggie May
John Peel
Jack Jones

6.3 The non-equi-join

So far we have looked at equi-joins, i.e. we have joined tables on the basis of equality between common attributes. The non-equi-join, which must be used carefully, is a join based on any valid comparison operator, such as <>, > ,=<. It is equivalent to taking the product of two relations and then performing the appropriate restriction on the result. Examples may involve recursive relationships, e.g. Which cleaners have a lower salary than cleaner Betty?

In SQL:

```
select c1.cName
from Cleaner c1, Cleaner c2
where c2.cName = 'Betty'
and c1.cSalary < c2.cSalary;
```

CNAME
Doug

Subqueries and the non-equi join

Note that a common SQL error is to use a non-equi join where only a subquery will give the correct results. So, for example, if it is required to find the bus drivers who are not qualified to drive bus type 2, a programmer might write the query as follows:

```
select distinct bdName
from Busdriver bd, Training t
where tNo = '2'
and bd.bdNo <> t.bdNo;
```

BDNAME
Maggie May
Jack Jones
Jane Brown
Sally Smith
Peter Piper
James Bond
John Peel

The result here is all the bus drivers, which is not what the programmer expected. What the programmer has, in fact, done is to consider each bus driver in turn and compared this record with each one in the Training table. Those bus driver names are printed where there is a record in the Training table with type '2' that has a different bus driver number. All drivers fall into this category so the names of all bus drivers will be output. The correct solution is to use a subquery with NOT IN.

```
select bdName
from Busdriver
where bdNo not in
    (select bdNo
    from Training
    where tNo = '2');
```

BDNAME
Jack Jones
Peter Piper

As illustrated by the foregoing example we cannot use a non-equi-join in place of NOT IN, i.e. NOT IN does not have the same relationship to negative joins as IN does to the equi-join. NOT IN looks for no matches while the non-equi-join forms a product of the tables (i.e. every combination) and then eliminates those rows in the join condition.

6.4 Correlated subqueries

A correlated subquery is one where information from the outer SELECT statement is referenced in the subquery. The subquery is executed differently from the non-correlated subqueries we saw earlier. Then it was executed from the bottom up. With correlated subqueries, on the other hand, the outer SELECT is executed first and provides the values, one at a time, for the evaluation of the inner subquery.

Steps to execute a correlated subquery

1. The outer query fetches a row
2. The inner query is executed, using the value from the row fetched in step 1
3. Data from the row fetched in step 1 will be selected and output depending on the values returned by the execution of the inner query
4. Repeat until no rows (outer query).

Example of correlated subquery

We can use a correlated subquery, for example, to find cleaners who earn less than the average salary for their depot:

```
select cName
from Cleaner c1
where cSalary <
   (select avg(cSalary)
   from Cleaner c2
   where c1.dNo = c2.dNo);
```

CNAME
Jean
Betty
Doug

We can see that this is a correlated subquery, since we have used an attribute (c1.dNo) in the WHERE clause of the inner SELECT. The table c1 was, however, specified in the outer SELECT. Note that the alias is necessary only to avoid ambiguity in column names.

6.5 Set operators

We now look at the implentation in SQL of the RA set operators **union**, **intersection** and **difference**. It is useful sometimes to combine information of a similar type from more than one table. We can use the normal operations of union, intersection and difference to do this. For example, if we had two bus drivers' tables: one of current drivers; the other of drivers who have left the company:

- The **union** of the two tables would be everyone in both tables (people who had left the company or people who are currently employed)
- The **intersection** of the two tables would be only those people who were in both tables (people who had left the company and were now employed again)
- The **difference** of the two tables would be one of two alternatives: everyone in the current bus drivers' tables but not people who had left the company and were now re-employed; everyone in the 'old' bus drivers' table but not anyone who was now re-employed.

When using these set operators, the two tables involved must have the same structure – that is, the same number of columns of a compatible type. When this is the case, we say that the two tables are **union compatible**. Oracle uses the set operators UNION, INTERSECT and MINUS to perform these operations.

Union of tables

As an example, we might want to find all those bus drivers who are based at the Holloway depot, or those drivers who are qualified to drive a bus of type 'midibus', or both:

```
select  bdName
from Busdriver bd, Depot d
where bd.dNo = d.dNo
and dName = 'Holloway'
union
select  bdName
from Busdriver bd, Training t, Bustype bt
where bd.bdNo = t.bdNo
and t.tNo = bt.tNo
and tDescript = 'midibus';
```

BDNAME
Jack Jones
James Bond
Jane Brown
John Peel
Maggie May

Intersection of tables

In this example, we find all those bus drivers who are based at the Holloway depot, and are qualified to drive a bus of type 'midibus':

```
select  bdName
from Busdriver bd, Depot d
where bd.dNo = d.dNo
and dName = 'Holloway'
intersect
select  bdName
from Busdriver bd, Training t, Bustype bt
where bd.bdNo = t.bdNo
and t.tNo = bt.tNo
and tDescript = 'midibus';
```

BDNAME
Jack Jones

Difference of tables

In this example, we find all those bus drivers who are based at the Holloway depot, but are not qualified to drive a bus of type 'midibus':

```
select  bdName
from Busdriver bd, Depot d
where bd.dNo = d.dNo
and dName = 'Holloway'
minus
select  bdName
from Busdriver bd, Training t, Bustype bt
where bd.bdNo = t.bdNo
and t.tNo = bt.tNo
and tDescript = 'midibus';
```

BDNAME
Jane Brown

Alternatively, we could find all those bus drivers who are qualified to drive a bus of type 'midibus', but are not based at the Holloway depot:

```
select  bdName
from Busdriver bd, Training t, Bustype bt
where bd.bdNo = t.bdNo
and t.tNo = bt.tNo
and tDescript = 'midibus'
minus
select  bdName
from Busdriver bd, Depot d
where bd.dNo = d.dNo
and dName = 'Holloway';
```

BDNAME
James Bond
John Peel
Maggie May

6.6 Existential qualification

Exists

A particular case of a correlated query is one that includes the Boolean qualifier 'exists'. The EXISTS keyword is used for what is called the 'existence test' – to test for the existence or non-existence of data that meets the criteria of the subquery.

For example, find the names of cleaners who are responsible for at least one bus:

```
select cName
from Cleaner c
where exists
    (select *
    from Bus b
    where c.cNo = b.cNo);
```

CNAME
John
Betty
Vince
Jay

EXISTS tests for the presence or absence of 'the empty set' of rows returned by the subquery. If the subquery returns at least one row, then the subquery evaluates to true. If no rows are returned, the subquery evaluates to false. In this example, the subquery is evaluated in turn for each row in the Cleaner table. The first cleaner is John with cNo = '110'. The subquery checks to see if there are any rows in the Bus table where the cNo is 110. In this case the empty set is not present and 'true' is returned. Cleaner John is therefore included in the output. The process is repeated for each of the cleaners' names. With three of the iterations (for cleaners, Jean, Doug and Geeta) 'false' is returned and these cleaners are excluded.

Not exists

Similarly, NOT EXISTS tests for the presence or absence of 'the empty set' of rows returned by the subquery. In this case, if the subquery returns at least one row, then the subquery evaluates to false. If no rows are returned, the subquery evaluates to true. For example:

```
select cName
from Cleaner c
where not exists
    (select *
    from Bus b
    where c.cNo = b.cNo);
```

CNAME
Jean
Doug
Geeta

In this example, the subquery is evaluated in turn for each row in the Cleaner table. The first cleaner is John with cNo = '110'. The subquery checks to see if there are any rows in the Bus table where the cNo is 110. In this case the empty set is not present and 'false' is returned. Cleaner John is therefore not included in the output. The process is repeated for each of the cleaners' names. Only for three iterations, with cleaners Jean, Doug and Geeta, where the empty set is present, will 'true' be returned and the cleaner be included.

In the above examples where the operators EXISTS and NOT EXISTS have been used, these queries could have been formulated using subqueries (IN and NOT IN) instead. Another alternative, in the first example only (i.e. EXISTS), is that a join condition could have been used instead. In fact, it is usually always possible to perform the queries using alternative and simpler methods. There is one case where the use of EXISTS is mandatory – relational algebra divide.

Relational algebra division

We saw the relational algebra operation division in Chapter 2. Divide takes two relations: one binary, one unary and builds a relation consisting of all values of one attribute of the binary relation that match (in the other attribute) all values in the unary relation.

Figure 6.3: Examples of divide

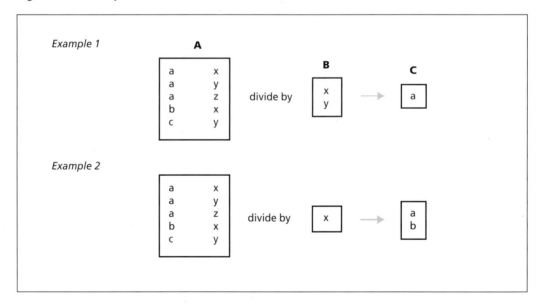

The division operation allows us to compare two relations to see if one is a subset of the other. This is what we would need to do to answer questions such as:

Find routes which allow buses of every type

or

Which bus drivers can drive all the buses based at the Holloway depot?

Double negative existential qualification

The double negative existential qualification is an SQL construct that allows us to directly compare two sets, as opposed to the set comparison operators such as IN, which allows us to compare a scalar [single] value with a set/relation. For example, if we wanted to find the names of bus drivers who could operate on every route:

```
select bdName
from Busdriver bd
where not exists
   (select *
   from Route r
   where not exists
      (select *
      from Ability a
      where bd.bdNo = a.bdNo
      and a.rNo = r.rNo));
```

The result, in this case, is 'no rows selected' as there is no driver in the database who operates every route.

Figure 6.4: Many-to-many relationship example

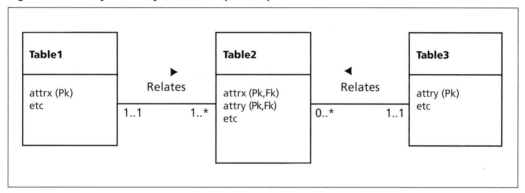

Given the many-to-many relationship as shown in figure 6.4, the following template can be used for 'relational algebra divide' queries:

```
select <attributes>
from  table1
where not exists
   (select *
   from   table3
   where not exists
      (select *
      from table2
      where table1.attrx = table2.attrx
      and table2.attry = table3.attry));
```

In more complicated queries involving RA divide, where there are more than three tables, then it will be necessary to join tables together, possibly within a VIEW (discussed in a later section), or within the nested subqueries to achieve the correct result.

6.7 Interactive queries

A very useful facility is provided to enable users to run the same query again, entering a different value of a parameter to a WHERE or HAVING clause. This is done by prefixing the column specification for which different values are to be supplied by the '&' sign. For example, we can easily find the number of buses of type 2. It is also possible to find the number of buses of any type by running the same query, in each case entering the value of the bus type number interactively.

```
select count(regNo) "buscount"
from Bus
where tNo = &tNo;
```

produced the following execution:

```
Enter value for tNo: 1
old 3: where tNo = &tNo
new 3: where tNo = 1
```

buscount
3

Thus it can avoid the need to recode in order to vary the values of interactively specified parameters.

6.8 SQL views

The permanent tables in the database are called the **base tables**. A view is derived from the base tables using any desired restriction, projection or join operations. It allows you to view the data that only concern you, and to create tables tailored to particular requirements. The data that is output when a view is executed is not what is actually stored when a view is created. It is a **virtual table**, which means it does not actually exist as a table in the database: only the view definition is stored. Views are dynamic – each time the view is used it is re-created from the base tables.

Views are used for a number of reasons:

- To enforce security by hiding data from certain users
- To simplify complex queries by providing intermediate answers which are dynamically updated and can be reused as input
- As input to utilities such as report generators.

You should consider using views when creating SQL queries – particularly when you have a complex query and you can produce an intermediate answer by, first of all, creating a view.

Creating views in SQL

Views are created using the CREATE VIEW statement. The syntax of this statement is very similar to that for creating tables using a SELECT. For example, to create a view showing the cleaner numbers and registration numbers of buses for which the cleaners are responsible:

```
create view CleanersAndTheirBuses
as select c.cNo, regNo
from Cleaner c, Bus b
where c.cNo = b.cNo;
```

To examine the structure of the view CleanersAndTheirBuses, we can use the describe command just as for table objects:

```
describe CleanersAndTheirBuses;
```

Name	Null?	Type
CNO	NOT NULL	VARCHAR2(5)
REGNO	NOT NULL	VARCHAR2(10)

To see the data in the view, we can issue a SELECT statement just as if the view CleanersAndTheirBuses is a table:

```
select *
from CleanersAndTheirBuses;
```

CNO	REGNO
110	A123ABC
110	D678FGH
112	D345GGG
114	H259IJK
113	P200IJK
113	P300RTY
110	R678FDS

6.9 PL/SQL

PL/SQL stands for **Procedural Language SQL** and is Oracle's procedural extension to SQL; it is used to access an Oracle database from various environments (e.g. Forms and Reports). PL/SQL, in some ways, is similar to a modern programming language as it includes features such as block structures, variables, constants, control structures (such as 'if' and loops), functions and procedures. It is, however, integrated with the database server; it is not a standalone language. It allows the user to store compiled code in the database, thus permitting the sharing of the same subprograms by multiple applications. PL/SQL is used for the following:

- To add programming logic to the execution of SQL commands (e.g. 'if' statement, 'for' and 'while' loops)
- To trigger database events to occur, such as referential constraints
- To store procedures which enforce business rules and application logic.

Any SQL statement (apart from CREATE TABLE) can be used in a PL/SQL program without any special pre-processing. PL/SQL can be considered as a superset of SQL. It allows the storage of compiled code in the database, enabling different applications to share functions and procedures. For example, PL/SQL can be used to implement program logic embedded within applications such as those for manipulating forms. In this brief introduction to the language, instead of presenting a formal syntax for PL/SQL, a number of examples are used to illustrate various features of the language.

Program structure – blocks

PL/SQL is grouped into units called **blocks**. Blocks can be **standalone** or **nested**. A block will take the form:

```
declare
<declarations section>
begin
<executable commands>
exception
<exception handling>
end;
```

Keywords are in bold. Variables, with their types, constants, cursors and local subprograms, are declared in the declaration section.   Variables are used to temporarily store values. The executable section contains the program statements. When an error occurs, an exception is raised and program control transfers to the exception handling section (optional). There are predefined and user-defined errors.

Simple example program

Note: when executing the sample PL/SQL programs within SQL*Plus, you should type in the command **'set serveroutput on'**. It allows the user to display information to the session's output device (screen). This needs to be entered only once per session.

The program in example 6.1 adds two numbers together and displays the sum.

Example 6.1: Simple PL/SQL block and execution

```
-- pl/sql program to add numbers and print message
declare
    num1        number:= 7;
    num2        number:= 5;
    totNum      number;

begin
-- main block
    totNum := num1 + num2;
    dbms_output.put_line('The number is ' || totNum );
end;


The number is 12

PL/SQL procedure successfully completed.
```

This is an example of an **anonymous block**, i.e. an unnamed block. PL/SQL programs comprise one or more blocks. These blocks can be separate or nested. Besides anonymous blocks there are also procedures and functions which we will look at later in this chapter. Anonymous blocks are declared in an application at the point where they are to be executed. They are passed to the PL/SQL engine for execution at runtime.

In the example, in the declaration section, we have declared three variables num1, num2 and totnum. These variables can hold data of type number. The initial value of any variable, regardless of its type, is NULL. We can assign values to variables, using the ":=" operator. The assignment can occur either immediately after the type of the variable is declared (as in the example), or anywhere in the executable portion of the program.

In the main block, num1 and num2 are added together and the total stored in totnum. 'Dbms_output.put_line' is used in a PL/SQL program to output to the screen. Note that the lines of code starting with two dashes (--) are comments.

Executable commands

Like any other high-level programming language, PL/SQL provides the following:

- The assignment statement (in the example above, 'totnum := num1 + num2')
- Conditional statements (if-then and variants)
- Loops (for, while)
- Procedures and functions.

Example including SQL SELECT INTO and UPDATE statements

The code below relates to our bus depots' database case study. This program increases bus driver Maggie May's salary by 10% if she earns less than 2500. The results of the execution are shown:

Example 6.2: PL/SQL block

```
--pl/sql program to update a busdriver salary by 10% if she earns less than 2500 –
includes SQL SELECT INTO, UPDATE statements and exceptions handling

declare
   tempSal      number(6,2);
   minSal       number(6,2) := 2500;
   driver       varchar2(20) := 'Maggie May';
begin
--main block
   select bdSalary into tempSal
   from BusDriver
   where bdName = driver;
   if tempSal < minSal then
      update BusDriver set bdSalary = (tempSal *1.1)
      where bdName = driver;
      dbms_output.put_line(' Bus driver '|| driver || ' salary updated to ' ||
      tempSal*1.1 );
   else
      dbms_output.put_line(' Bus driver '|| driver || ' earns' || tempSal );
   end if;
   commit;

   exception
   when no_data_found then
   dbms_output.put_line(' Maggie May record not found ');
end;
```

The following SQL*Plus session illustrates the execution:

```
Bus driver Maggie May salary updated to 2420
PL/SQL procedure successfully completed.
```

The SELECT INTO statement is used in the above example. It states where the returned data values, found in the database table, are to be stored. In the above example, the database value of 'bdSalary' is stored in the variable 'tempSal'. The INTO clause is mandatory for SELECT statements within PL/SQL blocks (which are not within a cursor definition).

Notice the IF THEN ELSE statement control structure, which is found in many procedural languages. So far, all examples have been processed sequentially. The IF THEN ELSE construct alters the order in which statements are executed depending on certain conditions. The condition 'tempSal < minSal' tests to see if the Maggie May's salary is less than minSal, which has been set to 2500. If true, her salary is updated by 10%; otherwise a message stating her current salary is output.

Exception handling is also illustrated in this example. Blocks have the ability to trap and handle local error conditions. You may also self-generate explicit exceptions that deal with logic and data errors. Block execution is terminated after an exception handling routine is executed.

Example using a procedure

The example below accepts a driver number '009' as input to a prodedure, and returns the driver's name and driver's depot name.

Example 6.3: PL/SQL block with procedure

```
--pl/sql program block to call procedure from main program
declare
bdrNo           BusDriver.bdNo%type := '009' ;
bdrName         BusDriver.bdName%type;
depName         Depot.dName%type;
status          boolean;

procedure getDriversDepot(
driverNo in      BusDriver.bdNo%type,
driverName out   BusDriver.bdName%type,
depotName out    Depot.dName%type,
status out        Boolean) is
begin
   select bdName, dName
   into driverName, depotName
   from BusDriver b, Depot d
   where b.bdNo = driverNo
   and b.dNo = d.dNo;
   status := true;

   exception
   when no_data_found then
   status := false;
end;

begin
--main block
   getDriversDepot (bdrNo,bdrName,depName,status);
   if (status) then
   dbms_output.put_line(' Bus driver   ' || bdrNo || ' ' || bdrName || ' works at ' ||
   depName );
   else
   dbms_output.put_line (' Bus driver   ' || bdrNo || ' not  found');
   end if;
end;
```

Output from running the code within SQL*Plus is as follows:

```
set serveroutput on

Bus driver 009 Jack Jones works at Holloway
PL/SQL procedure successfully completed.
```

This example includes a procedure. A procedure is a type of **subprogram.** Subprograms are named PL/SQL blocks that can take parameters and are one of two types: procedures or functions. A procedure is used to perform an action. A function is similar to a procedure, except that a function *must* compute and return a single value.

In the foregoing program, the procedure is called getDriversDepot and is specified in the declare section. The table below has been drawn to show how the different sets of data names relate to one another. Different names have been used for the two sets of variables to aid understanding of the purpose of the various variables. Two variables can, in fact, have the same name, provided that they are defined in different blocks. Variables names should be different from the names of attributes in the table.

Description	Database attribute name	Main program variables	Procedure variables (parameters)
Bus driver number	bdNo	bdrNo	driverNo
Bus driver name	bdName	bdrName	driverName
Depot name	dName	depName	depotName

Also in the declaration sections, the variables are declared with their types. For example, Boolean (true or false) is the type for status, and busDriver.bdNo%type is the type for bdrNo. The latter is called an **anchored data type** – the type for bdrNo is determined by looking up the bdrNo in the Busdriver table (varchar2(5)).

The main block calls the procedure getDriversDepot passing the bus driver's number bdrNo = '009'. In the procedure, notice the SQL SELECT statement. If the driver is found, 'status' is returned as *true*, and the details will be printed, otherwise it is false and an error message will be printed.

6.10 PL/SQL cursors

Almost any SQL statement can be used in a PL/SQL statement, including UPDATE, DELETE and INSERT. However, a SELECT INTO statement (as in the example above) cannot be used to return more than one row. When more than one row is required, PL/SQL provides **cursors**. This allows rows of a query result to be accessed one row at a time. The cursor can be thought of as a pointer, which points to a particular row of a query result.

A cursor must be declared. It is opened, used and then closed when no longer required (using the OPEN, FETCH INTO and CLOSE statements). The FETCH statement, when executed, puts the 'current' row pointed at by the cursor into a record or variable list. Information from a cursor that is being processed can be obtained by using **cursor attributes**. An example, in the following sample code, is %FOUND which returns *true* if a record was successfully fetched from the cursor. Another example is ROWCOUNT which returns the total number of rows returned so far.

PL/SQL cursor example

This example lists all the drivers by name with their depot.

Example 6.4: PL/SQL cursor

```
--pl/sql program to list all drivers and their depots, using a cursor
declare
cursor  driverCursor is
   select bdNo,bdName,dName
   from BusDriver b, Depot d
   where b.dNo = d.dNo;
driverCursorRec driverCursor%rowtype;

begin
   open driverCursor;
   fetch driverCursor into driverCursorRec;
   while driverCursor%found loop
      dbms_output.put_line( driverCursorRec.bdNo || ' ' ||
      driverCursorRec.bdName|| ' ' || driverCursorRec.dName ||' depot '  );
      fetch driverCursor into driverCursorRec;
   end loop;
   close driverCursor;
end;
```

Output from running the code within SQL*Plus is as follows:

```
001 Jane Brown Holloway depot
007 James Bond Hornsey depot
008 Maggie May Hornsey depot
009 Jack Jones Holloway depot
010 Peter Piper Islington depot
011 John Peel Hornsey depot
PL/SQL procedure successfully completed.
```

Notice the WHILE loop above. There are three kinds of loops in PL/SQL:

- **Loop** – the loop body is executed repeatedly until an exit statement
- **For loop** – the loop body is executed a specific number of times
- **While loop** – the loop body executes as long as a condition is true.

In the example, the first record is fetched into the driverCursorRec variable and then the WHILE loop is performed while '%FOUND' returns *true*. If there are no records returned, then the WHILE loop will not be executed.

6.11 PL/SQL stored procedures and functions

Stored procedures

The procedure that we looked at in an earlier example was declared and called from within the PL/SQL program. It is possible to store procedure and function definitions **in the database**, and to have them invoked from various environments that have access to the database. This allows code that enforces business rules to be moved from the application to the database. Some of the most important advantages of using stored procedures are summarised as follows:

- The code can be stored once for use by different applications. Since the procedural code is stored within the database and is fairly static, applications may benefit from the reuse of the same queries within the database
- The use of stored procedures can make the application code more consistent and easier to maintain. This principle is similar to the good practice in general programming, in which common functionality should be coded separately as procedures or functions
- Because the processing of complex business rules may be performed within the database, significant performance improvement can be obtained in a networked client/server environment.

Stored functions

In Oracle, a procedure is implemented to perform certain operations when called upon by other application programs. Depending on the operations, it may not return any value, or it might return one or more values via corresponding variables when its execution finishes. Unlike procedures, a **function** always returns a value to the caller as a result of completing its operations. It is also worth mentioning that a function may be invoked by code within a procedure, and a procedure may be called from within a function. Again, we use an example to illustrate how to create a function. This stored function takes as input a bus registration number, and returns the type (description) of that bus:

Example 6.5: Stored function

```
--pl/sql stored function to return the bus type for a given bus
create function getBusDescription(busReg in bus.regNo%type)
   return busType.tDescript%type as
   typeDesc busType.tDescript%type;
begin
   select tDescript
   into typeDesc
   from Bus b, BusType bt
   where b.tNo=bt.tNo
   and regNo = busReg;
   return (typeDesc);
end;

Function created.
```

The stored function is created within SQL*Plus in the same way that a table or view is created. The CREATE FUNCTION clause defines the function's name (e.g. 'getBusDescription') as well as input variables. Note that CREATE OR REPLACE can be used to overwrite previously created functions with the same name. The cause defines an input variable, together with its data type (in this case, the type is the same as the regNo in the Bus relation, i.e. varchar2(10)).

The RETURN keyword specifies the data type of the function's return value, which can be any valid PL/SQL data type. Every function must have a return clause, because the function must, by definition, return a value to the calling environment.

The function can now be called from a number of environments such as an SQL statement, another stored procedure or function, or a database trigger (see the next section in this chapter). The following is a call made to the function 'getBusDescription' within an SQL query:

select regNo, getBusDescription(regNo)
from Bus
where dNo = '101';

REGNO	GET_BUS_DESCRIPTION(REGNO)
A123ABC	doubledecker
D678FGH	metrobus
D345GGG	doubledecker

6.12 Database triggers

What is a trigger?

A trigger defines an action the database should take when a modification is made to the database. They are associated with a single table within the database, and are specific to an UPDATE, INSERT or DELETE operation, or a combination of these, against rows in the table. The database stores triggers in the same way that it stores normal data. The execution of triggers is transparent to the user. They are automatically executed whenever a specified event occurs and a condition is satisfied. They may be used to:

- Maintain database integrity
- Enforce complex business rules
- Audit changes to data.

Examples of how triggers are used include:

- To enforce referential integrity. For example, when a cascading delete is required if a 'BusDriver' record is deleted with all the 'Training' details linked to that driver
- When a bus driver's PCV (passenger carrying vehicle) driving test date is earlier than a certain date, a trigger could create a training record automatically to indicate that certain training is due
- To recalculate ongoing tallies. For example, year-to-date information relating to bus drivers' salaries.

Triggers can be used to supplement database integrity constraints. However, they should not be used to replace the constraints. When enforcing business rules in an application, the declarative constraints available with the DBMS (e.g. Oracle) should be used. Triggers should then be created to enforce rules that cannot be coded through declarative constraints. The reason for this is that the enforcement of the declarative constraints is more efficient than the execution of triggers.

Triggers in Oracle

In Oracle, an SQL trigger automatically executes a PL/SQL block (the trigger action) when a triggering event (UPDATE, INSERT or DELETE) occurs on a table. We say that the trigger is **fired** when the triggering event occurs.

To design a trigger, we need to specify the following:

- When the trigger is to be executed
- The actions which need to be taken when the trigger executes.

Example trigger

Instead of presenting a formal syntax for creating triggers, a number of examples are used to illustrate how different types of triggers are created. An example of a trigger is given below. It enforces the constraint that a cleaner cannot be responsible for more than four buses.

Example 6.6: Trigger example

```
--pl/sql trigger  to enforce constraint cleaner cannot be responsible for
--more than four buses.

create or replace trigger overworked
before insert or update on Bus
for each row
declare
   cleanerCount number;
   ex            exception;

begin
   select count(*) into cleanerCount
   from Bus
   where cNo  = :new.cNo;
   if cleanCount < 4 then
     dbms_output.put_line('Row added to bus table successful');
   else
     raise ex;
   end if;

   exception
   when ex then
     raise_application_error(-20000, 'Cleaner'||:new.cNo|| 'already
        responsible for 4 buses');
end;

Trigger created.
```

In our example, the trigger will fire BEFORE (timing) any INSERT or UPDATE (event) operation on the Bus table. Timing could also be AFTER, and event could also be DELETE. FOR EACH ROW means that this is a **row trigger** which is fired once for each row that is affected by the triggering event.

The last part of a trigger definition is the BEGIN/END block containing PL/SQL code. It specifies what action will be taken after the trigger is invoked. In this block we use the RAISE_APPLICATION_ERROR procedure (system provided) to generate an error message and stop the execution of any Insert or Update on Bus operation which may result in a cleaner being responsible for more than four buses.

In RAISE_APPLICATION_ERROR, the number '–20000' is a user-defined error number for the condition (the number must be between –20000 and –20999), and the text in single quotes is the error message to be displayed on the screen.

The special variables 'new' and 'old' are used to refer to new and old rows respectively. The row that is currently being processed can be accessed through using the words 'old' and 'new' – for example, :new.cNo, :old.cNo. The variable **:old** refers to the data as it existed prior to the transaction (before an update or delete). The **:new** values are the data values that the transaction creates (such as the columns in an inserted record).

Note that in the trigger body, 'new' and 'old' must be preceded by a colon (:). An exception to this is in the WHEN clause, where a preceding colon is not used, as in the next example.

Trigger execution

A program block which inserts new values into the Bus table is created for testing the trigger. The following SQL*Plus session illustrates the execution to test the trigger 'overworked':

```
insert into bus  values ( 'S123ABC','Daf','1','102', '113');

1 row created.

insert into bus  values ( 'T123ABC','Daf','1','102', '113');

1 row created.

insert into bus  values ('T124ABC','Daf','1','102', '113');

ERROR at line 1:
ORA-20000: Cleaner113already responsible for 4 buses
ORA-06512: at "PATRICIA.OVERWORKED", line 17
ORA-04088: error during execution of trigger 'PATRICIA.OVERWORKED'
```

Row-level and statement-level triggers

Database triggers are classified as follows:

- **Row-level triggers** include the clause FOR EACH ROW in the CREATE TRIGGER statement. They fire once for each row affected by the SQL statement. The example above is a row-level trigger, with the FOR EACH ROW statement defining it as such. They are the most common type of triggers. These triggers execute once for each row operated upon by a SQL statement and can access the original (old) and new column values processed by the SQL statement. For example, if an UPDATE statement updates 100 rows in the BusDriver table, the row-level trigger for that table would be executed 100 times

- **Statement-level triggers** are the default trigger and do not include the clause FOR EACH ROW in the CREATE TRIGGER statement. A statement-level trigger fires only once for each triggering statement. They do not have access to the column values of each row that the trigger affects. For example, if an UPDATE statement updates 100 rows in the BusDriver table, the statement-level trigger of that table would only be executed once.

Row-level triggers are typically used when you need to know the column values of a row to implement a business rule as in the trigger example above. Statement-level triggers are used to process information about the SQL statement that caused the trigger to fire and may be used to enforce additional security measures on a table.

The WHEN option in row-level triggers

For row-level triggers, there is another optional clause which can be used to further specify the conditions that must be met for the trigger to fire. The WHEN clause is used to specify the exact condition for the trigger to fire. The condition can be a complex Boolean expression connected by AND/OR logical operators. For the trigger to fire, the condition must be evaluated to true. If it is evaluated to false or does not evaluate because of NULL values, the trigger will not fire. For example, if we want to take some action when a cleaner is moved to the Holloway depot, we can define a trigger as follows:

Example 6.7: Trigger illustrating WHEN option

```
--pl/sql row-level trigger  with when option
create or replace trigger HollowayDepotTrigger
after update of dNo on Cleaner
for each row
when (new.dNo = '110')
begin
    dbms_output.put_line('warning message - new cleaner at Holloway depot');
end;

Trigger created.
```

Here the condition to be met is "new.dNo = '110' ". So if the new record used to update the Cleaner table has a depot number of '110', i.e. it evaluates to true, then the message will be printed.

Triggers and referential integrity

In example 6.6, we saw how a trigger could be used to maintain a business rule (i.e. that cleaners were responsible for no more than four buses). We now look at examples of how triggers can be used to maintain referential integrity. In Chapter 5 in the introduction to SQL you learned that the foreign key constraint in the CREATE TABLE statement is often used for ensuring the referential integrity among parent and child tables. However, the foreign key constraint can only enforce standard integrity rules:

- The foreign key column in the child table cannot reference unmatched rows in the parent table
- If the Delete Cascade option is chosen, then all matching rows in other tables are deleted (child rows) as well as the target row (parent row)
- If the Delete Cascade option is not chosen, a row in the parent table that is being referenced via a foreign key column cannot be deleted.

When non-standard referential integrity rules have to be specified as well, then **triggers are created**. For example:

- Set the foreign key column to NULL for updates and deletes
- Cascade updates – this means update all matching rows in other tables referenced by foreign keys as well as the target rows
- Set a default value to the foreign key column on updates and deletes. Such a default value might be a code number such as '999'.

Note that if we are implementing non-standard referential integrity constraints then the foreign key constraint must not be declared in the CREATE TABLE statement. This is because the standard foreign key constraint will override the trigger and the trigger will therefore not work.

In this section, we are going to see two examples of using triggers to implement the Delete Cascade rule and the Update Cascade rule. The two tables we will use to illustrate this are Depot and Bus:

```
Depot(dNo, dName, dAddress)
Bus(regNo, model, ......dNo,.....)
```

We know that dNo in Bus is a foreign key linking to Depot. To create the trigger to cascade deletes see the following example.

Example 6.8: Trigger cascade deletes

```
--pl/sql trigger to demonstrate cascade deletes
create trigger cascadeDeletesDepotBus
before delete on Depot
for each row
begin
delete from Bus
where bus.dNo = :old.dNo;
end;

Trigger created.
```

It can be seen from the above example that, before the parent row is deleted from the Depot table, all the child rows in the Bus table are deleted. This maintains the referential integrity. (In the PL/SQL code, ':old.dNo' represents the dNo of the row in the Depot table, which is to be deleted.)

To create the trigger to cascade updates:

Example 6.9: Trigger cascade updates

```
--pl/sql trigger to demonstrate cascade updates
create trigger cascadeUpdatesDepotBus
after update of dNo on Depot
for each row
begin
update Bus
set Bus.dNo = :new.dNo
where Bus.dno = :old.dNo;
end;

Trigger created.
```

Again it can be seen from example 6.9, that after the parent row is updated in the Depot table, all the child rows in the Bus table are updated accordingly. This maintains referential integrity.

Listing triggers and removing triggers

It is sometimes useful to list the triggers that you have created for a table. Make sure the table name is in upper case.

```
select trigger_name
from user_triggers
where table_name = 'BUS';
```

TRIGGER_NAME
OVERWORKED

Existing triggers can be deleted via the DROP TRIGGER command. For example, the 'overworked' trigger is removed from the Bus table in the following way:

```
drop trigger overworked;
```

6.13 Summary

In this chapter we discussed in more detail the SQL query language. We introduced some advanced features of SQL including self-joins, subqueries, correlated queries, the EXISTS operator and views. We continued our discussion of how the relational algebra operators are implemented in SQL, namely union, intersection, difference and divide.

We also focused on the Oracle procedural extension to SQL, namely PL/SQL. We introduced the PL/SQL block and the stored procedure and function.

Finally, the chapter described the use of database triggers in providing an automatic response to the occurence of specific database events.

6.14 Review questions

 Review question 6.1   Examine the following query involving a self-join. Give the English meaning of the query. What is the purpose of each of the tables?

> **Select** b2.regNo
> **From**   Bus b1, Bus b2,
>   Depot d1, Depot d2
> **Where** b1.regNo = 'P200IJK'
> **And**   b1.dNo = d1.dNo
> **And**   d1.dAddress = d2.dAddress
> **And**   d2.dNo = b2.dNo;

 Review question 6.2   Examine the following query involving a self-join. Rewrite the question using nested selects (subqueries) instead.

> **Select** b2.regNo
> **From**   Bus b1, Bus b2,
>   Depot d1, Depot d2
> **Where** b1.regNo = 'P200IJK'
> **And**   b1.dNo = d1.dNo
> **And**   d1.dAddress = d2.dAddress
> **And**   d2.dNo = b2.dNo;

 Review question 6.3   State whether you think the pair of SQL statements below are equivalent:

> **select** distinct c.cNo, cName
> **from** Cleaner c, Bus b
> **where** c.cNo = b.cNo
> **and** model like 'Daf%';

> **select** cNo, cName
> **from** Cleaner
>   **where** cNo in
>   (**select** cNo
>   **from** Bus
>   **where** model like 'Daf%');

Explain your answer.

 Review question 6.4   State whether you think the pair of SQL statements below are equivalent:

> **select** distinct c.cNo, cName
> **from** Cleaner c, Bus b
> **where** c.cNo <> b.cNo
> **and** model like 'Daf%';

> **select** cNo, cName
> **from** Cleaner
> **where** cNo not in
>   (**select** cNo
>   **from** Bus
>   **where** model like 'Daf%');

Explain your answer.

 Review question 6.5   The following relation diagram concerns patients who have been admitted to hospital and given various treatments. For each patient's admission, the date admitted is held, plus the doctor who authorised the admission. Each time a patient is treated this is recorded, along with the doctor who authorised the treatment and the date.

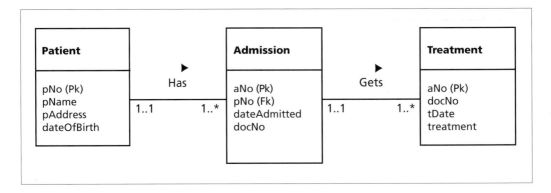

Give the English meaning of the following SQL command:

```
select p.pName
from Patient p, Admission a
where p.pNo = a.pNo
and not exists
    (select * from Treatment t
    where t.aNo = a.aNo
    and  t.docNo = a.docNo);
```

 Review question 6.6   Given the following relation diagram concerning patients who have been admitted to various hospitals:

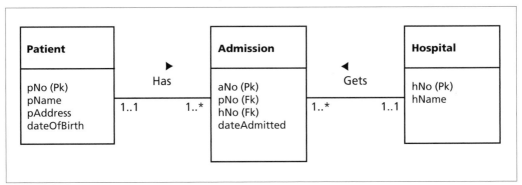

describe what the following statement does and outline how it achieves it:

```
select pName
from Patient
where not exists
    (select * from Hospital
    where not exists
        (select *
        from Admission
        where patient.pNo = admission.pNo
        and hospital.hNo = admission.hNo));
```

Review question 6.7   An SQL programmer wanted to find (as in review question 6.6) the names of patients who have been admitted to every hospital. He did this by using the COUNT function to count the total number of hospitals each patient had been admitted to and then comparing this with the total number of hospitals in the database, i.e.:

```
select  distinct pName, count (hNo)
from Patient p, Admission a
where p.pNo = a.pNo
group  by pName,hNo
having count(hNo) =
    (select count(hNo)
    from Hospital);
```

Is this a valid way of tackling this query?

Review question 6.8   Explain the purpose of *views* in SQL. Give an example in SQL of a view, again using the sample Bus Depots' Database database. You should create a view, and then illustrate how it might be used.

Review question 6.9   What is PL/SQL?

Review question 6.10 Describe the structure of a PL/SQL block.

Review question 6.11 What is the purpose of cursors in PL/SQL?

Review question 6.12 Why are stored procedures useful in databases?

Review question 6.13 What is a database trigger?

Review question 6.14 Triggers can be used to:

- Supplement declarative constraints to maintain database integrity
- Enforce complex business rules
- Audit changes to data.

Give examples (other than the ones given in this chapter) for each of these.

Review question 6.15 Should triggers be used to replace declarative constraints and, if so, why?

Review question 6.16 When and how do we use triggers to maintain referential integrity?

Query processing and optimisation

OVERVIEW

When users submit queries to a DBMS, they expect a response that is not only correct and consistent for a particular instantiation of the database; but also timely, that is, it is produced in an acceptable period of time. However, queries can be written in a number of different ways, many of them being inefficient. In this chapter we look at the stages of query processing: in particular, we look at **query decomposition** and **optimisation**, where the high-level SQL query is transformed into relational algebra. We examine the **heuristic approach** to query optimisation where transformation rules are used to achieve an efficiently executed query.

| **Learning outcomes** | On completion of this chapter, you should be able to: |

- Understand the purpose of query processing and optimisation

- Understand why DBMSs incorporate optimisers

- Describe the stages of query processing and optimisation

- Understand how SQL queries are translated into relational algebra during query decomposition

- Explain how to apply heuristic transformation rules to improve the efficiency of a query.

7.1 Introduction

When a query is submitted to a DBMS, the response should be produced in an acceptable period of time. However, queries can be written in a number of different ways, many of them inefficient. Therefore, the DBMS should take a query and, before it is run, prepare a version that can be executed efficiently. This process is known as **query optimisation**.

As it is usually impossible to produce an optimal version of a query within a short period of time (due to the underlying intractability of the problem), a fairly efficient version, generated quickly, is acceptable. It is clear that it would not be appropriate to spend thirty minutes optimising a query that only takes two minutes to execute in an unoptimised form! Thus, in reality, we are concerned with the improvement of execution strategy, rather than finding the most efficient version (which is effectively impossible for most queries).

Note that current RDBMS optimisers are complex pieces of software and will vary in design. The optimisers are based on rules, and in this chapter we give a simplified version of a typical execution plan which is not based on particular database management software. The rules are often expressed using a symbolic notation: here we present the relational algebra and the heuristic rules informally.

SQL query example

Consider a simple query using the bus depots' database: display the route descriptions that bus driver Jack Jones can operate. There are a number of ways to evaluate this simple query and each may be significantly different in terms of execution time and memory used.

This query involves three tables: BusDriver, Ability and Route:

- BusDriver (bdNo, bdName, bdSalary, dNo)
- Ability (bdNo, rNo)
- Route (rNo, rDesc, dNo).

In order to achieve the result, we would need to join these tables together and restrict the answer to Jack Jones. If, for instance, there were three hundred bus drivers, fifty possible routes and thousands of rows in the Ability table, then a join of the three tables would produce a very large intermediate table held in main memory. Rather than start by joining the three tables together, the DBMS optimiser could first restrict the BusDriver table to Jack Jones's, and thus reduce the BusDriver table to one row before joining the result to the other two tables.

We will see that it is not our job to worry about the efficiency of the SQL code that we write: the DBMS considers various alternatives and opts for a good execution strategy. The choice of the strategy, as we have seen in the example, can have a dramatic impact on the size of the intermediate tables and thus on execution time.

7.2 Relational algebra

Before examining the topic of query optimisation in detail, we need to look again at **relational algebra**. We saw in Chapter 1 that many high-level data manipulation languages are based on either (or both as in the case of SQL) **relational algebra** or **relational calculus**, both of which were defined by E F Codd. They are theoretical languages – formal and non-user-friendly. They illustrate the basic operations required by any data manipulation language such as SQL. The algebra also serves as a convenient basis for optimisation.

Relational algebra (RA) operators again

We saw in Chapter 2 how each relational algebra operator takes one or more relations as its input, and produces a new relation as output. Codd originally defined eight operators. In this chapter, we will limit our discussion to the special relational operators **restrict**, **project** and **join**.

Being a high-level symbolic language, RA expressions can be easily rewritten in equivalent forms.

For example:

        R1 = BusDriver Join Ability where BusDriver bdNo = Ability bdNo
        R2 = Restrict from R1 where rNo = '10'
        R3 = Project over R2 [bdName]

is equivalent to:

        R1 = Restrict from Ability where rNo = '10'
        R2 = BusDriver Join R1 where BusDriver bdNo = R1 bdNo
        R3 = Project over R2 [bdName]

The relational algebra above is used to find the names of bus drivers who can operate on route number ten. If you wish to remind yourself of theses relational algebra syntax examples, re-read Chapter 2, section 2.4.

Examining the first set of RA expressions above:

- Firstly there is a join on the two tables BusDriver and Ability
- Followed by a restrict (rNo ='10')
- Finally a project of bdName.

The second set of expressions is executed in the following order:

- Firstly there is a restrict (rNo = '10') on the Ability table
- Followed by a join on the 2 tables Busdriver and restricted Ability
- Finally a project of bdName.

In both cases the output will be identical, but the way that each query has been executed will differ. Rewriting RA expressions serves as the basis for optimisation.

7.3 Why do DBMSs incorporate optimisers?

Optimisation is required if a DBMS is to perform a query in a reasonable period of time. The larger a database becomes, the greater the need for an optimiser. As many databases may contain over a million records, even a modest improvement in efficiency would have a dramatic effect on response times. It is one of the strengths of relational databases that query optimisation can be done automatically by a software optimiser included within the DBMS software.

A software optimiser is superior to a human optimiser for the following reasons:

- A software optimiser would have access to a wealth of statistical information not available to programmers (e.g. the cardinality of each domain, the cardinality of each table, and the number of times each different value occurs in each column). This information is kept in the **system catalog**
- A software optimiser can assess many more different forms of query than a human optimiser would be inclined to do, or capable of doing
- A software optimiser can embody the best optimising practices.

7.4 Query processing and optimising

Phases of query processing

Figure 7.1: Stages in processing an SQL query

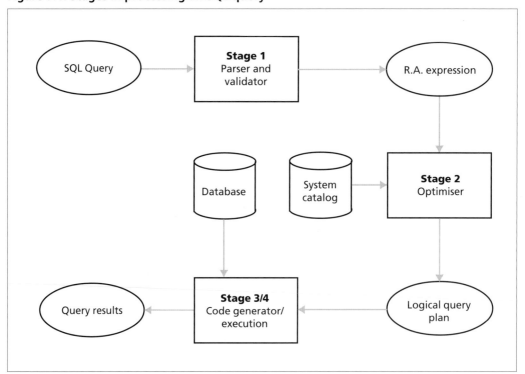

We can see from figure 7.1 that query processing consists of four main phases. In this chapter we concentrate on the first two phases. These phases can be further subdivided.

7.5 Stages 1 and 2: parsing and optimising

Stages 1 and 2 can be divided into several distinct substages including:

1.1. Syntactic and semantic checking.

1.2. Casting the query into some internal representation: the query is converted into a form more suitable for machine manipulation, such as relational algebra.

2.1. Heuristic optimisation: this involves reorganising the query into a more efficient form.

2.2. Systematic optimisation: next the query optimiser must consider how to retrieve the information physically from the database. It must, therefore, generate a query plan using access routines for the various operations. There may be a variety of access routines that can perform the same activity – for example, a join can be evaluated using either nested loop (used for small relations) or sort merge (for large relations), each with its own cost function.

2.3. Selection of the cheapest plan: having generated several access plans, the systemic optimiser would then choose the cheapest.

This is then coded for execution at the appropriate time to retrieve the required data from the database. We will now look at the first three substages above in more detail.

Stage 1.1: Syntactic and semantic checking

A query is expressed in a high-level query language (SQL) and parsed to check if it is **syntactically** correct (i.e. obeys the rules of SQL grammar). The query is then validated to see if it is **semantically** correct (i.e. verified to see that the attributes, tables, views and other objects actually exist in the database).

Syntactic checking example

Assume the relation:

BusDriver (bdno varchar2(5), bdname varchar2(50), ...)

and the query:

    select d_no
    from BusDriver
    where d_no = 007;

Why would this query be rejected? It is rejected on two (syntax) grounds:

- d_no is not defined for the BusDriver relation (it should be bdNo)
- The bdNo is defined as type varchar, so the comparison 'bdNo = 007' does not have matching types. Whether it is rejected or not (for this reason) will depend on the particular DBMS. For example, Oracle will not reject the query on these grounds and will find 007's details even when the comparison is 'bdNo = 7'.

Semantic checking example

Assume the relation:

    BusDriver (bdNo, bdName, bdSalary, dNo)
    Depot(dNo, dName, dAddress)

And the query:

```
select bdNo, bdName
from BusDriver,  Depot
where bdSalary >5000 and dName = 'Hornsey'
and BusDriver.dNo = Depot.dNo
and bdSalary < 2000;
```

Why is the query incorrect? It is incorrect on semantic grounds:

- We cannot have a salary that is both greater than 5000 and less than 2000.

Ideally, a DBMS should reject incorrectly formulated queries such as the one above. However, many will not, including Oracle.

Stage 1.2: Casting the query into some internal representation

The query is converted into a form more suitable for machine manipulation. This form should be rich enough to be capable of representing all possible queries in a DBMS query language and should be neutral (i.e. it should not prejudice any subsequent choices in the optimisation process). In relational data models, the form is based on relational algebra or relational calculus. This chapter assumes the use of relational algebra, which is usually manipulated in the form of a parse tree.

Parse tree example

Given tables Cleaner and Bus:

```
Cleaner (cNo, cName, cSalary, dNo)
Bus (regNo, model, tNo, dNo, cNo)
```

Our query is to 'Get names of Cleaners who are responsible for bus H259IJK'. In SQL we might write it as:

```
select cName
from Cleaner c, Bus b
where c.cNo = b.cNo
and regNo = 'H259IJK';
```

In relational algebra:

```
R1 = Cleaner Join Bus where Cleaner cNo = Bus cNo
R2 = Restrict from R1 where regNo = 'H259IJK'
R3 = Project over R2 [cName]
```

As a parse tree:

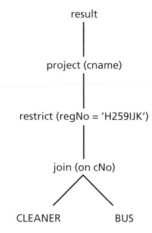

Note that the tree is inverted:

- The bottom level (the leaves) contains the relations in the query
- The middle layer contains relational algebra operations to be performed on the relations or results of previous operations
- The top level (the root) is a single operation that produces the final result.

When viewing the tree, you should understand that it is executed from the bottom right-hand side. When creating your own trees in the various exercises in this chapter, you should draw them starting from the bottom right-hand side.

Stage 2.1: Heuristic optimisation (converting to a more efficient form)

Heuristic optimisation depends on the syntax and not the semantics of the database. It is based only on the general qualities of the relational algebra expressions, and involves substituting relational algebra with more efficient expressions, using **equivalence-preserving transformation rules**. This results in more efficient evaluation. It may include the reordering of expressions, or the removing of redundant or useless operations.

The equivalence-preserving transformation rules are not independent of each other. Given a particular expression to transform, the application of one rule might generate an expression that is susceptible to transformation, after the application of another equivalence rule. The optimiser applies transformation rules until it finally results in an acceptable version of the query. There are many equivalence rules. Here we present a set of **heuristics** (rules of thumb) that are known to produce more efficient queries.

Heuristics used to optimise queries

The **first principle of heuristic optimisation** is to minimise disk input/output and processing by reducing the size of intermediate tables in a query. The earlier the tables appear in the processing, then on balance, the greater is the advantage in reducing their size. This is an important principle. Firstly, it means that processing time is reduced.

Secondly, it may be possible to process a small table in main memory, whereas large tables may be too big to fit into main memory and would require expensive reading and writing to secondary memory. Therefore, the operations that tend to reduce the size of tables (e.g. select, project) are performed before operations that could produce large tables (e.g. union, Cartesian product).

The **second principle of heuristic optimisation** bears more directly on the amount of computation involved. It is sometimes possible to reduce the complexity of queries by rewriting them in a simpler form.

The **third principle of heuristic optimisation** is that it is sometimes possible to rewrite expressions in a form, which although not simpler, is less computationally demanding.

We will now look at examples of rules that fall into each of these categories.

Rules that tend to reduce the size of intermediate tables

These are the rules of thumb that tend to reduce the size of intermediate tables and that we are going to use in our examples:

- Perform restriction as early as possible
- Rearrange leaf nodes so that the leaf with the most restrictive restriction operates first
- Perform projection as early as possible.

Query optimisation example

The tables used to demonstrate heuristic processing are:

Table name	Attributes
STUDENT	sNo, sName, sAddress
REGISTRATION	sNo, cNo, cDate
COURSE	cNo, cName, instructor

Our example query is 'List the registration numbers and names of students registered on the database course'. In SQL we might write it as:

```
select sNo, sName
from Student s, Registration r, Course c
where s.sNo = r.sNo
and r.cNo = c.cNo
and cName = 'Database';
```

Converting from SQL to relational algebra, we have the following:

```
R1 = Student Join Registration where Student sNo = Registration sNo
R2 = R1 Join Course where R1 cNo = Course cNo
R3 = Restrict from R2 where cName = 'Database'
R3 = Project over R3 [sNo, sName]
```

As a parse tree:

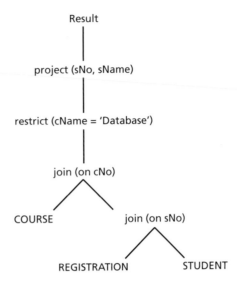

In this case we have joined the REGISTRATION to STUDENT as the first join, followed by joining the result of this to COURSE.

Rule 1: Perform restriction as early as possible

This rule reduces the cardinality (number of tuples) of the resulting relation, and therefore reduces subsequent processing time. For example, if a restriction is performed before a join, then this reduces the size of the input to the join, as it reduces the amount of data to be scanned in performing that join. It also reduces the size of the output, which could make a difference, keeping the output in main memory and not having to spill it out onto disk.

Therefore, the restriction operator is pushed as far down the parse tree as possible. At intermediate nodes, the operators are pushed down the appropriate branches. In this case it is not applicable to pass restriction down the STUDENT branch, as STUDENT does not contain the cName attribute. This reasoning does not apply to the other branch.

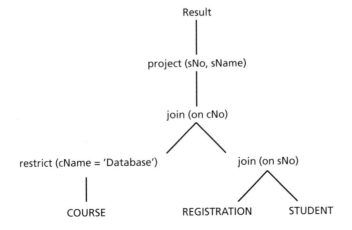

Rule 2: Rearrange leaf nodes so that the most restrictive restriction operates first

Our previous rule **'Perform restriction as early as possible'** pushed 'restrict cName = Database' down the tree just above the COURSE leaf. This means the restriction will only occur after REGISTRATION has been joined to STUDENT. Remember that execution occurs from the bottom right of the tree to the top. If there are thousands of student records, then the intermediate joined table will be huge. So, instead of the above arrangement, a better option is to first rearrange leaf nodes so that the leaf with the restriction operates first; that is, restrict the COURSE table to 'database' tuples only, before performing joins. Therefore the tree above is transformed to:

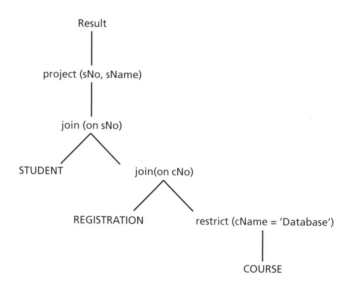

Where there is more than one restriction in the query, the query optimiser will calculate, using information from the system catalog, which restriction to operate first.

Rule 3: Perform projection as early as possible

Under certain conditions projection may be commuted with a Cartesian product (or join). However, a projection cannot be simply moved down the tree. When a projection is preceded by a join, it is possible to push the projection down before the join. As the projection is pushed down the tree it will acquire new attributes; therefore the original projection must be performed after the join. Unless the cardinalities of the intermediate relations are reduced, the usefulness of pushing a projection down before a join is questionable.

Our example query as before is 'List the numbers and names of students registered on the Database course'. With this rule we take each attribute, one by one, in the original projection. This simplified algorithm will try to push the projection of the attribute down the tree as far as possible. It will not always produce the optimum version of the query. We begin by considering the first attribute sNo.

As a parse tree:

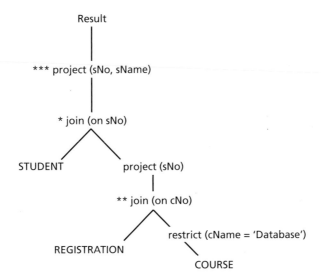

Here, we have pushed the projection of the attribute sNo down the tree before the join (*). Remember that the tree is executed from the leaves (at the bottom of the tree) to the root (at the top of the tree) as shown in the following diagram.

In order to push the projection further down the tree, the projection has to acquire a new attribute cNo so that the join at (**) is to be performed. The original projection (***) is still performed after the join. Here we have succeeded in reducing the cardinalities of the intermediate relations attributes, such as registration date, which is no longer needed and has not been included in the join.

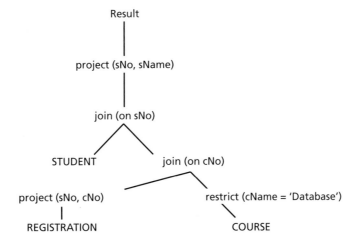

Our projection project (sNo, cNo) has been pushed down the tree as far as possible. Note that, with this rule of thumb, projections of more than one attribute are moved as a whole and are not split into sub-projections. We now consider pushing the next attribute in our original projection, sName, as far down the tree as possible:

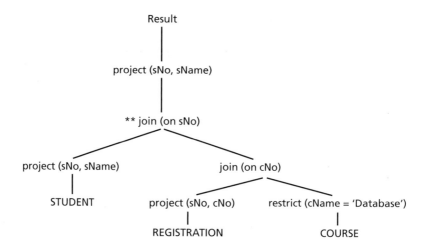

Note that as the projection 'project (sName)' is pushed down the tree, it acquires a new attribute (sNo) in order that the Join can take place at **. Expressed back in relational algebra form:

R1 = Restrict from Course where cName = 'Database'
R2 = Project over Registration [sNo, cNo]
R3 = R1 Join R2 where R1 cNo = R2 cNo
R4 = Project over Student [sNo, sName]
R5 = R3 Join R4 where R3 sNo = R4 sNo
R6 = Project over R3 [sNo, sName]

We have thus succeeded in reducing the size of the intermediate tables created during the execution of the query.

Rules that tend to directly reduce the amount of computation involved: part I

The following rules make expressions simpler:

- Combine a cascade of restrictions into one restriction
- Combine a cascade of projections into one projection.

Combine a cascade of restrictions into one restriction

Example query:

Get the full details of courses with course Database where the instructor is Smith. Expressed in relational algebra:

> R1 = Restrict from Course where instructor = 'Smith'
> R2 = Restrict from R1 where cName = 'Database'

can be converted to:

> R1 = Restrict from Course where instructor = 'Smith' and cName = 'Database'

Combine a cascade of projections into one projection

> R1 = Project over Course [cName, instructor]
> R2 = Project over R1 [cName]

can be converted to

> R1 = Project over Course [cName]

In fact, in a sequence of projections, all but the last can be ignored.

Rules that tend to directly reduce the amount of computation involved: part II

The following rule involves rewriting the query in a less computationally demanding form:

- Any restriction condition is converted into conjunctive normal form.

Conjunctive normal form (CNF) is a sequence that is made up of components joined by the 'and' operator. Each component, called a conjunct, consists of one or more terms connected by the 'or' operator. By converting a query to CNF, manipulation of complex queries is made easier.

For example, given the restriction:

> where P OR (Q AND R)

can be rewritten as:

> where (P OR Q) AND (P OR R)

This transformation is desirable as it reduces computation: if P is false, then the former version will usually involve more work. Consider the truth tables:

P	Q	P AND Q	P OR Q
T	T	T	T
T	F	F	T
F	T	F	T
F	F	F	F

Conjunctive normal form is desirable for the following reason. A condition that is in conjunctive normal form evaluates to true only if every conjunct evaluates to true, equivalently. It evaluates to false if any conjunct evaluates to false. Thus, if a conjunct of statements has an equal chance of being true or false, on average for a true result, all conjuncts must be evaluated; for a false result only half need to be evaluated. This emphasis on efficient evaluation of false conditions is preferable, if the majority of tuples that are to be tested are likely to evaluate to false, which is the case for most queries submitted to a database.

In a parallel processing system, moreover, it might be possible to evaluate all the conjuncts simultaneously, each one on a different processor, and terminate the entire evaluation as soon as any one of them returns a false. A statement in **disjunctive normal form**, on the other hand, evaluates to false only if all disjuncts are false, and true if at least one conjunct is true. This is less efficient if the majority of tuples that are to be tested are likely to evaluate to false.

Activity 7.1

Query optimisation exercise

Given the following database where patients are assigned to a ward and may have operations given by one surgeon:

Table	Attrib 1	Attrib 2	Attrib 3	Attrib 4
Ward	wardNo	wardName		
Patient	patNo	patName	wardNo	patAddress
Surgeon	surgNo	surgName		
Operation	opNo	patNo	surgNo	opDate

a. Write the following query in SQL (in an inefficient form). Display patient numbers and surgeon names for operations which have taken place since 1st March 2001, for patients in the Alexandra Ward.

b. Now convert the query into relational algebra form.

c. Draw a parse tree for the expression you have produced.

d. Use heuristic rules, which reduce the size of intermediate tables, to transform the relational algebra query into a more efficient form. At every step indicate the rule you are applying.

7.6 Summary

In this chapter, students were introduced to query processing. The focus was particularly on the first stages of query processing – parsing and optimisation. It was shown how a query could be converted into relational algebra form and how heuristic transformation rules can be applied to improve the efficiency of a query.

7.7 Review questions

 Review question 7.1   Given the following database:

Table	Attrib 1	Attrib 2	Attrib 3	Attrib 4
Supplier	sNo	sName	city	status
Part	pNo	pName	description	
Shipment	sNo	pNo	quantity	

a. Write the following query in SQL – display part number (pNo) and names for part supplied by suppliers who are located in Manchester.

b. Now convert the query into relational algebra form.

c. Try doing questions a) and b) again but this time reorder the statements in your clause.

Review question 7.2   Why is a software query optimiser superior to a human optimiser?

Review question 7.3   Explain why database management systems incorporate optimisers.

Review question 7.4   What is heuristic optimisation?

Review question 7.5   Given the following database as in review question 7.1:

Table	Attrib 1	Attrib 2	Attrib 3	Attrib 4
Supplier	sNo	sName	city	status
Part	pNo	pName	description	
Shipment	sNo	pNo	quantity	

and the following RA expression, to display part numbers and part names for parts supplied by suppliers who are located in Manchester:

F1 = Part Join Shipment where Part pNo = Shipment pNo
F2 = F1 Join Supplier where F1 sNo = Supplier sNo
F3 = Restrict from F2 where city = 'Manchester'
F4 = Project over F3 [pNo, pName]

Draw a parse tree for this.

Review question 7.6   Now apply heuristic rules to the parse tree in review question 7.5, which reduce the size of intermediate tables to transform the relational algebra query into a more efficient form. The first rule is to 'perform restriction as early as possible'.

Review question 7.7   Now continue with the optimisation example, by taking the parse tree in review question 7.6 and using the rule, if necessary, to rearrange the leaf nodes so that the leaf with the most restrictive restriction operates first.

Review question 7.8   Now continue with the optimisation example, by taking the parse tree in review question 7.7, and use the rule, if necessary, to 'perform projection as early as possible'. Consider only the first attribute to be projected, 'pNo'.

Review question 7.9   Take the parse tree in review question 7.8, and transform it back into algebraic form.

Review question 7.10 Give examples of heuristic rules which reduce the size of intermediate tables.

Review question 7.11 Give examples of heuristic rules that tend to directly reduce the amount of computation involved.

7.8 Feedback on activity

Activity 7.1: Query optimisation exercise

a. We have deliberately started with an inefficiently written query – the SQL is written with the restriction last. Note that the user need not worry about the efficiency of the SQL code as it is the job of the DBMS optimiser to transform the query.

Select patNo, surgName
from Surgeon s, Operation o, Patient p, Ward w
where p.wardNo = w.wardNo
and p.patNo = o.patNo
and o.surgNo = s.surgNo
and wardName = 'Alexandra'
and opDate > '01-03-2001';

b.

F1 = Ward Join Patient where Ward wardNo = Patient wardNo
F2 = F1 Join Operation where F1 patNo = Operation patNo
F3 = F2 Join Surgeon where F2 surgNo = Surgeon surgNo
F4 = Restrict from F3 where wardName = 'Alexandra'
F5 = Restrict from F4 where date > '01-03-2001'
F6 = Project over F5 [patNo, surgName]

c.

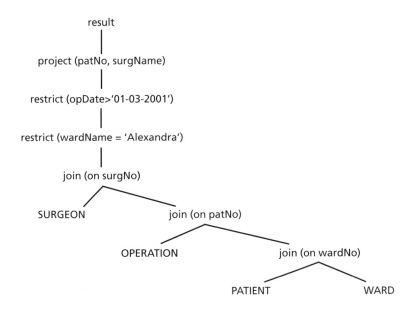

d. Rules to reduce the size of intermediate tables:

Perform restriction early as possible: therefore, push the restrict operator as far down the tree as possible.

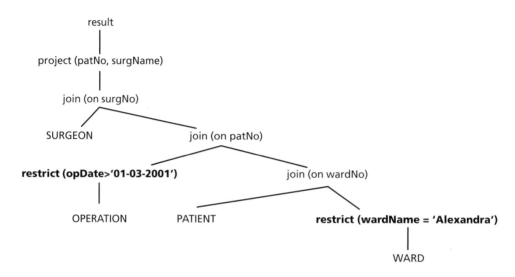

Rearrange the leaves of the tree so that the leaf node with the most restrictive restriction is executed first: consider the rule to increase optimisation by rearranging the leaves of the tree so that the leaf node with the most restrictive restriction processes is executed first. In this example there are two restrictions which affect two different tables (Operation and Ward). During execution the optimiser can work out which restriction is more restrictive by looking up data in the system catalog. In the above solution we will assume that we have already obeyed the rule by joining a restricted WARD table first of all.

Perform projection as early as possible: when a projection is preceded by a join, it is possible to push the projection down before the join. As the projection is pushed down the tree, it may acquire new attributes, therefore the original projection must be performed after the join.

We will consider here only the first attribute to be projected, 'patNo'. We have pushed the attribute patNo down the tree, before the join on SURGEON. The original projection is still performed after the join in order that we can output the two required attributes (patNo, surgName).

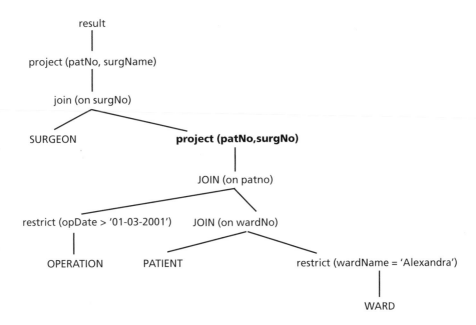

In order to push the projection patNo down the tree, the projection has to acquire a new attribute 'surgNo' so that the join with SURGEON can be performed.

Our projection 'project (patNo, surgNo)' is now pushed down the tree as far as possible. Note that with this rule of thumb, projections of more than one attribute are moved as a whole, and are not split into sub-projections. Here, we have succeeded in reducing the cardinalities of the intermediate relations – attributes such as 'opDate' are no longer needed and have not been included in the join.

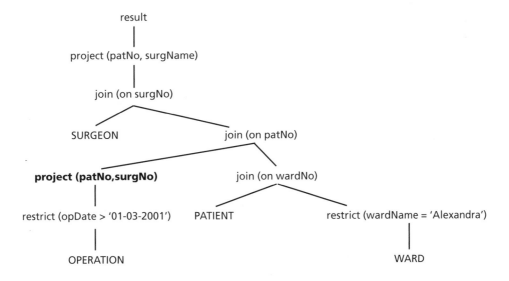

On the next page you can see this transformed query expressed in algebraic form.

F1 = Restrict from Ward where wardName = 'Alexandra'
F2 = F1 Join Patient where F1 wardNo = Patient wardNo
F3 = Restrict from Operation where date > '01-03-2001'
F4 = Project over F3 [patNo, surgNo]
F5 = F2 Join F4 where F2 patNo = F4 patNo
F6 = F5 Join Surgeon where F5 surgNo = Surgeon surgNo
F7 = Project over F6 [patNo, surgName]

Consider any additional transformation which might be introduced to further restrict intermediate tables, for example performing project (surgName) as early as possible.

Object-oriented and object-relational models

OVERVIEW

Object-oriented (OO) concepts are influencing the development of information systems in general and database systems in particular. Many relational DBMS vendors are now offering OO features, and the ISO SQL standard SQL3, released in 1999, has added features to support object-oriented data management. At the same time there is often confusion as to what object-oriented actually means and, unlike the relational model, there is no internationally agreed standard for the critical elements underlying OO database systems. Nevertheless, there is a consensus as to the key elements of an OO data model. This chapter attempts to examine some of these elements.

After introducing the basic concepts of relational databases and entity-relationship modelling in Chapters 2 and 3, we now discuss **object-oriented data models** and **OO database systems**. Relational data models and systems have been very successful for the development of databases used by traditional business applications. We saw in Chapter 2 that there are certain shortcomings in relational databases. These become particularly important when we need to design databases for more complex applications. Some examples of these advanced database systems are described and their requirements examined. These new applications were the major motivation for **enhanced entity-relationship modelling** and later OO databases. We will examine elements of the object-oriented programming model that object-oriented database systems provide for, and discuss two additional concepts in the enhanced entity-relationship model, specialisation and generalisation, which are relevant to object-oriented modelling . This section sets the scene for the next, which examines a methodology for object-oriented database conceptual design.

Finally, we look at how relational database vendors, such as Oracle, have recognised the need for additional data modelling features and have incorporated many OO elements in their products. Specifically, we examine the extensions to the relational model and the features which characterise those products generally known as **object-relational DBMSs.**

Learning outcomes   On completion of this chapter, you should be able to:

- Investigate alternative strategies for developing an object-oriented database system

- Understand the components which make up an OODBMS

- Understand the common elements in the OO programming model (class, inheritance, instances, object identity, encapsulation, methods)

- Describe two concepts in the enhanced entity-relationship model: specialisation and generalisation

- Understand the basics of object-oriented database design

- Explain how the relational model has been extended in Oracle to support advanced database applications.

8.1 Introduction

In Chapter 2 we looked at the disadvantages of relational databases systems. In this chapter we will see that relational database systems cannot meet the more demanding requirements of applications whose needs are quite different from those of traditional business database applications such as order processing and stock control. These new applications are often termed **advanced database applications**. Among the applications that have proved difficult to support within the relational environment are those involved in the storage and manipulation of design data. Examples of such applications include computer-aided design (CAD), computer-aided manufacture (CAM), geographic information systems (GISs), databases to support CASE tools and image processing applications.

These new applications were the major motivation for the development of object-oriented databases. Another reason for their creation is the increasing use of OO programming languages in developing software applications. Traditional databases (i.e. relational) are more difficult to use when embedded in OO languages such as C++ or Java. In this chapter, we will look at some of the **components** which make up an **object-oriented database system** and examine those elements of the object-oriented programming model that object-oriented database systems provide for, in addition to the traditional DBMS functionality. Traditionally, database management and software engineering have emphasised different approaches: database management has been concerned with the static aspects of storing information; software engineering has been concerned with the more dynamic aspects of the software. With the adoption of many of the concepts of software engineering and, in particular, object-oriented programming, the two disciplines have come together.

From Chapter 3 you may recall that data modelling is concerned with the design of the data content and structure of the database. So far we have looked at the more traditional approach of the entity-relationship model. As with any data modelling activity, object-oriented data modelling gives us a formal model of an organisation. The process is very similar, but OO design requires the schema to include both a description of the object data structure and constraints, and the object behaviour. The easiest way to begin to build an object model is to use some of the methods already developed for entity-relationship modelling and **enhanced** entity-relationship modelling. The latter includes **generalisation** and **specialisation** and refers to abstraction mechanisms which enable more complex applications to be represented in semantic models.

Relational database vendors such as Oracle have recognised the need for additional data modelling features and have incorporated many OO features in their products. We next examine the extension to the relational model and the features which characterise those products generally known as object-relational DBMSs.

8.2 Advanced database applications

Among the applications that have proved difficult to support within the relational environment are those involved in the storage and manipulation of design data. Design data is often complex, variable in length, and may be highly interrelated. Its structure may evolve rapidly over time, though previous versions may have to be maintained and may involve longer-duration transactions. Examples of applications that have proved difficult to implement in relational systems include computer-aided design (CAD), computer-aided manufacture (CAM), geographic information systems (GISs), databases to support CASE tools, digital publishing, office information systems (OISs) and multimedia systems.

Geographic information systems

Geographic information systems (GISs) provide the functions and tools needed to store, analyse, and display spatial information. Spatial data covers multidimensional points, lines, polygons, cubes and other geometrical objects. A spatial object is characterised by its location and boundary.

The key components of GIS software are:

- Tools for entering and manipulating spatial data such as geographic information like addresses or political boundaries
- A database management system (DBMS)
- Tools that create intelligent digital maps you can analyse, query for more information, or print for presentation
- An easy-to-use graphical user interface (GUI).

Computer-aided design

Two other applications which involve spatial data are CAD and CAM (computer-aided manufacture). These were the major motivation for object-oriented databases. A CAD database stores data relating to mechanical and electrical design for buildings, cars, integrated circuits, etc. Designs of this type have some common characteristics:

- Data have many types, each with a small number of instances
- Designs may be very large, with maybe millions of parts and often there will be interdependent subsystem designs
- They evolve through time
- Updates are far-reaching – one change may effect a large number of design objects

- Various versions of designs must be maintained, with many staff working on these versions at the same time. There needs to be version control and the final product must be consistent and coordinated.

Consider, for example, a CAD database for an electronic circuit. A circuit uses many parts which are of different types. Each part may refer to other parts, and some of these parts may also be connected to one another. Each part of a type will have the same properties. The design of the circuit may change over time and updates may affect many of the interconnected parts.

8.3 Object-oriented systems overview

Object orientation has its roots in the SIMULA language (late '60s), which incorporated some OO concept such as objects and classes. In the '70s, SMALLTALK was developed which in addition incorporated concepts such as inheritance. Later the programming language C was extended to incorporate OO concepts and C++ came into being. More recently, Java, suitable for sharing programs across the World Wide Web, has been widely adopted.

Many object-oriented databases have their origin in OO programming languages. An **object** used by such languages is similar to (but not the same as) a program variable and exists only during program execution. The important difference between OO programming languages and more traditional programming languages is that the software should be constructed from reusable components. **Object-oriented database management systems** (OODBMSs) have incorporated the features of the OO programming model. Also an OO database extends the existence of objects so they are stored permanently – in other words, OO databases store **persistent data**. In contrast to OO programming languages' variables, OODBMs data is stored on secondary storage and can be shared by many programs and applications.

With relational and previous generation databases the concentration was on the static aspects of the information system – that is, only the structure of the data, and the data itself was stored in the database. The dynamic aspects of the software (the actual programs) were stored separately. An object has two components:

- **State** (value)
- **Behaviour** (operations).

Thus, in an object-oriented database system, both the data and the processes acting on the data are incorporated.

8.4 Alternative strategies for developing an OODBMS

There are a number of approaches to developing an OODBMS (Khoshafian and Abnous, 1990). Most approaches do not start from scratch but extend existing data models or languages. For example:

- Extend an existing OO programming language (such as C++ or Java) with database capabilities. This is exactly the approach taken by the OODBMS Gemstone
- Embed OO database language constructs in a conventional host language. This was the approach taken by the OODBMS O2, which provides embedded extensions in C. Relational databases have a similar approach when SQL is embedded in a host language

- Extend an existing language (such as SQL) with OO capabilities. This approach has been taken by both RDBMSs and OODBMSs. Later in this chapter we will also look Object-Relational Oracle which supports some object-oriented features. Also Versant and other vendors provide a version of Object SQL (OQL), the object database standard query language.

8.5 Object-oriented components and concepts

OODBMSs combine the following:

- **Many of the features of the OO programming model**
  Note that there is no common OO programming model to use as a point of reference, no formal foundation for the concepts described, and, as yet, no standard for object-oriented models. Each OODBMS provides its own interpretation of base functionality. In the next section we will examine some of the common features including classes, objects and attributes, inheritance, methods and object identity
- **Traditional DBMS facilities**
  DBMSs traditionally provide support for persistence, sharing, querying, transaction and concurrency control, recovery, security, integrity and scalability. These are the facilities that are usually available in a DBMS.

In this chapter we concentrate on the first component above (i.e. those common elements in OO programming models). The second component (traditional DBMS facilities) is examined in other chapters in this book, when we look at transaction and concurrency control and query processing.

Objects, classes and attributes (instance variables)

- **Objects:** an object is similar to the idea of an entity occurrence in entity-relationship modelling but there is an important difference. An entity models only the state (the structure of the data). However, an object encapsulates both data and functions into a self-contained package. Thus, objects that have the same structure and behaviour can be grouped together to form a **class**. An example of an object might be an instance of the class BusDriver
- **Classes:** these are blueprints for defining a set of similar objects (i.e. an object is an instance of a class). The structure and behaviour (defined as we will see by attributes and methods respectively) are defined once for the class rather than separately for each object. Each instance has its own value(s) for each attribute, but shares the same attribute names and methods with other instances of the class
- **Attributes:** the current state of an object is described by one or more attributes (also called instance variables). There are various classifications of attributes (e.g. simple, complex and reference) – we will examine these in detail next.

Example attributes for BusDriver instance

name	John
dateOfBirth	19/01/63
address	......
salary	35000
busTypes	type1, type3, type4

Note that name and salary in the above example are simple attributes, as they cannot be broken down further and contain primitive types (e.g. integers or literals); dateofBirth, busTypes and, possibly, address are complex attributes. busTypes is also a reference attribute because it contains a value (or collection of values in this case) which are themselves objects.

Methods and messages

Methods: these are fragments of program code or procedures which are used to carry out operations relevant to the object in question. They are internal to each object and may alter an object's private state. By 'state' we mean the values of the data items of the object in question. Examples of methods for the BusDriver class are AddNewBusType and GiveRise.

Methods are activated by **messages** passed between objects. A message may be viewed as a request from one object (the sender) to another object (the receiver) asking the second object to execute one of its methods. If object A in the database wants object B to do something, it sends B a message. The success or failure of the requested operation may be conveyed back from object B to object A, via a further message. In general, each object has a set of messages that it can receive and a set of replies it can send. An object does not need to know anything about the other objects that it interacts with, other than what messages can be sent to them. The internal workings are thus encapsulated into the definition for each object.

Example of a method

```
method void updateSalary (float increment)
    {       salary = salary + increment;
    {
```

In this example a method consists of two parts: a name, and a body. The body performs the behaviour associated with the method name and consists of a block of code that carries out the required functionality. For example, the method updateSalary has code, which takes the input parameter increment and adds it to the instance variable salary to produce an updated salary. The name of the method, known as the message, is updateSalary. The keyword 'void' denotes that updateSalary does not return a value.

Example of method execution

```
BusDriver.updateSalary(1000)
```

In the above example: execute updateSalary method on a BusDriver object and pass the method, an increment of 1000 is given.

Example of the class BusDriver

The structural component of a class is implemented as **instance variables** (the attributes). For the class BusDriver these are *name, salary, depot, busTypes...* The behavioural component is defined by the **methods** of the class BusDriver including the operator updateSalary which has, as an argument (or parameter), the increment (incr) to be allocated to the driver. Thus methods can (among other things) be used to change the object's state by modifying its attribute values.

Figure 8.1: The private and public components of a class

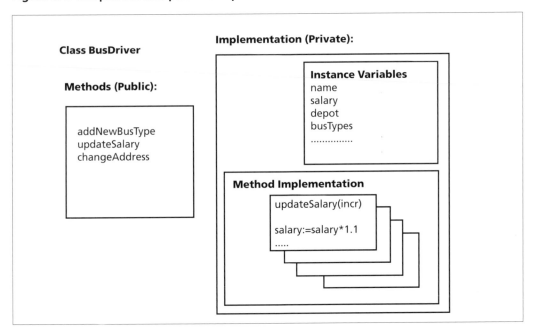

In figure 8.1, all instances (objects) of the class BusDriver will always have these variables and methods, and a single code base implements the operator which is always invoked when an instance (e.g. John Smith) is sent the message. For instance, John's internal representation consists of his description (name, salary, etc) and the bus types he has had training to drive. Some of the values that describe John might also describe other objects: for example, John shares his depot with his co-worker Jim, so the depot is a shared value. The aggregation of the full set of these values captures the state of John as an instance of BusDriver. In relational DBMS terms these instances would represent rows in at least one table. Although the values of the variables in the internal representation vary for each instance of a class (i.e. they may be in different states), all instances will be of the same class.

Encapsulation and information hiding

Encapsulation means the packaging together of both the data structure and the methods that are used to manipulate the object. The term implies that the internal structure and methods are packaged in such a way that other objects cannot see them. Classes distinguish between the public interface and the private internal implementation and components. The private internal representation is not available to other objects. The public interface is composed of the methods 'understood' by that object. The only way that an object can be manipulated or accessed is through the public interface, with the attributes on the inside protected from the outside by the methods. This concealing of the internal structure, with its inherent complexity, is known as **information hiding**.

In database systems, encapsulation and information hiding ensure that application programmers have access only to the interface part, and thus they provide a form of **logical data independence** – we can change the internal implementation of a class without changing any of the applications using that class. Encapsulation allows the internal details of an object to be changed without affecting the external details. These concepts simplify the construction and maintenance of database applications through modularisation. An object is a 'black box' that can be constructed and modified independently of the rest of the system, provided the public interface is not changed.

Example class definition

The class definition is like a template which defines the set of data items and methods available to all instances of that class of object. Some object database systems also allow the definition of database constraints within class definitions, but this feature will be ignored here. For example, consider the object type Book as might exist in a library database. Information to be held on a book includes its title, date of publication, publisher and author. Typical operations on a book might be:

- Take a book out on loan
- Reserve a book for taking out on loan when available
- A Boolean function which returns true if the book is currently on loan and false otherwise.

These operations will be implemented as methods of class 'book'. The class 'book' may be defined by the following structure:

Example of class book defined by structure

```
class  Book
     properties
          title:                  string;
          dateOfPublication:      date;
          publishedBy:            Publisher;
          writtenBy:              Author;
     operations
          create () -> Book;
          loan (Book, Borrower, dateDue);
          reserve (Book, Borrower, dateReserved);
          onLoan (Book) -> Boolean;
end Book;
```

The notation used in the class definition will be explained later in this chapter. An important point to note here is that data abstraction, as provided by the class mechanism, allows one to define properties of classes in terms of other classes. Thus we see from the above example that the properties publishedBy and writtenBy are defined in terms of the classes 'Publisher' and 'Author' respectively. This will also be explained more fully later in this chapter.

Class definitions for Author and Publisher

Outline class definitions for Author and Publisher could be as follows:

```
class    Author
          properties
               name:             string;
               nationality:      Country;
               yearOfBirth:      integer;
               yearOfDeath:      integer;
          operations
               create () -> Author;
end Author.
```

```
class    Publisher
         properties
                name:        string;
                location:    City;
         operations
                create () -> Publisher;
end Publisher.
```

Inheritance

Inheritance allows one class to be defined as a special case of a more general class. These special cases are known as **subclasses**, and the more general cases are known as **superclasses**. By default, a subclass inherits all the properties (both state and behaviour) of its superclass, and it also defines its own unique properties. In addition, a subclass can redefine inherited methods. If class B is a subclass of class A, then if class B inherits the characteristics of class A, every instance of B is automatically an instance of A. However, the reverse is not true.

Example of inheritance hierarchy

Consider the hierarchy of people illustrated in figure 8.2.

Figure 8.2: Classes and the inheritance hierarchy

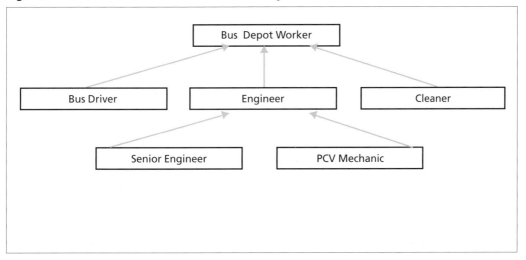

In figure 8.2, Bus Drivers, Engineers and Cleaners are subclasses of Bus Depot Workers. Senior Engineers and PCV Mechanics further specialise Engineers. The class Bus Depot Worker is a superclass of Bus Driver, Engineer and Cleaner.

The advantages of inheritance

All OODBMSs provide inheritance of some sort. The main advantages of inheritance are:

- **Reusability:** through the inheritance mechanism, the characteristics of an object can be made available to other objects. Depending on the system, this may involve both state (data) and behaviour (methods) of objects

- **Extensibility:** another aspect of the mechanism is that it provides a natural way for applications or systems to evolve. As new features, data, or program code are added, these can be defined in terms of new objects. These inherit the already tested characteristics of the earlier part of the system. This will include both the behaviour (operations, methods, etc) and the representation (instance variables, attributes, etc) from existing classes.

Object identity

OIDs

An OO database system provides a unique identity for each independent object stored in the database. This identity is implemented via a unique system-generated object identifier (OID). The use of primary keys (as used in relational databases) is not a satisfactory means for identifying objects in databases. For a database table storing 'bus depot worker', for example, the identifier key might be an employee name (lastname, firstname). The use of primary keys from home relations as foreign keys in referencing relations has intrinsic problems. These lead to drawbacks such as:

- The need to use inefficient joins to retrieve object data
- A primary key is only unique within a relation, but not across an entire system
- A primary key is generally chosen from the attributes of a relation, making it dependent upon object state. If a candidate (potential) key is subject to change, identity has to be simulated by unique identifiers, such as the employee number, but as these are not under system control there is no guarantee of protection against violations of identity.

In the case of the OID, its value is not visible to the external user, but is used internally by the system to identify each object uniquely. The OID is unique to that object. Each identifier can be associated with one, and only one, object. Also, the OID is invariant, in the sense that it cannot be altered during its lifetime. The OID will not be reused by another object, even after an object has been removed. An important advantage is that objects can use it to contain or refer to other objects.

An OODBMS must have some mechanism for generating OIDs. It is not usually the physical address of the OID but, more often, a long integer is used which maps to the physical address. It is therefore independent of the values of any of its attributes (that is, its 'state'). An object identity is permanent, whereas the state of an object (the values of its instance variables) can change arbitrarily; thus, a bus depot worker's address can change, but the identity remains the same. Object-oriented systems that support this strong built-in identity also allow the object to undergo structural modifications (i.e. change its class) without any changes in its identity. Another consequence of this independence is that two objects could have the same state but would have different identities.

Object identity advantages

Object identity offers several advantages in OODBMSs:

- They are efficient: OIDs require little storage within a complex object
- As they cannot be modified by the user, the system can ensure entity and referential integrity more easily, and users do not need to maintain referential integrity
- They help locate objects quickly, as the OIDs point to an actual address or to a location within a table that gives the address of the referenced object
- They do not depend upon the data contained in the object in any way. This allows the value of every attribute of an object to change, but for the object to remain the same object with the same OID.

Complex objects

Conventional relational databases allow a fixed number of types for their attributes (e.g. reals, integers, strings, and dates). Many advanced DB applications include data which have many types. Modern systems must be able to handle freeform text, photographs, audio, video, etc. Data (e.g. designs in a CAD system) may be very large, with many interdependent subsystems. Fixed structure (horizontal and vertical homogeneity) of the relational model is too restrictive for many objects that have a complex structure. OO systems offer a rich collection of types in addition to the basic ones. Importantly, these additional types include other objects.

8.6 The object-oriented database system manifesto

The OODB manifesto (Atkinson et al, 1989) proposed thirteen mandatory features for an object-oriented DBMS. It is still generally agreed that an OODBMS should support these features. Eight of these apply to OO concepts; the rest to features one would expect to find in any DBMS. The features are listed below in no particular order:

- OODBMSs should allow **complex objects:** we will see next that OO systems offer a rich collection of types, in addition to the basic ones, such as integers and strings. Importantly, these additional types include other objects

- **Encapsulation** must be supported: the state and behaviour of an object are encapsulated, that is, not visible outside of the object. This is achieved by ensuring that programmers have access only to the interface specification of methods. It means that the internal details can be changed without affecting the applications that use it

- **Classes** must be supported: the blueprint for creating objects; defines static and dynamic properties of an object (attributes and methods); organised in a hierarchy of classes

- The DML must be **computationally complete:** the DML should be a general-purpose programming language (not the case with SQL2), otherwise there will be impedance mismatch problems

- **Data persistence** must be supported: data must persist after the application that created it has terminated

- **Large databases** must be supported: OODBMSs (as well as conventional DBMSs) have indexes, buffers, etc to manage secondary storage – these are transparent to the user

- **Concurrent users** should be supported

- An efficient, application-independent ad hoc **query language** should be supported

- Classes must be able to **inherit from their ancestors:** a subclass will inherit attributes and methods from its superclass – this can greatly reduce redundancy

- **Recovery mechanisms** should exist

- **Dynamic binding** must be supported: methods are not linked to their associated code until an application is invoked. This is known as dynamic binding. When dynamic binding occurs, the systems binds message selectors to their methods at run time instead of at compile time

- The set of **data types must be extensible:** the user should be able to build new types from the set of predefined types and these should be indistinguishable in usage from system-defined types

- **Object identity** must be supported: all objects must have a unique identity which is independent of its attribute value – this means fast and efficient locating of objects.

8.7 Comparison of OODBMSs and RDBMSs

In the past few years, object-oriented (OO) concepts have been applied to many areas of computer science and this has led to the widespread use of object-oriented programming languages such as C++ and Java. However, OO database systems have been relatively slow to be adopted. We have seen that relational data models and systems have been very successful for the development of databases used by traditional business applications. Also, OO techniques are sometimes favoured in database applications because the OO model is semantically much richer than earlier data models, thus a database based on the OO model is more capable of storing data that accurately reflects 'real world' information.

We saw previously that there are certain shortcomings to relational databases when we need to design databases for advanced database systems. In activity 8.1 we again look at these shortcomings and consider how the OO model has overcome these disadvantages.

Activity 8.1

Comparing the relational model and OO model

Examine the following tables:

Weaknesses of RDBMSs:

- Poor representation of 'real world' entities
- Semantic overloading
- Poor support for integrity and enterprise constraints
- Homogeneous data structure
- Limited operations
- Difficulty handling recursive queries
- Impedance mismatch.

Advantages of OODBMSs:

- Enriched modelling capabilities
- Extensibility
- Removal of impedance mismatch
- More expressive query language
- Support for schema evolution
- Support for long-duration transactions
- Applicablility to advanced database applications
- Improved performance.

Examine the **weaknesses of RDBMSs** above. If you have forgotten the details, look at Chapter 2. Also examine the **advantages of OOBDMSs** above, which have been discussed throughout this chapter. Now produce a grid with two columns. On the left-hand side, list the shortcomings of the relational approach and, on the right-hand side, explain how the OO approach might overcome these problems.

8.8 **Enhanced entity relationship modelling**

In Chapter 3 we examined the development of a database using entity-relationship modelling. The **enhanced entity relationship model** was proposed to include features suitable for applications with more complex requirements, such as the advanced applications described earlier in this chapter. Two of the most important extensions are relevant to the OO approach. These are **specialisation** and **generalisation**. The process of forming a superclass is referred to as generalisation and the process of forming a subclass is known as specialisation. We now discuss these in more detail.

Specialisation

Most existing object-oriented systems allow developers to extend an application by specialising existing components (in most cases, classes) of their applications. Software extensions are achieved by creating subclasses of existing classes.

Figure 8.3: Specialisation

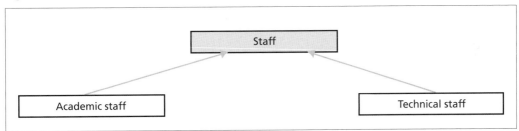

Specialisation is illustrated in figure 8.3, in which the class with the shaded background is an 'older' existing class, and the classes with a white background are created by inheriting structure and behaviour from existing classes. Therefore, specialisation is a **top-down approach** to software development. We start with a general class hierarchy (the top-level superclasses) and extend it by the creation of subclasses (the classes that are the leaves, or at the bottom of the hierarchy). Specialising an existing class can be achieved by adding instance variables, restricting existing instance variables, adding methods, overriding existing methods, and so on.

Generalisation

Generalisation is the complement of specialisation. It uses a **bottom-up approach** by creating classes that are generalisations (or superclasses) of existing subclasses. This is illustrated in figure 8.4. Here, the new class (which is at the top of the hierarchy), is created by extracting common structures, including instance variables and methods of existing, more specialised classes, from existing classes (which are at the bottom of the hierarchy).

Figure 8.4: Generalisation

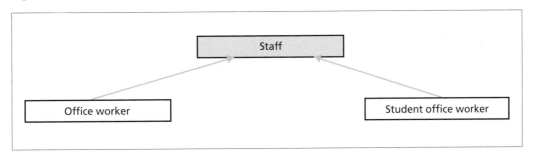

As an example of generalisation, assume that we have two existing classes, 'Lecturer' and 'Student'.

Lecturer has the following attributes:

name
telephoneNumber
address
salary
employeeNumber
worksFor

Student has the following attributes:

name
studentNumber
address
telephoneNumber
advisor

These existing classes have a common structure and behaviour. In order to abstract this common structure and behaviour, we need to generalise the two classes in class 'UniversityMember' with attributes:

name
telephoneNumber
address

Once UniversityMember is created, it can be used as a superclass of other classes that could be constructed by specialising UniversityMember.

UML inheritance hierarchy diagram

Inheritance, as we saw earlier in this chapter, is relevant to the object-oriented model. The UML (unified modelling language) notation was introduced in Chapter 2 for entity-relationship diagrams. We now show how inheritance is included in the diagram, i.e. by using the open arrow to indicate inheritance. The diagram is similar to the entity-relationship diagram, but in this case each rectangle denotes a superclass or subclass that includes entity name, attribute names and methods. An example is given in figure 8.5.

Figure 8.5: Inheritance hierarchy diagram example

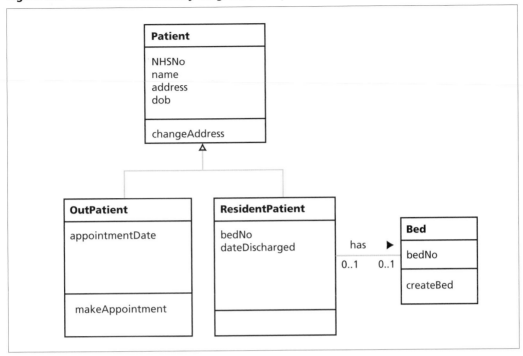

Here each subclass (OutPatient, ResidentPatient) participates in different relationships – an outpatient is not assigned to a bed, whereas all other patients are. Also, each entity subclass may have different attributes (e.g. ResidentPatient may have 'dateDischarged' as an attribute; OutPatient might have 'appointmentDate').

8.9 Object-oriented data modelling

Object-oriented data modelling gives us a formal model of an organisation, in a similar way as the entity-relationship model did. In the entity-relationship model the schema includes both a description of the object data structure and constraints. OO design requires these, but in addition the object behaviour is identified and mapped to a set of methods that are unique for each class.

In this section we will show how the enhanced entity-relationship model when mapped to a relational model can be amended to complete the design of the data structure part of the OO model. 'Behaviour modelling', a technique that identifies and documents the behaviour of each class in the model, is not covered in this section.

Representing relationships

Here we examine the way that relationships are represented in OODBMSs. The representation of relationships is one of the most fundamental ways in which data models differ. Before we look at this representation, it is useful to explore how types are created and several relevant varieties of variables: reference, collection and derived attributes.

Creating types

Creating types in an OODBMS is far more flexible than is the case for relational databases. In the relational model, there is only one category of type that a user may create – the table. The definitions of a table's attributes (columns) are the type definition, and the rows of a table are instances of the type. An important restriction on the table is that attributes of the table must be the system-defined literal types. User-defined types cannot be used as attribute types. Hence, for example, an attribute may not have another table as an attribute. OODBMSs typically allow more flexibility in the types of attribute values permitted: object attributes may have complex values, such as sets or references to other objects. Like the attributes of relational records, attributes (instance variables) of OODBMS objects have names, and they are generally referenced by a 'dot' notation. For example, the revision attribute of a document d may be referenced as d.revision. Attributes that contain literal values are called simple attributes. There are three kinds of complex attributes: **references**, **collections** and **procedures**.

Reference attributes

Reference attributes, or associations, are used to represent relationships between objects. They take on values that are objects, that is, references to entities. For example, referring to a document tracking application, we might define two classes, Document and Chapter. Instead of using a foreign key as in the relational model, we could define a 'Document' reference attribute of 'Chapter' to indicate to which document a chapter belongs:

Example 8.1

```
class  Chapter
      properties
          title          string;
          number         Number;
          doc            Document;
```

Note that methods (operations) are not included in the examples in this section.

Collection attributes

The second kind of complex attribute is one that represents a collection of objects or literals. The object model specifies five built-in collections subtypes including **set** (unordered collection/ no duplicates), **bag** (unordered collection/duplicates allowed) and **list** (ordered collection/ duplicates allowed). As in example 8.2, we can define two collection-valued attributes of the 'Document' object type in our example database:

Example 8.2

```
class Document
      properties
          title          string;
          revision       date;
          keywords       SET [string]
          chaps          LIST [Chapter];
```

The first collection, 'keywords', is a set of keyword strings (i.e. literals) associated with the document, perhaps used to look up documents associatively by subject matter. The second collection, 'chaps', is a list of chapter objects (i.e. an object) for this document. Note that we chose to make the keywords a set, since there is no particular reason to order them, but we chose to make the chapters a list, rather than sorting by a chapter number when retrieving them. It is important to note that relational first normal form does not permit collection-valued attributes (as this would constitute a repeating group); in contrast, most of the OODBMSs we discuss do allow collections. Thus, we diverge in an important way from the relational model on this point: sets and lists of objects are important concepts in the data model.

Representing binary relationships

Relationships are represented in an object-oriented data model using the complex attributes described in the previous section: references and collections of references. The representation used depends on both the multiplicity and the degree of the relationship. Binary relationships can be represented as follows:

Example 8.3

```
class Document
    properties
        title       string;
        revision    date;
        chaps       LIST [Chapter] <-> doc;
        authors     LIST[Person] <-> pubs;
        index       Index <-> for;

class Chapter
    properties
        title       string;
        number      number;
        doc         Document <-> chaps;

class Index
    properties
        entries     number;
        for         Document <-> index;

class Person
    properties
        name        string;
        pubs        LIST [Document] <-> authors;
```

Example 8.3 shows how binary one-to-one, one-to-many and many-to-many relationships may be represented. In all these cases the relationship is manifested as a new attribute of an object that references the associated object, and a new attribute of the associated object that provides a 'back reference', using the '<->' symbol.

Names of attributes

Names must be given to the new attributes used to represent relationships, analogous to the names given to attributes representing relationships in the relational model. For example, in the class examples above, the relationship between documents and chapters is represented by the 'chaps' attribute of the document objects, and by the 'doc' attribute of the chapter objects.

Inverse attributes

Note that the syntax of the class examples specifies both the doc attribute and the inverse attribute (the chaps attribute of document objects), using a double arrow: doc: Document <-> chaps. Conversely, the inverse attribute is defined with a similar syntax in the Document declaration: chaps: LIST[Chapter] <-> doc. The inverse attribute pairs must be kept consistent. For example, if we add another chapter to a document by setting the chapter's doc attribute, the OODBMS must add the chapter to the document's chaps list. If a chapter is moved to another document, then both attributes must likewise be updated. The problem of synchronising inverse attributes is a form of referential integrity (i.e. maintaining the correctness of references when an object is deleted or a relationship is changed).

Creating an object-oriented schema from a relational model

We now outline a simplified methodology for converting an relational schema to an object-oriented schema. We will use an example concerning internal candidates for job interviews within an organisation.

The relational model

The following is a relational schema for part of a database concerning personnel who are applying for internal promotion within a company. Interviews are held for a number of jobs; candidates can take part in more than one interview. Some employees are asked to be members of the interview panel, so that a number of employees will interview a particular candidate for a particular job.

Candidate (cNo char5, cName char20, deptNo char5, cTel char15, presentPosition char15)

PanelMember (pmNo char5, pmName char20, deptNo char5, pmtel char15, lastSatOnPanel date)

Job (jobNo char5, jobTitle char15, startSalary number, deptNo char5)

Interview (intNo char5, jobno char5, cno char5, intdate date)

Panel (intNo char5, pmno char5)

Department (deptNo char5, deptName char15, deptHead char20)

Given the above relational schema, we will construct an equivalent object-oriented database schema. For this exercise we will ignore methods. Note that attributes with the same name have attribute values that are pooled from the same domain.

The relation diagram

It is helpful to start by drawing a relational model for the above. Note the assumptions that have been made about optional/mandatory relationships.

Figure 8.6: Relation diagram for personnel database

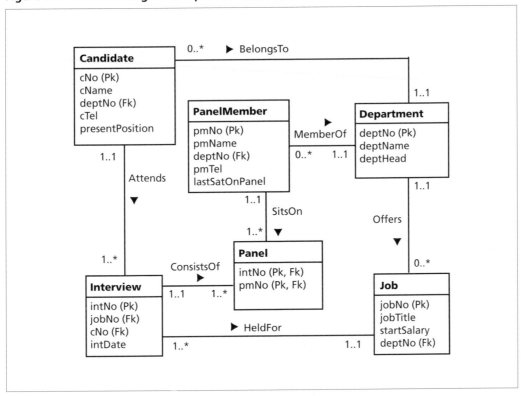

A simplified methodology

Using the following methodology we convert the relation diagram to the object-oriented schema below as follows:

1. We examine the relations in figure 8.6 with their attributes in order to see if any superclasses can be created from these entities using the **generalisation** process. Observe that 'name', 'department number' and 'telephone number' are in both the Candidate and PanelMember relations. Thus we create a superclass which we name Employee. Note that the subclasses Candidate and PanelMember inherit the attributes (and methods) of the superclass Employee.

2. Next we create **classes** for all entities. An exception to this is any 'link entities' that had previously been created from the decomposition of many-to-many relationships (in the example Panel and Interview entities). Notice that Panel has no non-key attributes. In our example the Panel disappears, with both the Interview and PanelMember classes having references to each other. Interview has attributes in its own right. Later we will look at incorporating Interview as a structure in one of the classes to which it relates.

3. Next we consider the properties or attributes of each class. In this simplified methodology we will consider only reference and collection attributes: derived attributes are not included. Looking at **reference attributes**, then all foreign keys in the relation model will become reference attributes in the object model. Thus the class Employee includes an attribute 'dept' which references the Department class. This means that an object Employee will 'include' all attributes and methods for its department as well as the attributes name and tel.

4. The next step is to consider one-to-many and many-to-many relationships in our relation model. Entities involved in such relationships may include **collection attributes**. For two entities, which are associated by a **many-to-many relationship**, then each class will have an

additional collection entity. So both PanelMember and Interview will have new collection entities 'pmInterviews' and 'iPanelMembers' respectively.

5. For all **one-to-many relationships** in the relation model, where one X entity occurrence corresponds to many Y entities, a new collection entity will be included in the X entity (class). For example the 'Cinterviews' collection attribute will be included in the Candidate class to incorporate the set of interviews which each candidate will be attending.

The object-oriented schema

```
class Employee
   properties
      name            char20
      dept            Department
      tel             char15;

class Candidate inherits Employee
   properties
      candNo          char5
      presentPosition char15
      cInterviews     set [Interview];

class PanelMember inherits Employee
   properties
      pmNo            char5
      lastSatOnPanel  date
      pmInterviews    set [Interview];

class Job
   properties
      jobNo           char5
      jobTitle        char15
      startSalary     number
      jobDept         Department
      jInterviews     set [Interview];

class Interview
   properties
      intNo           char5
      intDate         date
      iJob            Job
      cand            Candidate
      iPanelMembers   set [PanelMember];

class Department
   properties
      deptNo          char5
      deptName        char15
      deptHead        Employee
      deptMembers     set [Employee]
      availableJobs   set [Job];
```

Note that the state of the classes are considered only (methods have been left out). Also we ignore inverse attributes and the back reference symbol <->.

The inheritance hierarchy diagram

We can now draw an inheritance hierarchy diagram based on our object-oriented schema. Attributes have been omitted for simplicity.

Figure 8.7: Inheritance hierarchy diagram

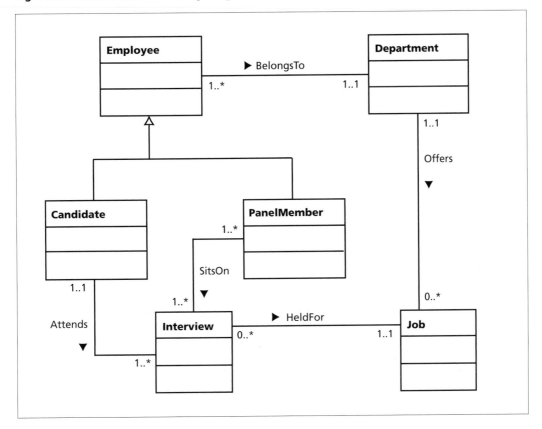

An alternative solution: structured complex objects

As mentioned earlier, Interview, like Panel, is the 'link entity' from a decomposed many-to-many relationship. Note that Panel was not included in our list of classes. In the case of Interview there are non-key attributes (intDate) as part of the class. We could not simply lose the class Interview as we need to include the non-key attribute intDate in our database. An alternative to the previous solution is to incorporate the attribute 'interviews' as a **structure** within one of the classes (for example, in class Job).

Thus:

```
class Employee
    properties
        name            char20
        dept            Department
        tel             char15;

class Candidate inherits Employee
    properties
        candNo          char5
        presentPosition char15;

class PanelMember inherits Employee
    properties
        pmNo            char5
        lastSatOnPanel  date;


class Job
    properties
        jobNo           char5
        jobTitle        char15
        startSalary     number
        jobDept         Department
        interviews      set  [intDate  date
                             cand       Candidate
                             panel      set [PanelMember]  ];

class Department
    properties
        deptNo          char5
        deptName        char15
        deptHead        Employee
        deptMembers     set [Employee]
        availableJobs   set [Job];
```

In our example, retaining the interview class is perhaps a better option but in many cases the use of structures provides a means of modelling complex and interrelated objects.

Referential integrity

You may remember that the referential integrity of a relational database will not be violated if a foreign key in one table matches a primary key in its 'parent' table, or be wholly null. For example, in the Candidates' relation model, a 'deptNo' (department number) in the Candidate entity must match a 'deptNo' in the Department relation or else be null. In the object-oriented model there are several ways of dealing with referential integrity, and different techniques have been implemented by different vendors. They vary on the amount of control the user has in explicitly deleting objects. For example, allow the user to delete and modify objects and relationships when no longer required. Here the system takes care of referential integrity. If we have a relationship from department to candidate and from candidate to department, when a Department object is deleted it is easy for the system to adjust the reference in the Candidate object (for example by setting the reference to null).

Comparison of relationships in relational and OO databases

Consider the most obvious differences between the relational and the object-oriented representation of relationships:

- References are represented using primary keys instead of OIDs in the relational model, although all the models use references as the basis to represent relationships
- Relationship (or link) tables are approximately equivalent to the intermediate objects introduced to represent relationships in an object-oriented model. However, in the relational model, far more are required to satisfy relational normalisation (e.g. when representing many-to-many binary relationships)
- The object-oriented models 'package' all the relationships in which an object type participates as attributes associated with the object. In our previous example, all the relationships for a Department object are shown in the object definition. In the relational model, it is necessary to examine the entire schema to determine which tables have foreign keys involving an entity table such as the Employee table
- Object-oriented models allow manual ordering of relationships using lists
- The access syntax and semantics are quite different.

Problems with the OO model

One of the key arguments against OO databases is that databases are usually not designed to solve specific problems, but we need to be able to use them to solve many different problems – some not always apparent at the design stage of the database. It is for this reason that OO technology and its use of encapsulation can often limit its flexibility. Indeed, the ability to perform ad hoc queries can be made quite difficult, although some vendors do provide a query language to facilitate this.

The use of the same language for both database operations and system operations can provide many advantages, including that of reducing impedance mismatch (the difference in level between set-at-a-time and record-at-a-time processing). C J Date, however, does not agree that this is best achieved by making the database language record-at-a-time; he even goes as far as to say that 'record-at-a-time is a throwback to the days of pre-relational systems such as IMS and IDMS'. Instead, he proposes that set-at-a-time facilities be added to programming languages. Nonetheless, it could be argued that one of the advantages of pre-relational systems was their speed. However, the procedural nature of OO languages can still lead to serious difficulties when it comes to optimisation.

Another problem associated with pure OO databases is that a large proportion of organisations do not currently deal with the complex data types for which OO technology is ideally suited, and therefore they do not require complex data processing. It is rather like using a sledgehammer to crack a nut. For these companies there is little incentive to move towards object technology, when relational databases and online analytical processing tools will be sufficient to satisfy their data processing requirements.

8.10 Oracle and the object-relational model

The **object-relational model** aims to address some of the problems of pure OO technology such as the poor support for ad hoc query languages, and open database technology, and provide better support for existing relational products, by extending the relational model to incorporate the key features of object-orientation. The object-relational model also provides scope for those using existing relational databases to migrate towards the incorporation of objects, and this perhaps is its key strength, in that it provides a path for the vast number of existing relational database users gradually to migrate to an object database platform, while maintaining the support of their relational vendor.

A major addition to the relational model is the introduction of a stronger type system to enable the use of complex data types, which still allow the relational model to be preserved. Several large database suppliers including IBM, Informix and Oracle, have embraced the object-relational model as the way forward. Here we look at some of the object-relational features of Oracle.

Object-relational features in Oracle

Many of the object-oriented features that appear in the ISO SQL standard SQL3 (1999) have been incorporated into Oracle. We shall examine the facilities originally incorporated in Oracle 8 and subsequent versions – these provide a good example of how one of the major database vendors is seeking to increase the level of object support within the DBMS, while still maintaining support for the relational model. Oracle support for OO constructs includes:

- **Abstract data types** – this is discussed further in this section
- **Collection types or collectors** – sets of elements which are treated as a single row. Oracle currently supports array types and nested table – discussed further in this section
- **Object tables** – these are used to store objects while providing a relational view of the attributes of the object – discussed further in this section
- **Object view** – these provide a virtual object table view of data stored in a regular relational table. They allow data to be accessed or viewed as if they were object-oriented tables, even if the data is really stored in relational format
- **Methods** – written in PL/SQL, Java or C.

Note that methods are omitted in the following examples.

Abstract data types

Abstract data types (ADTs) are data types that consist of one or more subtypes. These are provided to enable users to define complex data types – structures consisting of a number of different elements, each of which uses one of the base data types provided within the Oracle product. For example, an abstract data type could be created to store addresses. Such a data type might consist of three separate subtypes such as varchar or number. From the time of its creation, an ADT can be referred to when creating tables in which the ADT is to be used.

The address ADT would be established with the CREATE TYPE definition:

```
Create type AddressType as object
(street      varchar2(30),
 city        varchar2(30),
 country     varchar2(30) );
```

ADTs can be **nested** (their definitions can make use of other ADTs). For example, if we wished to set up an ADT to describe customers, we could make use of the address ADT above as follows:

```
Create type CustomerType as object
(custNo      number(6),
name         varchar2(50),
birthDate    date,
gender       char,
address      AddressType );
```

The advantages of ADTs are that they provide a standard mechanism for defining complex data types within an application, and facilitate reuse of complex data definitions.

Object tables

These are tables created within Oracle 8 (and subsequent versions) which have column values that are based on ADTs. Therefore, if we create a table which makes use of the customer and address ADTs described in the previous example, the table will be an object table. The code to create such a table would be as follows:

```
Create table OTCustomer of CustomerType;
```

Note that this CREATE TABLE statement looks rather different to those encountered in Chapter 5 on SQL data definition language (DDL). It is very brief, because it makes use of the previous work we have done in establishing the customer and address ADTs. It is extremely important to bear in mind the distinction between object tables and ADTs:

- **ADTs** are the building blocks on which object tables can be created. ADTs themselves cannot be queried, in the same way that the built-in data types in Oracle such as number and varchar2 cannot be queried. ADTs simply provide the structure which will be used when objects are inserted into an object table
- **Object tables** are the elements that are queried, and these are established using a combination of base data types such as varchar2, date, number and any relevant ADTs as required.

Example of inserting data into object tables

Consider the ADTs AddressType and CustomerType and the object table OTCustomer above.

To insert data into the OTCustomer table we use the SQL INSERT statement, but also need to include the attributes that make up the ADT (street, city country) surrounded by brackets and prefixed by the name of the ADT, 'AddressType'. So, for example:

```
Insert into OTCustomer values('123','Harjinder', '01-jan-80', 'm',
AddressType('17 High Road', 'New Tow', 'England'));
```

To display the customer number and street:

```
Select custNo, c.address.street
From customer c;
```

Note alias 'c' is needed here.

Nested tables

A nested table is a 'table within a table'. It is a collection of rows, represented as a column in the main table. For each record in the main table, the nested table may contain multiple rows. This can be considered as a way of storing a one-to-many relationship within one table. For example, if we have a table storing the details of departments, and each department is associated with a number of projects, we can use a nested table to store details about projects within the department table. The project records can be accessed directly through the corresponding row of the department table, without needing to do a join. Note that the nested table mechanism sacrifices first normal form, as we are now storing a repeating group of projects associated with each department record. This may be acceptable, if it is likely to be a frequent requirement to access departments with their associated projects in this way.

For example, we could create a table of pet owners which includes data about the owners' pets. Using a nested table, the information about both owners and pets can be stored.

```
Create  or replace type PetType as object
    (petNo        number(6),
    name          varchar2(50),
    birthDate     date,
    gender        char,
    breed         varchar2(30) );
```

Note the optional use of OR REPLACE in the CREATE statement, which ensures that existing tables of this name are deleted first.

To use this ADT as the basis for a nested table we now need to create a new ADT thus:

```
Create or replace type PetNestedtable as table of PetType;
```

The AS TABLE clause tells Oracle that the type created will be the basis of a nested table. We now create a table of pet owners. The third column of this table 'pets' has a type which is a nested table.

```
Create table Owner
    (ownerNo    number(6),
    name        varchar2(50),
    pets        PetNestedtable)
    nested table pets store as PetNestedtable_tab;
```

Thus, the data in the pets column will be stored in one table and the data in the other columns (ownerNo, name) will be stored in a separate table with pointers between the tables. In the example, the nested table will be stored in PetNestedtable_tab.

Varying arrays

A varying array, **varray**, is a collection of objects, each with the same data type. The size of the array is preset when it is created. The varying array is treated like a column in a main table. Conceptually, it is a nested table, with a preset limit on its number of rows. Varrays also then allow us to store up to a preset number of repeating values in a table. The data type for a varray is determined by whatever the type of data that is to be stored.

A varying array is based on either an ADT or one of Oracle's standard data types. Oracle suggests that if the array you wish to create is based on more than one column it is better to use nested tables instead. In the example we will create a varying array which stores pet names in an owner table. We start by creating a new data type PetNamesType:

```
Create type PetNamesType as object
   (petName varchar2(50) );
```

To use this ADT in varying array we will need to decide on the maximum number of pets per owner – assume ten. Now we create the varying array:

```
Create type PetNamesVA as varray(10) of PetNamesType;
```

Now we create an Owner table with a varying array of type PetNamesType for its Pet column:

```
Create table Owner
   (ownerNo    number(6),
    name       varchar2(50),
    pets       PetNamesVA);
```

Listing types and removing types

It is useful to list the types you have created in your Oracle area.

```
SQL> select type_name
2  from user_types;

TYPE_NAME
AddressType
CustomerType
......
```

Existing types can be deleted using the DROP TYPE command, for example:

```
SQL> drop type AddressType;
```

But note that you cannot drop a type if a table which you have created depends on it.

Object-oriented data modelling

We have already looked at the case study concerning Middlesex Transport, which is responsible for running a fleet of buses throughout North London. The scenario is given in Chapter 4 and the relation model is repeated below.

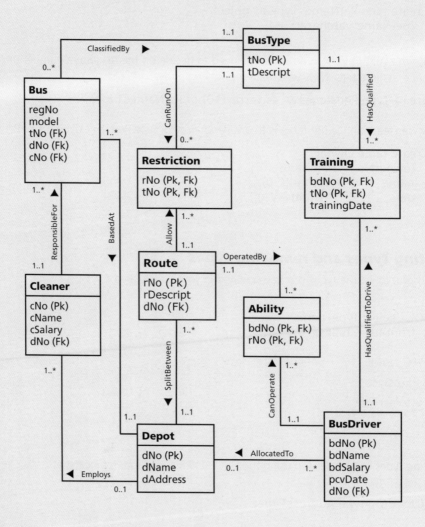

Remind yourself of the details of the scenario and consider the previous diagram. Now construct an equivalent object-oriented database schema in the form:

```
Class   ClassName
        properties
        name        char12
        address     address
        etc
```

Note: predefined types (such as characters and numbers) can be omitted.

Activity 8.3

Further development of objects in Oracle

Visit the website **http://Oracle.com** and find out about further aspects of object support within the Oracle10g database and later systems. Much of this information is included within white papers. In particular, look for summaries of new features, and a paper on Objects and the Extensibility option.

8.11 Summary

In this chapter, we introduced the enhanced entity-relationship, object-oriented and object-relational models. Object-oriented concepts, which are part of the object-oriented programming model, were examined and their importance as part of the object-oriented database model was emphasised. We introduced a methodology for converting a relational model to object-oriented. Next the focus was on object-relational databases, and some of Oracle's object-oriented database extensions were studied and practised.

8.12 Review questions

Review question 8.1   Using the template below, fill in the **Relational** column to compare the characteristics of CAD and CAM systems with conventional relational databases.

CAD/CAM	Relational
Data has many types, each with a small number of instances	
Designs may be very large, with maybe millions of parts and often there will be interdependent subsystem designs	
They evolve through time	
Updates are far-reaching – one change may affect a large number of design objects	
Various versions of designs must be maintained, with many staff working on these versions at the same time. There needs to be version control and the final product must be consistent and coordinated	

Review question 8.2   Suggest three or four classes that might be needed for the personnel department of a university. Now create two or three instances for each of your university classes.

Review question 8.3   One approach to developing an OODBMS is to extend an existing OO programming language (such as C++ or Java) with database capabilities. Describe three other approaches.

Review question 8.4   Describe the difference between methods and messages in object-oriented systems.

Review question 8.5   What are the advantages of inheritance?

Review question 8.6   Define each of the following concepts:

1. Object
2. Attribute
3. Object identity
4. Complex object

Review question 8.7   What are the advantages of OIDs compared with primary keys in relational databases?

Review question 8.8   The OODB Manifesto proposed thirteen mandatory features for an object-oriented DBMS. Eight of these features apply to OO concepts; the rest to features one would expect to find in *any* DBMS. Can you identify the eight?

Review question 8.9   What is meant by generalisation, and what is its importance to the object-oriented data model?

Review question 8.10   Assume that there are two existing classes, Supplier and Customer, with attributes:

1. Supplier (sno, companyName, address, telephoneNo, contactPerson, balanceOwing)

2. Customer (cno, companyName, address, telephoneNo, balanceOwed)

Use the bottom-up approach of generalisation to create a class or classes from these existing classes.

Review question 8.11 (i)   Consider a subset of a hospital information system with the following characteristics:

- Patients can either be resident patients or outpatients

- For both types of patients we will need to hold the name, telephone number, date of birth and the patient's doctor (GP)

- For a resident patient we will need to hold the ward name in which the patient is currently residing, the admission date of the patient, and also information about any operations that the patient has had

- The operation information will include the date and time of the operation, the surgeon (assume one) who carried out the operation, plus the theatre where the operation took place

- For both GPs and surgeons we will hold the name and telephone number; in addition we will hold the surgeon's specialism (e.g. ear, nose and throat) – assume one per surgeon

- For outpatients we will need to hold information about the outpatients' appointments: the appointment date and time.

Draw an entity-relationship diagram for the above case, making any assumptions that you need to make about optional/mandatory relationships. Indicate primary and foreign keys. You can omit the type for each attribute. Map this ERD to a relational model.

Review question 8.11 (ii)   Now construct an equivalent object-oriented database schema including any structured attributes. In this case include the type of the attributes, but only those that are specific to the object-oriented schema.

Review question 8.11 (iii)   Now draw a class diagram based on your object-oriented schema in question 8.11 (ii).

Review question 8.12 (i)   Consider an Employee Database. The entities are given below:

Employee (eNo: varchar(10), eName: varchar(20), deptNo: varchar(10), presentPosition: varchar(20))

Department (deptNo: varchar(10), deptName: varchar2(20), deptHead: varchar2(20))

Write Oracle abstract data type definitions for the Candidate and Department entities and try running these in Oracle SQL*Plus.

Review question 8.12 (ii)   Now create object tables based on these ADTs. State the difference between the object tables and the ADTs.

Review question 8.12 (iii)   Suppose that employees are assigned to projects: one project per employee. A project will have a number of employees working on the project. A project includes a project number, description and expected number of days for completion. Create the table for the project (called OTProject) which includes a nested table of employees who work on the project (i.e. use the EmployeeType type definition created in question 8.12(i) as the basis of a nested table in a project table).

Review question 8.13   Students taking a course can do up to ten assessments. Suggest a table definition for a Student object which holds registration number, name, email address and grades. Include any necessary type statements in your answer.

8.13 Feedback on activities

Answer 8.1 Your grid should look something like:

Shortcomings of the relational approach	Advantages of OODBMSs
Poor representation of 'real world' entities; only one construct for representing both entities and relationships: the relation (semantic overloading)	Enriched modelling capabilities: both state and behaviour encapsulated. More natural representation of the real world
Homogeneous data structure; all attribute values must be atomic	Objects store the relationship it has with other objects; many-to-many relationships supported. Objects can be formed into complex objects
Poor support for integrity and no support for enterprise constraints	Better support for integrity and enterprise constraints
Limited operations; most DMLs lack computational completeness	More expressive query language. Most OODBMSs provide a DML that is computationally complete
Impedance mismatch – inefficiencies occur when mapping a declarative language such as SQL to a procedural language such as C	Removal of impedance mismatch – OO languages are row level (rather than set level)
	Improved performance, although this is arguable
	Extensibility – new types built from existing types
	Reduced redundancy and reusability – forming a superclass involves factoring out common properties of several classes and through this inheritance mechanism the state and behaviour of an object can be made available to other objects
Schema changes difficult	Support for schema evolution.
Difficulty in modelling complex applications	Applicability to advanced database applications

cont...

Answer 8.2 Note that system types such as characters and numbers have been omitted.

Class Employee
   properties
      eNo
      eName
      eSalary
      eDepot   **Depot**

Class BusDriver inherits Employee
   properties
      pcvDate
      bdAbility   **set[Route]**
      bdTraining   **set[Training]**

Class Cleaner inherits Employee
   properties
      cBuses   **set[bus]**

Class Route
   properties
      rNo
      rDescipt
      rDepot   **Depot**
      rRestrictions   **set[BusType]**
      rAbility   **set[BusDriver]**

Class Bus
   properties
      regNo
      model
      bType   **Bustype**
      bDepot   **Depot**
      bCleaner   **Cleaner**

Class Bustype
   properties
      tNo
      tDescript
      tRestrictions   **set[Route]**
      tTraining   **set[Training]**
      tBuses   **set[Bus]**

Class Depot
   properties
      dNo
      dName
      dAddress
      dRoutes   **set[Route]**
      dEmployees   **set[Employee]**
      dBuses   **set[Bus]**

Class Training
   properties
      tDriver   **BusDriver**
      tType   **BusType**
      tTrainingdate

Transaction management and concurrency control

OVERVIEW

The purpose of this chapter is to introduce the fundamental technique of **concurrency control**. This provides database systems with the ability to handle many users accessing data simultaneously. Problems arise from the fact that users wish to query and update stored data at the same time. If these operations are not controlled, then the database may become inconsistent. This chapter helps you understand the functionality of database management systems, with special reference to **online transaction processing** (OLTP).

These topics fit closely with the next chapter – on backup and recovery – so you may want to revisit this chapter later to review the concepts here. It will become clear that there are a number of circumstances where recovery procedures may need to be invoked to salvage previously executed or currently executing transactions.

Learning outcomes On completion of this chapter, you should be able to:

- Understand the purpose of concurrency control

- Explain what a transaction is, its properties and the reasons for designing databases around transactions

- Analyse the problems of data management in a concurrent environment

- Critically compare the relative strengths of different concurrency control approaches.

9.1 Introduction

This chapter describes the problems that arise from the fact that users wish to query and update stored data at the same time. It examines the **concurrency control techniques** that are used to ensure the non-interference of concurrently executing transactions. Central to the understanding of concurrency control is the concept of the **transaction**. We therefore examine its importance and function. If concurrent operations are not controlled, then the database may become inconsistent. We will be looking at a number of concepts that are technical and unfamiliar. You will be expected to be able to handle these concepts, but not to have any knowledge of the detailed algorithms involved.

We will be examining particular concurrency control problems which occur when multiple transactions, submitted by various users, interfere with one another in a way that produces incorrect results. We will look at ways in which such problems might be addressed, and explore the protocols, or sets of rules, which can be applied to prevent conflict when transactions are executing concurrently. One important set of protocols we will be covering employs the technique of **locking data items** to prevent multiple transactions from accessing the items concurrently. This chapter also looks at the particular problem of **deadlock** and examines ways in which it can be resolved.

9.2 Transactions

What is a transaction?

A transaction is the execution of a program that accesses or changes the content of a database. It may be the entire program, a portion of a program or a single command. It may be distributed (i.e. available on different physical systems or different logical subsystems) and use data concurrently with other transactions.

A transaction has a clear start and finish. The assumption is that it will start its execution on a consistent database, and if it runs to completion then the transaction is said to be **committed** and the database will be in a new consistent state. Once a transaction is committed, the transaction manager knows that the database is (or should be) in a **consistent state** again and all of the updates made by that transaction can now be made permanent. If the changes are made permanent, then the database has reached a **new synchronisation point**.

The other possibility is that the transactions do not commit satisfactorily (i.e. do not reach their end). In this case, the transaction is **aborted** and the incomplete transaction is **rolled back** (the exact way in which this is done will be considered in the backup and recovery chapter) and the database restored to the consistent state it was in before the transaction started. In an SQL database, an entire program or user session is regarded as one transaction; however, the user may explicitly force a commit or rollback using the 'commit' or 'rollback' commands.

Desirable properties of transactions

The acronym ACID indicates the properties of well-formed transactions. Any transaction that violates these principles will cause concurrency problems.

Properties of transactions:

- **Atomicity:** a transaction is an atomic unit of processing; all of the tasks of a transaction are performed or not performed at all. A transaction does not partly happen
- **Consistency:** the database state is consistent at the end of a transaction
- **Isolation:** a transaction should not make its updates visible to other transactions until it is committed This property, when enforced strictly, solves the temporary update problem and makes cascading rollbacks of transactions unnecessary
- **Durability:** when a transaction has made a change to the database state and the change is committed, this change is permanent and should be available to all other transactions.

Transaction operations

For recovery purposes, a system always keeps track of when a transaction starts, terminates, and commits or aborts. Hence, the recovery manager keeps track of the following transaction states and operations (these keywords are indicative of many data manipulation languages):

- **BEGIN_TRANSACTION:** this marks the beginning of transaction execution
- **READ or WRITE:** these specify read or write operations on the database items that are executed as part of a transaction
- **END_TRANSACTION:** this specifies that READ and WRITE operations have ended and marks the end limit of transaction execution. However, at this point it may be necessary to check whether the changes introduced by the transaction can be permanently applied to the database (committed) or whether the transaction has to be aborted because it violates concurrency control or for some other reason (rollback)
- **COMMIT_TRANSACTION:** this signals a successful end of the transaction so that any changes (updates) executed by the transaction can be safely committed to the database and will not be undone
- **ROLLBACK:** this signals that the transaction has ended unsuccessfully, so that any changes or effects that the transaction may have applied to the database must be undone.

In addition to the preceding operations, some recovery techniques require additional operations that include the following:

- **UNDO:** similar to rollback, except that it applies to a single operation rather than to a whole transaction
- **REDO:** this specifies that some of a transaction's operations must be redone to ensure that all the operations of a committed transaction have been applied successfully to the database.

Transaction states

This section describes how a transaction moves through its execution states. A transaction goes into an **active state** immediately after it starts execution, where it can issue READ and WRITE operations. When the transaction ends, it moves to the **partially committed state**. At this point, some concurrency control techniques require that certain checks are made to ensure that the transaction did not interfere with other executing transactions. In addition, some recovery protocols are needed, to ensure that a system failure will not result in an inability to record the changes of the transaction permanently.

Once both checks are successful, the transaction is said to have reached its **commit point** and enters the **committed state**. Once a transaction enters the committed state, it has concluded its execution successfully.

However, a transaction can go to the **failed state** if one of the checks fails, or if it aborted during its active state. The transaction may then have to be rolled back to undo the effect of its WRITE operations on the database. The **terminated state** corresponds to the transaction leaving the system. Failed or aborted transactions may be restarted later, either automatically, or after being resubmitted as brand-new transactions.

9.3 Read and write operations

From the point of view of interaction with data in a database, the DBMS activities with which we are concerned will be simplified. There are only two activities.

The database item can be read:

> read_item(x)

which reads a database item named x into a program variable x;

and it can be written:

> write_item(x)

which writes the value of a program variable x into the database item named x.

Transaction theory and practice is about ensuring that data is read accurately and written accurately, though, as you will see, there may be compromises to make.

Read and write operations of a transaction

In order to recover successfully, many recovery mechanisms keep a log of certain operations. These key database access operations are:

read_item(x)

This includes the following steps:

1. Locate disk sector   Compute the address of the disk block that contains item x.
2. Copy item(x)   Copy the disk block into a memory buffer
   (if that disk block is not already in some main memory buffer).
3. Copy item(x)   Copy item x from the buffer to the variable named x.

write_item (x)

This includes the following steps:

1. Locate disk sector	Find the address of the disk block that contains item x.
2. Copy disk block into memory	Copy that disk block into a buffer in main memory (if that disk block is not already in some main memory buffer).
3. Copy application variable x to item x in main memory	Copy item x from the program variable named x into its correct location in the main memory buffer either immediately or at some later point in time.
4. Store sector to disk	Store the updated block in the buffer back to disk either immediately or at some later point in time.

In this and subsequent chapters, it is assumed that the read statement 'read(a)', executed by a transaction, has the effect of copying the contents of the field 'a' in the database into the variable 'a' in the transaction. Similarly, a write statement 'write(a)', executed by a transaction, has the effect of copying the variable 'a' in the transaction into the field 'a' in the database.

The database buffer

Note that transactions read and write to a database buffer rather than directly to the disk itself. It is this buffer that transactions read from and write to directly: the buffer in turn reads from and writes to disk. The use of a database buffer dramatically improves processing performance. As we shall see in Chapter 10 on recovery, the buffer is not necessarily changed immediately after a program variable is changed. It may not be carried out immediately after a write is issued, but may be deferred while other transaction operations are performed. Usually, the decision is determined by the recovery manager of the DBMS. If the writes are not written directly to the database on disk and transaction failure occurs, then this is a problem that the recovery manager has to solve. For the purposes of this chapter, however, we assume that changes made by an application program are made immediately to the buffer.

9.4 **Concurrent access of data**

Many computer systems can be used simultaneously by more than one user. This is made possible by **multiprogramming**, a technique that allows the computer to run multiple programs (or transactions) at the same time. If, as is usually the case, only one CPU exists, then only one program can be processed at a time. Therefore, to avoid excessive delays for an individual user, multiprogramming systems give all users equal time slices on the CPU, executing commands from all queued processes for short, interleaved periods.

Due to the speed at which these commands are executed, the impression of concurrent use is given to the users. This process is known as **interleaving**. This uses the CPU efficiently by allowing it to run a portion of another program, when the program currently running on the CPU requires some input or output to secondary storage (such a disk access). An important issue is that more than one application may attempt to access the same data item. As a result, data stored in a multi-user DBMS can be damaged or destroyed. To overcome this problem, **concurrency control techniques** have been developed to protect data from incorrect changes caused by transactions running simultaneously.

Scheduling transactions problems

Scheduling of transactions is under the control of a transaction manager and may involve different users submitting transactions that execute concurrently, for example accessing and updating the same database records. The transaction manager is responsible for interleaving different transactions.

If transactions do not use the same database items, then there are no concurrency problems. However, if transactions do use the same database items, there are various ways in which a transaction, though correct in itself, can nevertheless produce an inconsistent database. This section examines three problems that can occur when concurrent transactions execute in an uncontrolled manner:

- The lost update problem
- The uncommitted dependency problem
- The inconsistent analysis problem.

These problems are described in the following scenarios in which bank accounts undergo credits, debits or money transfers.

The lost update problem

Interleaved use of the same item can be a problem where one update overwrites another. This is known as a **lost update**. Consider the following situation:

In example 9.1, there are two transactions (T1 and T2). These are submitted at approximately the same time. In our bank scenario, there may be an attempt to update a balance field in an account record by two different transactions simultaneously. Suppose that their operations are interleaved by the operating system, as shown in the example.

Example 9.1: Lost update problem

Time	Transaction T1	Transaction T2	Comments
1	read_item(x)		Read operation is performed in transaction T1 at time 1
2	x:=x–40	read_item(x)	At time 2 the value of data item x is modified by T1. A read operation is performed in transaction T2
3	write_item(x)	x:=x+20	At time 3 a write operation is performed in transaction T1. The value of data item x is modified by T2
4		write_item(x)	Write operation is performed in transaction T2 at time 4

Note that transaction operations BEGIN_TRANSACTION, END_TRANSACTION, COMMIT, etc have been omitted from the example above (and subsequent examples). The lost update problem occurs when two transactions, which access the same database items, have their operations interleaved in a way that makes the value of some database item incorrect.

The above interleaved operation will lead to an incorrect value for data item x, because at time 2, T2 reads in the original value of x, which is before T1 changes it in the database, and hence the updated value resulting from T1 is lost. For example, if x = 100 at time 1, (i.e. the balance on the account is 100), T1 reduces x by 40 and therefore, at time 3, 60 is written to the database.

At time 4, T2 writes an updated version of x to the database but this is based on the original value of x. The final result should be x = 100 – 40 + 20 = 80; but in the concurrent operations in our example, it is x = 120 because the update at time 3 by T1 was lost.

The uncommitted dependency problem

An uncommitted dependency problem occurs when a transaction is allowed to retrieve – or worse, update – a record that has been updated by another transaction, but has not yet been committed by that other transaction. This is because if it has *not yet* been committed there is always a possibility that it will *never* be committed, and that it will be rolled back instead. In this case the first transaction will have used some data that is now incorrect. Consider the following situation:

Example 9.2: Uncommitted dependency problem

Time	Transaction T1	Transaction T2	Comments
1		read_item(x)	
2		x:=x–20	
3		write_item(x)	x is temporarily updated
4	read_item(x)	...	
5	...	**ROLLBACK**	T2 fails and must change the value of x back to its old value; meanwhile T1 has read the temporary incorrect value of x

At time 3, transaction T2 has updated the value of x. Transaction T1 fetches the result of an uncommitted update at time 4. That update is then undone at time 5. Transaction T1 is therefore operating on a false assumption, namely, that item x has the value at time 3, whereas x has whatever value it has at time 1. As a result, transaction T1 may well produce incorrect output. There are a number of reasons for a transaction rolling back; for example, rollback of transaction T2 may be due to a system crash, and transaction T1 may already have terminated by that time, in which case the crash would not cause a rollback to be issued for T1.

Consider the following, even more unacceptable, situation:

Example 9.3: The dirty read

Time	Transaction T1	Transaction T2	Comments
1		read_item(x);	
2		x:=x–20;	
3		write_item(x)	x is temporarily updated
4	read_item(x)		
5	x:=x+100;		
6	write_item(x)		
7	**COMMIT**		
8	Read_item(y)	... **ROLLBACK**	T1 depends on uncommitted value and loses an update

In this case, not only does transaction T1 become dependent on an uncommitted change at time 4 but it also loses an update at time 7, because the rollback causes item x to be restored to its value before time 1.

This problem is also known as **the dirty read**. Data may be made available to one transaction before completion of the second transaction. If the second transaction does not complete successfully, and the original data is restored, the first transaction may continue with inaccurate data.

The inconsistent analysis problem

The inconsistent analysis problem occurs when a transaction reads several values, but a second transaction updates some of these values during the execution of the first. This is significant, for example if one transaction is calculating an aggregate summary function on a number of records, while other transactions are updating some of these records. The aggregate functions may calculate some values before they are updated, and others after they are updated. Therefore, different summaries (SUMs, and COUNTs for example) may be inconsistent.

Consider the following situation in which a number of Account records have the following values:

ACC1	ACC2	ACC3
40	50	30

If 10 is transferred from ACC 3 to ACC 1, while concurrently calculating the total funds in the three accounts, the following sequence of events may occur:

Example 9.4: Inconsistent analysis problem

Time	Transaction T2	Transaction	Comments
0	sum = 0	...	
1	read_item(ACC1)		
2	sum:= sum+ ACC1		
3	read_item (ACC2)		
4	sum:= sum+ACC2		Sum is now 90
5		read_item (ACC3)	
6		read_item (ACC1)	
7		ACC3 = ACC3–10	
8		ACC1 = ACC1+10	
9		write_item (ACC3)	ACC3 is now 20
10		write_item (ACC1)	ACC1 is now 50
11		**COMMIT**	
12	read_item (ACC 3)		T1 has value 20 for ACC3
13	sum:= sum+ACC3		Sum is now 110 which is incorrect!

The two transactions are operating on account (ACC) records: transaction T1 is summing account balances; transaction T2 is transferring an amount 10 from ACC3 to ACC1. The result produced by transaction T1 (110) is obviously incorrect: if T1 were to write that result back into the database, it would leave the database in an inconsistent state. Transaction T1 has seen an inconsistent state of the database, and therefore performed an inconsistent analysis.

Note the difference between this example and the previous one: there is no question in this case of T1 being dependent on an uncommitted change, since T2 commits all its updates before T1 fetches the value in ACC3.

Lost update problems

Given the following transactions and assume that x = 5 and m =10:

Transaction T1	Transaction T2
read_item(x);	read_item(x);
x:=x–m;	x:=x+m;
write_item(x);	write_item(x);

Generate a schedule of operations that illustrates the lost update problem.

Activity 9.2

Uncommitted dependency problem

Given the following transactions and assume that x = 5, m = 10, n = 15:

Transaction T1	Transaction T2
read_item(x);	read_item(x);
x:=x–n;	x:=x+m;
write_item(x);	write_item(x);
	ROLLBACK

Generate a schedule of operations that illustrates the uncommitted dependency problem.

Activity 9.3

Inconsistent analysis problem

Given the following transactions and assume that x = 5, y = 20, z = 30:

Transaction T1	Transaction T2
read_item(x);	sum:=0
read_item(y);	read_item(x);
read_item(z)	sum:=sum+x;
y:=y*z	read_item(y);
write(y)	sum:=sum+y;
x:=x*z	write_item(sum)
write(x)	

Generate a schedule of operations that illustrates the inconsistent analysis problem.

Serial schedules

An obvious way to overcome the problems described earlier is for transactions to be scheduled serially. A schedule S is **serial** if, for every transaction T participating in the schedule, all of the operations of T are executed consecutively in the schedule. In other words, **serial execution of transactions** means transactions are performed one after another without any interleaving of operations. If we have two transactions, A and B, then there are only two possible serial schedules: completing all operations of A then all operations of B, or completing all operations of B then all operations of A. Although in many cases all possible serial schedules will leave databases in identical states, there is no guarantee that this will be the case. Pragmatically, this may be very important. In banking, for example, it matters whether interest for an account is calculated before or after a large deposit. However, as far as the DBMS is concerned, no serial execution will allow the database to be left in an inconsistent state, and every serial execution is considered to be correct even though different results may be produced.

In this case, the validity of the sequence of the calculations is the responsibility of the application software, not the DBMS.

Non-serial schedules

The major problem with serial execution is that it is inefficient. Concurrent processing, in which the operations of transactions are interleaved, is far more efficient. These kinds of schedules are termed **non-serial schedules**. However, when operations may be interleaved, there will be many possible orders (or schedules) in which the system can execute the individual operations of the transactions. This is a more flexible approach, but some constraints must be applied if the resulting schedule is to be correct.

Serializable schedules

Intuitively, it is obvious that the schedules shown in the previous examples are 'wrong' in some way. It is also clear that there is a need for a formal definition for the correctness of schedules, as this formal definition can be used to verify the validity of scheduling algorithms. An important area of concurrency control, called **serializability theory**, attempts to determine which schedules are correct and which are not – and to develop techniques that only allow correct schedules. If a set of transactions executes concurrently, we say that the schedule is correct if it produces the same results as some serial execution. Such a schedule is called **serializable**. It is essential to guarantee serializability in order to ensure database correctness.

Figure 9.1: Relationship between non-serial and serializable schedules

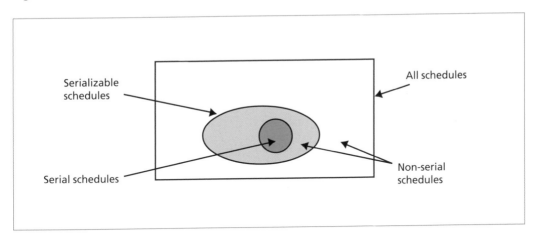

With reference to figure 9.1, the grey areas indicate all serializable schedules, that is, those schedules which produce consistent and correct results. Notice that this includes the darker grey area – serial schedules.

In determining strategies to generate serializable schedules, the following factors are significant:

- If two transactions are only reading a variable, they do not conflict and order is not important
- If two transactions read or write completely separate variables, they do not conflict and order is not important
- If one transaction writes to a variable and another either reads or writes to the same variable, the order of execution is important.

Serializability can be achieved in several ways, but most systems use either **locking** or **time stamping**. Usually, the DBMS has a concurrency control subsystem that is part of the DBMS package, and is not directly controllable by either the users or the DBA. The task of the DBMS is to 'select' an efficient serializable schedule from the huge potential pool of schedules, many of which will be inefficient or incorrect (or both).

9.5 Locking

Aim of locking

One way of providing serializable execution of transactions is by means of a locking mechanism. A **lock** is a variable associated with a data item in the database, and it describes the status of that data item with respect to possible operations that can be applied to the item. The overall aim of locking is to obtain maximum concurrency and minimum delay in processing transactions. The idea of locking is simple: when a transaction needs an assurance that some object it is accessing, typically a database record, will not change in some unpredictable manner while the transaction is not running on the CPU, it acquires a lock on that object. The lock bars access to the object by other transactions. Thus the first transaction can be sure that the object in question will remain in a stable state, as long as the transaction needs it. One important lock is the multiple-mode lock, which can apply an **exclusive** (write) or **shared** (read) lock onto the object to be locked, before the corresponding database read or write operation is performed.

Granularity of locks

Locks have **granularity**: the size of the object locked may vary, it may be the entire database, a whole file, a disk block, a database record, or a field value of a database record. Locks with a large granularity are easy to administer but cause frequent contention for items. Locks with small granularity are difficult to administer (they may involve many more details for the DBMS to keep track of and check) but conflict is less frequent. In examples in this chapter, we are deliberately vague and assume that the granularity is a 'data item'.

Shared locks (S locks)

If a DBMS wishes to read an item, then a **shared lock** may be placed onto that item. If a transaction has a shared lock on a database, it can read the item but not update it. If a transaction A holds a shared lock on record R, then a request from transaction B for an S lock on R will be granted (that is, B will now also hold an S lock on R). However, a request from transaction B for an X lock on R will cause B to go into a wait state (and B will wait until A's lock is released).

Exclusive locks (X locks)

If a DBMS wishes to write an item, then an **exclusive lock** may be placed onto that item. If a transaction has an exclusive lock on an item, it can both read and update it. To prevent interference from other transactions, only one transaction can hold an exclusive lock on an item at any given time. If a transaction A holds an exclusive lock on record R, then a request from transaction B for a lock of either type on R will cause B to go into a wait state (and B will wait until A's lock is released).

This can be summarised in the table 9.1 (if transaction A holds the lock specified along the top of the table, then the matrix indicates whether transaction B can request the types of locks indicated down the left):

Table 9.1: Exclusive and shared locks

	Type of lock that A holds on R Exclusive lock	Shared lock	No lock
Type of lock on R that B requests			
Exclusive lock	N	N	Y
Shared lock	N	Y	Y
No lock	Y	Y	Y

Acquiring and removing locks

Locking is usually achieved by inserting a flag into the field record page, or similar field, to indicate that part of the database is locked. Transaction requests for record locks are normally **implicit** (at least in most modern systems). In addition, a user may specify **explicit** locks. When a transaction successfully retrieves a record, it automatically acquires a **shared lock** on that record. When a transaction successfully updates a record, it automatically acquires an **exclusive lock** on that record. If the transaction already has a shared hold on the record, then the update will promote the shared lock to the exclusive level, as long as T is the only transaction with a shared lock on X at the time. Exclusive and shared locks are normally held until the next **synchronisation point:** where all of the updates made by the transaction can now be made permanent, and the database is in a consistent state. However, a transaction can explicitly release locks that it holds prior to termination using the 'Unlock' command.

Use of locking

In the following section, the use of exclusive and shared locks to guarantee serializability will be examined. In the following examples, locks are assumed to be implicit and unlocking is not allowed.

We will examine the three problems of:

- Lost update
- Uncommitted dependency
- Inconsistent analysis

... and consider if the use of such locks will resolve these problems.

Lost update problem

Table 9.2: Deadlock

Time T1	Transaction T2	Transaction	Comments
1	read_item(x) (acquires S lock on x)		Implicit locks are acquired before a read. Read operation is performed in transaction T1 at time 1
2	x:=x–40	read_item(x) (acquires S lock on x)	At time 2 the value of data item x is modified by T1. A read operation is performed in transaction T2
3	write_item(x) (request X lock on x)	x:=x+20	The value of data item x is modified by T2. Also at time 3 there is a request for an X lock on data item x by T1, but T1 must wait for release of S lock by T2
4	Wait	write_item(x) (request X lock on X)	At time 4 there is a request for an X lock on data item x by T2, but T2 must wait for release of S lock by T1
5	Wait	Wait	Both transactions waiting for S locks on x to be released

Consider the lost update problem presented earlier, amended to illustrate the use of locking. At time 3 there is no possibility of T1 acquiring an X lock on x, as there already exists an S lock on x, therefore it has to wait. Transaction T2 at time 4 also tries to get an X lock on x, but is unable to, as T1 itself has an S lock on it, therefore both wait fruitlessly for the other to release a lock. This situation is known as a deadly embrace or **deadlock**. The lost update problem does not occur, but the problem of deadlock now exists which we will discuss later.

The uncommitted dependency problem

Table 9.3: Uncommitted dependency with locking

Time T1	Transaction T2	Transaction	Comments
1		read_item(x); (acquire S lock on x)	
2		x:=x–20;	
3		write_item(x) (acquire X lock on x)	
4	read_item(x) (request S lock on x)		At time 4 there is a request for an S lock on data item x by T1, but T1 must wait for release of X lock by T2
5	Wait		
n	resume: read_item(x) (acquire S lock on x)	Commit (release X lock on x)	
n+1	...		

Table 9.3 shows what happens to the interleaved executions of the uncommitted dependency problem, but with the addition of a locking mechanism. Transaction T1's operation at time 4 is not accepted because it involves an implicit request for an S lock on x, and an X lock is already held by T2, so T1 goes into a wait state. It remains in that wait state until T2 reaches a synchronisation point (either commit or rollback) when T2's lock is released, and T1 is able to proceed. At that point T1 sees a committed value – the pre-T2 value if T2 terminates with a rollback, or the post-T2 value otherwise. Either way, T1 is no longer dependent on an uncommitted update. So in this case, locking solves the problem.

9.6 Guaranteeing serializability

Unlocking

To overcome the problem of deadlock it is tempting to allow **unlocking** to occur. If items to be used are locked, accessed and unlocked in a contiguous sequence of operations in a schedule, then the deadlocking impasse can be avoided. However, another important problem is then encountered: if unlocking is allowed, then the serializability of schedules in which transactions participate cannot be guaranteed. Thus, these schedules of transactions may result in incorrect states of the database. For example:

Transaction T1	Transaction T2
read_lock(y)	read_lock(x)
read_item(y)	read_item(x)
unlock(y)	unlock(x)
write_lock(x)	write_lock(y)
read_item(x)	read_item(y)
x:=x+y	y:=x+y
write_item(x)	write_item(y)
unlock(x)	unlock(y)

Initial values: x = 20, y = 30

Results of serial schedule **transaction T₁** followed by **transaction T₂**: x = 50, y = 80

Results of serial schedule **transaction T₂** followed by **transaction T₁**: x = 70, y = 50

Consider the interleaved schedule S:

T1	T2
read_lock(y)	
read_item(y)	
unlock(y)	
	read_lock(x)
	read_item(x)
	unlock(x)
	write_lock(y)
	read_item(y)
	y:=x+y
	write_item(y)
	unlock(y)
write_lock(x)	
read_item(x)	
x:=x+y	
write_item(x)	
unlock(x)	

Result of schedule S: x = 50, y = 50. This **schedule is not serializable** because the item y in transaction T1, and x in transaction T2, were unlocked too early.

Guaranteeing serializability

We have seen that using locks in themselves does not guarantee serializability. To guarantee serializability, an additional protocol must be included. This protocol concerns the positioning of locking and unlocking operations in every transaction and is known as **two-phase locking (2PL)**.

There are a number of variations including:

- Basic 2PL
- Conservative 2PL
- Strict 2PL.

Basic two-phase locking (2PL)

A transaction is said to follow the **basic two-phase locking** protocol if, within a transaction, all locking operations (read_lock, write_lock) precede the first unlock operation. A transaction which follows the protocol has two phases: the **expanding phase** or growing phase (during which new locks on items can be acquired but none can be released), followed by a **shrinking phase** during which existing locks can be released but no new locks can be acquired. It can be proved that if every transaction in a schedule follows the two-phase locking protocol, then the schedule is guaranteed to be serializable. Unfortunately, this protocol may reintroduce the problem of deadlock.

Two-phase locking may limit the amount of concurrency that can occur in a schedule. This is because a transaction T may not be able to release an item x after it has finished using x – if T needs to lock an additional item y later on. Conversely, T must lock the additional item y before it needs it so that it can release x. Hence, x must remain locked by T until all items that the transaction needs have been locked – only then can x be released by T. Meanwhile, another transaction waiting to access x may be forced to wait, even though T has finished using x. Conversely, if y is locked earlier than it is needed, another transaction wanting to access y is forced to wait even though T is not using y yet. This is the price for guaranteeing serializability of all schedules without having to check the schedules themselves. The benefit is the guaranteed correctness of the resulting permanent values in the database.

Transactions T1 and T2 of the previous figure do not follow the two-phase locking protocol, as the write_lock(x) operation follows the unlock (y) operation in T1, and similarly, the write_lock(y) operation follows the unlock(x) operation in T2. If we enforce two-phase locking, the transaction can be rewritten as T1' and T2':

T1'
read_lock(y)
read_item(y)
write_lock(x)
read_item(x)
x:=x+y
write_item(x)
unlock(x)
unlock(y)

T2'
read_lock(x)
read_item(x)
write_lock(y)
read_item(y)
y:=x+y
write_item(y)
unlock(y)
unlock(x)

The two transactions that follow the basic 2PL protocol interleaved are as shown:

Table 9.4: Basic 2PL example

Time T1	Transaction T2	Transaction	Comments
1	read_lock(y)		
2	read_item(y)		
3		read_lock(x)	
4		read_item(x)	
5	write_lock(x)		At time step 5, it is not possible for T1 to acquire an X lock on x as there is already an S lock on x held by T2
6	Wait		
7		write_lock(y)	At time step 7, it is not possible for T2 to acquire an X lock on y as there is already an S lock on y held by T1
8		Wait	Both transactions are waiting for the other to release a lock
	.....		.....

These transactions could result in the schedule above which clearly terminates in a deadlock.

Preventing the lost update problem using basic 2PL

We have looked at the lost update problem earlier where another user can override an apparently successfully completed update operation. A solution to the problem using the lost update problem example which we considered earlier is shown next using 2PL.

Table 9.5: Solving lost update problem

Time	Transaction T2	Transaction	Comments
T1			
1	write_lock(x)		X lock on data item x by T1
2	read_item(x)	write_lock(x)	Read operation is performed in transaction T1 at time 2. Also at time 2 request for an X lock on data item x by T2, but T2 must wait for release of X lock by T1
3	x:=x–40	Wait	
4	write_item(x)	Wait	The value of data item x is modified by T1
5	Commit/unlock(x)	Wait	X lock on data item x by T1 released. T2's request for X lock now granted
6		read_item(x) (acquires S lock on x)	A read operation is performed in transaction T2
7		x:=x+20	
8		write_item(x) (acquires X lock on x)	The value of data item x is modified by T2
9		Commit/unlock(x)	

Conservative two-phase locking

Conservative 2PL is a deadlock-free protocol. It requires a transaction to lock all the data items it needs in advance. If at least one of the required data items cannot be obtained, then none of the items are locked. Rather, the transaction waits and then tries again to lock all the items it needs. Although conservative 2PL is a deadlock-free protocol, this solution further limits concurrency.

Strict two-phase locking

In practice, the most popular variation of 2PL is **strict 2PL**, which guarantees strict schedules. **Strict schedules** are those in which transactions can neither read nor write an item x until the last transaction that wrote x has committed or aborted. In this variation, a transaction T does not release any of its locks until after it commits or aborts. Hence, no other transaction can read or write an item that is written by T unless T has committed, leading to a strict schedule for recoverability. Strict 2PL is not deadlock free.

Notice the difference between **conservative** and **strict 2PL**. The former must lock all items before it starts, whereas the latter does not unlock any of its items until after it terminates (by committing or aborting). Strict 2PL is not deadlock free unless it is combined with conservative 2PL. In summary, all type 2PL protocols guarantee serializability (correctness) of a schedule, but limit concurrency. The use of locks can also cause the additional problem of deadlock. Conservative 2PL is deadlock free.

9.7 Dealing with deadlock

Locking mechanisms, including basic and strict two-phase locking, can cause the additional problem of deadlock. We have seen a number of examples of deadlock. Deadlock is the situation where one transaction is waiting for a resource which is locked by another transaction. This transaction in turn is waiting for a resource which is locked by the first transaction (or possibly yet another transaction).

Deadlock may involve more than two transactions. It may be dealt with by using one of two approaches: preventing deadlock from happening or allowing deadlock to occur and then resolving it.

Preventing deadlock from happening

There are a number of methods of achieving this which include:

- Locking all data items at the beginning of transaction (conservative two-phase locking which we looked at earlier)
- Ordering data items using transaction timestamps. With timestamping, a unique identifier is given to each transaction indicating its start time. When transactions are executing concurrently, older transactions are given priority. When accessing the same data, newer transactions are rolled back.

Resolving deadlock

Some DBMSs allow deadlock to occur and then resolve the deadlock. If deadlock occurs, protocols for resolving it include: wait and retry, pre-empting one transaction in favour of another, aborting one or both transactions. A simple solution is based on **lock timeouts**. A transaction requesting a lock will wait for a system-defined period of time. If the request has not been granted within the period, the transaction is aborted and then restarted. The DBMS has assumed that there is a deadlock and is attempting to resolve it. This simple solution is used by a number of commercial DBMSs.

9.8 Oracle concurrency control

Oracle guarantees that users will see a consistent version of the database. If transactions are in progress which have not committed, then other transactions will not see any changes made by these uncommitted transactions.

Isolating transactions

We can use the following SQL SET TRANSACTION commands to isolate one transaction from other transactions.

- **SET TRANSACTION READ COMMITTED:** default command. Within a transaction a statement sees only the data which was committed before the statement started. This means that data may be changed by other transactions. This may cause inconsistent analysis problems
- **SET TRANSACTION SERIALIZABLE:** serialization is enforced at the transaction level. A transaction only sees data that was committed before the transaction began, as well as any changes made by the transaction through Insert, Update or Delete
- **SET TRANSACTION READ ONLY:** similar to the previous statement but data can be read only. A transaction only sees data that was committed before the transaction began.

The application of these commands can be seen with the following examples.

Airline reservation example

An airline reservation system might use the command SET TRANSACTION SERIALIZABLE. Assume we have two transactions running concurrently, each checking the availability of seats and making a reservation if possible. Assume that there is only one seat available.

Figure 9.2: SET TRANSACTION SERIALIZABLE

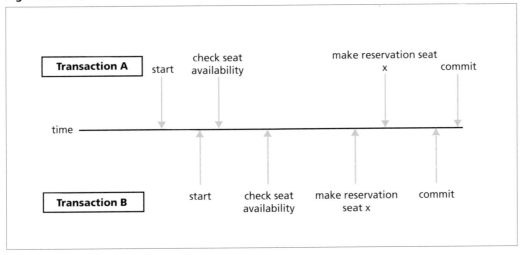

In figure 9.2, there is danger that the two transactions will double-book the same seat. However, if the transactions have been designated as SET TRANSACTION SERIALIZABLE it will not happen. Here, serialization is enforced at the transaction level. Both transactions only see data that was committed before the transaction began, as well as any changes made by that transaction through Insert, Update or Delete. Transaction B makes and commits a reservation on seat x before transaction A. When transaction A tries to commit, the database system recognises that data which it had used in its transaction has been changed (by transaction B). Transaction A will not be allowed to update seat x and therefore its changes will not be committed.

Online ordering example

Our second example, an online ordering system, might use the command SET TRANSACTION READ COMMITTED. Again we have two transactions running concurrently: one checking the price of an item and then making an order; the other changing the price of an item.

Figure 9.3: SET TRANSACTION READ COMMITTED

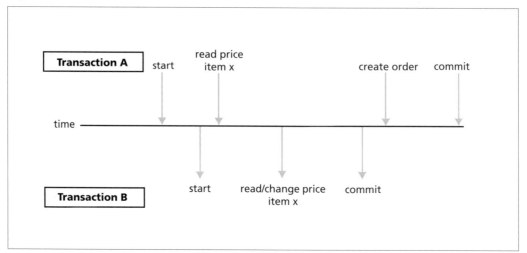

Figure 9.3 shows that there is a danger that in transaction A, an order will be created based on an old price. If the transactions have been designated as SET TRANSACTION READ COMMITTED, Oracle will allow this to happen. Here, serialization is enforced at the statement level. Therefore, transaction B changes price x and transaction A creates an order on the original price which user A has seen.

In our first example it is important that serializability is enforced at the transaction level, as it is critical that double-booking of airline seats is avoided. In the other applications, such as order entry, it may not be so important that transaction A, in our example, used an older price. In this case, increased concurrency of transactions might be more important.

Locks in Oracle

Locks are not placed on data for read operations – only for write operations. This means that a read operation never blocks a write operation. A user does not lock a data item explicitly – data locking will occur automatically for all SQL statements. A user is allowed, however, to lock data manually or change default-locking behaviour.

Deadlock in Oracle

Oracle will detect deadlock and it is automatically resolved when the statements involved in the deadlock are rolled back.

Activity 9.4

Serial schedules

Assuming that initially x = 3, y = 2:

Transaction T1	Transaction T2
read_lock(x)	read_lock(y)
read_item(x)	read_item(y)
x:=x+3	y:=2*y
write_lock(x)	write_lock(y)
write_item(x)	write_item(y)
unlock(x)	unlock(y)
read_lock(y)	read_lock(x)
read_item(y)	read_item(x)
y:= x+y	x:=x+y
write_lock(y)	write_lock(x)
write_item(y)	write_item(x)
unlock(y)	unlock(x)

Create all possible serial schedules and examine the values of x and y.

Activity 9.5

Checking for serializability

Assuming that initially x = 3, y = 2:

Transaction T1	Transaction T2
read_lock(x)	read_lock(y)
read_item(x)	read_item(y)
x:=x+3	y:=2*y
write_lock(x)	write_lock(y)
write_item(x)	write_item(y)
unlock(x)	unlock(y)
read_lock(y)	read_lock(x)
read_item(y)	read_item(x)
y:= x+y	x:=x+y
write_lock(y)	write_lock(x)
write_item(y)	write_item(x)
unlock(y)	unlock(x)

Create a non-serial interleaved schedule and examine the values of x and y. Is this schedule serializable?

The inconsistent analysis problem again

Consider the inconsistent analysis problem again. The example, as before, starts off with Account records having the following values:

ACC1	ACC2	ACC3
40	50	30

If 10 is transferred from ACC 3 to ACC 1 while concurrently calculating the total funds in the three accounts, the following sequence of events may occur:

Time	Transaction	Transaction T1	Comments T2
0	sum = 0	...	
1	read_item(ACC1)		
2	sum:= sum+ACC1		
3	read_item(ACC2)		
4	sum:= sum+ACC2		Sum is now 90
5		read_item(ACC3)	
6		read_item(ACC1)	
7		ACC3=ACC3–10	
8		ACC1=ACC1+10	
9		write_item(ACC3)	ACC3 is now 20
10		write_item(ACC1)	ACC1 is now 50
11		COMMIT	
12	read_item(ACC3)		T1 has value 20 for ACC3
13	sum:= sum+ACC3		Sum is now 110 which is incorrect!

Rewrite the above transaction T1 and transaction T2 but with the addition of a locking mechanism (do not include unlock at this stage). Check to see if your new schedule is serializable.

Solving the inconsistent analysis problem with 2PL

Consider the inconsistent analysis problem discussed in activity 9.6. Use the basic 2PL protocol to see if you can solve this problem.

2PL example

Given the schedules and assuming that initially x = 3, y = 2:

T1	T2
read_lock(x)	read_lock(y)
read_item(x)	read_item(y)
x:=x+3	y:=2*y
write_lock(x)	write_lock(y)
write_item(x)	write_item(y)
unlock(x)	unlock(y)
read_lock(y)	read_lock(x)
read_item(y)	read_item(x)
y:= x+y	x:=x+y
write_lock(y)	write_lock(x)
write_item(y)	write_item(x)
unlock(y)	unlock(x)

Show how the basic two-phase locking protocol would generate a serializable schedule.

Deadlock example

Explain how deadlock would occur, given the following non-serial schedule:

Line no	T1	T2
1	read_lock(x)	
2	read_item(x)	
3	x:= x+7	
4		read_lock(x)
5		read_item(x)
6		x:= x+x*2
7	write_lock(x)	
8	write_item(x)	
9	unlock(x)	
10		write_lock(x)
11		write_item(x)
12		unlock(x)

9.9 Summary

This chapter examined the purpose of the transaction manager in a database management system and how concurrency was controlled when more than one transaction accessed a database at the same time. It was shown that, although transactions working on their own can be correct in themselves, interleaving can create databases with inconsistent data. A number of potential problems caused by concurrency were examined and various approaches to concurrency control were described.

9.10 Review questions

Review question 9.1   Discuss the reasons for designing database systems around transactions.

Review question 9.2   Describe the so-called 'ACID' properties of database transactions.

Review question 9.3   Name and explain problems which can occur when transactions are scheduled.

Review question 9.4   Explain the following terms:

1. Dirty read

2. Serial schedule

3. Serializability.

Review question 9.5   Explain what is a locking mechanism, distinguishing between S (shared lock or read) locks and X (exclusive or write) locks.

Review question 9.6   What is two-phase locking protocol? How does it guarantee serializability? Distinguish between basic 2PL and conservative 2PL.

Review question 9.7   What is meant by the term 'deadlock'?

9.11 Feedback on activities

Answer 9.1 A possible solution:

Transaction T1	Time	Transaction T2	x
read_item (x);	t1		5
x:=x–m;	t2	read_item(x);	5
write_item(x);	t3	x:=x+m;	–5
	t4	write_item(x);	15

Here, T1 and T2 start at nearly the same time; both read x as 5. T1 reduces x by m and stores the update in the database (–5). Meanwhile, T2 increases its copy of x by m, giving a result of 15, which it stores in the database. The previous update is therefore overwritten or lost.

Answer 9.2 A possible solution:

Transaction T1	Time	Transaction T2	x
	t1	read_item(x);	5
	t2	x:=x+m;	5
	t3	write_item(x);	15
read_item(x);	t4		15
x:=x–n;	t5		15
write_item(x);	t6		0
	t7	**ROLLBACK**	5

This problem occurs when one transaction is allowed to see the intermediate results of another transaction before it is committed. T2 updates x to 15, but later it aborts the transaction so that x should be restored to its original value (5). In the meantime, T1 has read the new value of x and calculated the incorrect value of 0, instead of –10.

Answer 9.3 A possible solution:

Transaction T1	Time	Transaction T2	x	y	z	sum
	t1	sum:=0	5	20	30	
	t2	read_item(x);	5	20	30	
read_item(x);	t3		5	20	30	
read_item(y);	t4		5	20	30	
read_item(z)	t5		5	20	30	
y:=y*z	t6		5	20*	30	
write(y)	t7		5	600	30	
x:=x*z	t8		5*	600	30	
write(x)	t9		150	600	30	
COMMIT	t10		150	600	30	
	t11	sum:=sum+x;	150	600	30	
	t12	read_item(y);	150	600	30	
	t13	sum:=sum+y;	150	600	30	
	t14	write_item(sum)	150	600	30	605

Note: x, y and z in the fourth to sixth columns are the values of x, y, z on the database – not the internal values of the variables.

This problem occurs when a transaction reads values from the database (here T2 reads x), and a second transaction updates some of them during the execution of the first (here T1 updates x after T2 has read it). The result of sum is incorrect (the value of 605 should in fact be 750).

This is an example of a dirty read, where transactions are allowed to read partial results of incomplete transactions that are simultaneously updating the database.

Answer 9.4 A *serial schedule* is where transactions are performed one after another without interleaving. There are only 2 possible serial schedules: completing all operations of T1 and then all operations of T2, or vice versa. The first is given below:

Time	T1	T2	x	y
1	read_lock(x)			
2	read_item(x)		3	
3	x:=x+3			
4	write_lock(x)			
5	write_item(x)		6	
6	unlock(x)			
7	read_lock(y)			
8	read_item(y)			2
9	y:= x+y			
10	write_lock(y)			
11	write_item(y)			8
12	unlock(y)			
13		read_lock(y)		
14		read_item(y)		8
15		y:=2*y		
16		write_lock(y)		
17		write_item(y)		16
18		unlock(y)		
19		read_lock(x)		
20		read_item(x)	6	
21		x:=x+y		
22		write_lock(x)		
23		write_item(x)	22	
24		unlock(x)		

Answer 9.5 *Non-serial interleaved schedule* – there are many possible answers for this question. For example:

Time	T1	T2	x	y
1	read_lock(x)		3	2
2	read_item(x)		3	2
3	x:=x+3			
4	write_lock(x)			
5	write_item(x)		6	2
6	unlock(x)			
7		read_lock(y)	6	2
8		read_item(y)	6	2
9		y:=2*y		
10		write_lock(y)		
11		write_item(y)	6	4
12		unlock(y)	6	4
13		read_lock(x)	6	4
14		read_item(x)	6	4
15		x:=x+y		
16		write_lock(x)		
17		write_item(x)	10	4
18		unlock(x)	10	4
19	read_lock(y)		10	4
20	read_item(y)		10	4
21	y:= x+y			
22	write_lock(y)		10	10
23	write_item(y)		10	10
24	unlock(y)		10	10

This schedule gives an incorrect result at line 21: T1 has a value of 6 for x, but it had been changed by T2 to 10, so at line 21 y should have a value of 14. This is an example of the inconsistent analysis problem where T2 updates values used by T1 during T1's execution

Serializability – if a set of transactions executes concurrently, we say that the schedule is correct if it produces the same results as some serial execution. In this example the schedule is not serializable.

Answer 9.6 There are a number of solutions possible. For example:

Time	Transaction T1	Transaction T2	Comments
0	sum = 0		
1	read_item(ACC1) (40) (acquire S lock on ACC1)		
2	sum:= sum + ACC1		
3	read_item(ACC2) (50) (acquire S lock on ACC2)		
4	sum:= sum + ACC2		sum is now 90
5		read_item(ACC3) (30) (acquire S lock on ACC3)	
6		ACC3=ACC3–10	
7		write_item(ACC3): (20) (acquire X lock on ACC3)	
8		read_item(ACC1) (40) (acquire S lock on ACC1)	
9		ACC1=ACC1+10	
10		write_item(ACC1) (request X lock on ACC1)	X lock rejected as S lock acquired at time 1
11	read_item(ACC3) (20) (request S lock on ACC3)	Wait	S lock rejected as X lock acquired at time 7
12	Wait		

Transaction T2's update at time 10 is not accepted, because it is an implicit request for an exclusive lock on ACC1, and such a request conflicts with the shared lock already held by T1; so T2 goes into a wait state. Likewise, transaction T1's read at time 11 is also not accepted, because it is an implicit request for a shared lock on ACC3 and such a request conflicts with the exclusive lock already held by T2; so T1 also goes into a wait state. Once again therefore, locking solves the original problem by forcing a deadlock.

Answer 9.7 A possible solution:

Time	Transaction T1	Transaction T2	Comments
0	sum = 0		
1		write_lock(ACC3)	Acquire X lock on ACC3
2	read_lock(ACC3)	read_item(ACC3)	ACC3 is 30
3	wait	ACC3=ACC3-10	T1 must wait for S lock
4	wait	write_item(ACC3)	ACC3 is now 20
5	wait	write_lock(ACC1)	Acquire X lock on ACC1
6	wait	read_item(ACC1)	ACC1 is 40
7	wait	ACC1:= ACC1 + 10	
8	wait	write_item(ACC1):	ACC1 is now 50
9	wait	Commit/unlock (ACC1,ACC3)	
10	read_item(ACC3)		
11	sum:= sum + ACC3		Sum is now 20
12	read_lock(ACC2)		Acquire S lock on ACC2
13	read_item(ACC2)		
14	sum:= sum + ACC2		Sum is now 70
15	read_lock(ACC1)		Acquire S lock on ACC1
16	read_item(ACC1)		
17	sum:= sum + ACC1		Sum is now 120 which is correct

Answer 9.8 A transaction is said to follow the two-phase locking protocol if, within a transaction, all locking operations (read_lock, write_lock), precede the first unlock operation. This protocol, however, is prone to deadlock but not in the example below.

Time	T1	T2	x	y
1	read_lock(x)		3	2
2	read_item(x)		3	2
3	x:=x+3			
4	write_lock(x)			
5	write_item(x)		6	2
6	read_lock(y)			
7	read_item(y)			
8	y:= x+y		6	2
9	write_lock(y)			
10	write_item(y)		6	8
11	unlock(x)	read_lock(y)		
12	unlock(y)	read_item(y)	6	8
13		y:=2*y		
14		write_lock(y)		
15		write_item(y)	6	16
16		read_lock(x)		
17		read_item(x)		
18		x:=x+y		
19		write_lock(x)		
20		write_item(x)	22	16
21		unlock(y)		
22		unlock(x)		

In the above solution the transactions are pretty much serial. Consider the following possible solution – would this work?

Time	T1	T2	x	y
1	read_lock(x)		3	2
2	read_item(x)			
3	x:=x+3			
4	write_lock(x)			
5	write_item(x)		6	2
6		read_lock(y)	6	2
7		read_item(y)	6	2
8		y:=2*y	6	2
9		write_lock(y)	6	2
10		write_item(y)	6	2
11	read_lock(y)			wait
12		read_lock(x)		wait

In this example we have a deadlock.

Answer 9.9 At line 7 there is already a read/shared lock on transaction x. Definition of read lock: 'If a transaction has a shared lock on a database, it can read the item but not update it. If a transaction A holds a shared lock on record R, then a request from transaction B for an X lock on R will cause B to go into a wait state (and B will wait until A's lock is released). So at line 7 T1 will have to wait for the release of T2's read lock on x. The same applies at line 10. T2 cannot apply the write lock as T1 already has a read lock on it. It will have to wait.

Deadlock is the situation where one transaction (T1) is waiting for a resource which is locked by another transaction (T2). This transaction in turn is waiting for a resource which is locked by the first transaction. Deadlock may involve more than two transactions.

Backup and recovery

OVERVIEW

Recovery techniques are intertwined with transaction management and concurrency control which were discussed in Chapter 9. In this chapter we will look at some of the techniques that can be used to recover from transaction failures. We will first introduce some concepts that are used in recovery processes such as the **system log**, **checkpoints**, and **commit points**. After outlining the recovery procedures, the process of **rolling back** (undoing) the effect of a transaction will be discussed in detail. We will present recovery techniques based on **deferred update**, also known as NO-UNDO/REDO technique and **immediate update**, which is known as UNDO/REDO.

Learning outcomes	On completion of this chapter, you should be able to:

- Describe a range of causes of database failure and explain mechanisms available to deal with these

- Understand a range of options available for the design of database backup procedures

- Analyse the problems of data management in a concurrent environment.

10.1 Introduction

Database systems, like any other computer systems, are subject to failures. Despite this, any organisation that depends upon a database must have that database available when it is required. Therefore, any DBMS intended for a serious business or organisational user must have adequate facilities for fast recovery after failure. In particular, whenever a transaction is submitted to a DBMS for execution, the system must ensure that either:

- All the operations in the transaction are completed successfully and their effect is recorded permanently in the database

or

- The transaction has no effect whatsoever on the database or on any other transactions.

The understanding of the methods available for recovering from such failures is therefore essential to any serious study of database systems. This chapter describes the methods for recovering from a range of problems that can occur throughout the life of a database system. These mechanisms include **automatic protection mechanisms** built into the database software itself, and **non-automatic actions** available to people responsible for the running of the database system, both for the backing up of data and recovery from a variety of failure situations. Certain recovery techniques are best used with specific concurrency control methods. Assume for the most part that we are dealing with large multi-user databases: small systems typically provide little or no support for recovery – in these systems, recovery is regarded as a user problem.

10.2 Transaction problems

There are a variety of causes of transaction failure.

These include:

- **Concurrency control enforcement:** concurrency control method may abort the transaction, to be restarted later, because it violates serialisability (the need for transactions to be executed in an equivalent way as would have resulted if they had been executed sequentially) or because several transactions are in a state of deadlock

- **Local error detected by the transaction:** during transaction executions, certain conditions may occur that necessitate cancellation of the transaction (e.g. an account with insufficient funds may cause a withdrawal transaction from that account to be cancelled). This may be done by a programmed ABORT in the transaction itself

- **A transaction or system error:** due to some operation in the transaction that may cause it to fail, such as integer overflow, division by zero, erroneous parameter values or logical programming errors

- **System software errors:** that result in abnormal termination or destruction of the database management system

- **Crashes due to hardware malfunction:** resulting in loss of internal (main and cache) memory (otherwise known as system crashes)

- **Disk malfunctions:** such as read or write malfunction or a disk read/write head crash. This may happen during a read or write operation of the transaction

- **Natural physical disasters and catastrophes:** such as fires, earthquakes or power surges, sabotage, intentional contamination with computer viruses, or destruction of data or facilities by operators or users.

The last two types are far less common than the rest. Whenever a failure of the first five occurs, the system must keep sufficient information to recover from the failure. Disk failure or other catastrophic failures of the last two do not happen frequently. If these failures do occur, recovery is a major task.

10.3 A typical recovery problem

Data updates made by a DBMS are not automatically written to disk at each synchronisation point. Therefore, there may be some delay between the commit and the actual disk writing. If there is a system failure during this delay, the system must still be able to ensure that these updates reach the disk copy of the database. Conversely, data changes that may ultimately prove to be incorrect, made for example by a transaction that is later rolled back, can sometimes be written to the database. Ensuring that only the results of complete transactions are committed to the database is an important task, which if inadequately controlled by the DBMS may lead to problems, such as the generation of an inconsistent database. This particular problem can be clearly seen in the following example.

Suppose we want to enter a transaction into a customer order. The following actions must be taken:

START

1. Change the customer record with the new order data
2. Change the salesperson record with the new order data
3. Insert a new order record into the database

STOP

The initial values are shown in figure 10.1(a). If only operations 1 and 2 are successfully performed, this results in the values shown in figure 10.1(b).

Figure 10.1(a): Initial values of the database

CUSTOMER:

cNo	orderNo	description	cost
123	1000	400 Tennis balls	£2400

SALESPERSON:

name	totalSales
Jones	£3200

ORDER:

orderNo
1000
2000
3000
4000
5000

Figure 10.1(b): Values of the database after operations 1 and 2

CUSTOMER:

cNo	orderNo	description	cost
123	1000	400 Tennis balls	£2400
123	8000	250 Cricket balls	£6500

SALESPERSON:

name	totalSales
Jones	£9700

ORDER:

orderNo
1000
2000
3000
4000
5000

This database state is clearly unacceptable as it does not accurately reflect reality. For example, a customer may receive an invoice for items never sent, or a salesman may make commission on items never received. It is better to treat the whole procedure (i.e. from START to STOP) as a complete transaction and not commit any changes to the database until STOP has been successfully reached.

10.4 Transaction logging

System log

The recovery manager overcomes many of the potential problems of transaction failure by a variety of techniques. Many of these are heavily dependent upon the existence of a special file known as a **system log** (sometimes called a journal or audit trail). This contains information about the start and end of each transaction, and any updates which occur in the transaction. The log keeps track of all transaction operations that affect the values of database items. This information may be needed to recover from transaction failure. The log is kept on disk (apart from the most recent log block that is in the process of being generated; this is stored in the main memory buffers). Thus, the majority of the log is not affected by failures, except for a disk failure, or catastrophic failure. In addition, the log is periodically backed up to archival storage to protect against such catastrophic failures.

The types of entries that are written to the log are described below – in these entries, T refers to a unique transaction identifier that is generated automatically by the system and used to uniquely label each transaction:

- **start_transaction(T):** this log entry records that transaction T starts the execution
- **read_item(T, x):** this log entry records that transaction T reads the value of database item x

- **write_item(T, x, old_value, new_value):** this log entry records that transaction T changes the value of the database item x, from old_value to new_value. The old value is sometimes known as **before image of x**, and the new value is known as an **after image of x**
- **commit(T):** this log entry records that transaction T has completed all accesses to the database successfully, and its effect can be committed (recorded permanently) to the database
- **abort(T):** this records that transaction T has been aborted
- **checkpoint:** this is an additional entry to the log. The purpose of this entry will be described in a later section.

Some protocols do not require that read operations be written to the system log, in which case the overhead of recording operations in the log is reduced, since fewer operations (only write) are recorded in the log. In addition, some protocols require simpler write entries that do not include new_value.

Because the log contains a record of every write operation that changes the value of some database item, it is possible to **undo** the effect of these write operations of a transaction T, by tracing backward through the log and resetting all items changed by a write operation of T to their old_values. We can also **redo** the effect of the write operations of a transaction T by tracing forward through the log, and setting all items changed by a write operation of T to their new_values. Redoing the operations of a transaction may be required if all its updates are recorded in the log, but a failure occurs before we can be sure that all the new_values have been written permanently in the actual database.

Committing transactions and force-writing

A transaction T reaches its **commit point** when all its operations that access the database have been executed successfully – that is, the transaction has reached the point at which it will not abort (terminate without completing). Beyond the commit point, the transaction is said to be **committed**, and its effect is assumed to be permanently recorded in the database. Commitment always involves writing a commit entry to the log and writing the log to disk. At the time of a system crash, we search back in the log for all transactions T that have written a start_transaction(T) entry into the log but have not written commit(T) entry yet; these transactions may have to be rolled back to undo their effect on the database during recovery process. Transactions that have written their commit(T) entry in the log must also have recorded all their write operations in the log (otherwise they would not be committed), so their effect on the database can be redone from the log entries.

Notice that the log file must be kept on disk. At the time of a system crash, only the log entries that have been written back to disk are considered in the recovery process, because the contents of main memory may be lost. Hence, before a transaction reaches its commit point, any portion of the log that has not yet been written to the disk must now be written to it. This process is called **force-writing** the log file before committing a transaction. A commit does not necessarily involve writing the data items to disk; this depends on the recovery mechanism in use.

A commit is not necessarily required to initiate writing of the log file to disk. The log may sometimes be written back automatically when the log buffer is full. This happens irregularly, as usually one block of the log file is kept in main memory until it is filled with log entries. Then it is written back to disk, rather than writing it to disk every time a log entry is added. This saves the overhead of multiple disk writes of the same information.

Checkpoints

In the event of failure, most recovery managers initiate procedures that involve redoing or undoing operations contained within the log. Clearly, not all operations need to be redone or undone, as many transactions recorded on the log will have been successfully completed and the changes written permanently to disk. The problem for the recovery manager is to determine which operations need to be considered, and which can safely be ignored. This problem is usually overcome by writing another kind of entry in the log, the **checkpoint entry**.

The checkpoint is written into the log periodically, and always involves the writing out to the database on disk the effect of all write operations of committed transactions. Hence, all transactions that have their commit(T) entries in the log before a checkpoint entry will not require their write operations to be redone in the case of a system crash. The recovery manager of a DBMS must decide at what intervals to take a checkpoint. The intervals are usually decided on the basis of the time elapsed, or the number of committed transactions since the last checkpoint.

Performing a checkpoint consists of the following operations:

- Suspending executions of transactions temporarily
- Writing (force-writing) all modified database buffers of committed transactions out to disk
- Writing a checkpoint record to the log
- Writing (force-writing) all log records in main memory out to disk.

A checkpoint record usually contains additional information, including a list of transactions active at the time of the checkpoint. Many recovery methods (including the deferred and immediate update methods) need this information when a transaction is rolled back, as all transactions active at the time of the checkpoint, and any subsequent ones, may need to be redone.

In addition to the log, further security of data is provided by generating backup copies of the database (held in a separate location). This guards against destruction in the event of fire, flood, disk crash, etc.

Undoing

If a transaction crash does occur, then the recovery manager may **undo** transactions (that is, reverse the operations of a transaction on the database). This involves examining a transaction for the log entry write_item(T, x, old_value, new_value), and setting the value of item x in the database to old_value. Undoing a number of write_item operations from one or more transactions from the log must proceed in the reverse order from the order in which the operations were written.

Redoing

Redoing transactions is achieved by examining a transaction's log entry, and for every write_item(T, x, old_value, new_value) entry, the value of item x in the database is set to new_value. Redoing a number of transactions from the log must proceed in the same order in which the operations were written in the log. It is only necessary to redo the last update of x from the log during recovery, because the other updates would be overwritten by this last redo. The redo algorithm can be made more efficient by starting from the end of the log and working backwards towards the last checkpoint. Whenever an item is redone, it is added to a list of redone items. Before redo is applied to an item, the list is checked. If the item appears on the list, it is not redone, since its last value has already been recovered.

10.5 Recovery outline

Recovery from transaction failures usually means that the database is restored to some state from the past so that a correct state – one from close to the time of failure – can be reconstructed. To do this, the system must keep information about changes to data items during transaction execution outside the database. This information is typically kept in the system log. It is important to note that a transaction may fail at any point (e.g. when data is being written to a buffer or when a log is being written to disk). All recovery mechanisms must be able to cope with the unpredictable nature of transaction failure. Significantly, the recovery phase itself may fail and therefore the recovery mechanism must also be capable of recovering from failure during recovery. A typical strategy for recovery may be summarised, based on the type of failures.

Recovery from catastrophic failures

The main technique used to handle catastrophic failures, including disk crash, is that of **database backup**. The whole database and the log are periodically copied to secondary offline storage such as optical disks, flash memory devices or removeable hard drives. In case of a catastrophic system failure, the latest backup copy can be reloaded, and the system can be restarted. To avoid losing all the effects of transactions that have been executed since the last backup, it is customary to back up the system log by periodically copying it. The system log is usually substantially smaller than the database itself, and so can be backed up more frequently. When the system log is backed up, users do not lose all transactions they have performed since the last database backup. All committed transactions recorded in the portion of the system log that has been backed up can have their effect on the database reconstructed. A new system log is started after each database backup operation. Hence, to recover from disk failure, the database is first re-created on disk from its latest backup copy. Following that, the effects of all the committed transactions are reconstructed – those operations that have been entered in the backed-up copy of the system log.

Recovery from non-catastrophic failures

When the database is not physically damaged but has become inconsistent due to **non-catastrophic failure**, the strategy is to reverse the changes that caused the inconsistency, by undoing some operations. It may also be necessary to redo some operations that could have been lost during the recovery process (or for some other reason) in order to restore a consistent state to the database. In this case, a complete archival copy of the database is not required. Rather, it is sufficient that the entries kept in the system log are consulted during the recovery.

There are two major techniques for recovery from non-catastrophic transaction failures: **deferred updates** and **immediate updates**. The deferred update techniques do not actually update the database until after a transaction reaches its commit point. It is then that the updates are recorded in the database. Before commit, all transaction updates are recorded in the local transaction workspace. During commit, the updates are first recorded persistently in the log, and then written to the database. If a transaction fails before reaching its commit point, it will not have changed the database in any way, so UNDO is not needed.

It may be necessary to REDO the effect of the operations of a committed transaction from the log, because their effect may not yet have been written in the database. For this reason, deferred update is also known as the **NO-UNDO/REDO algorithm**. We will examine the deferred update technique in more detail later in this chapter.

In the immediate update techniques, the database may be updated by some operations of a transaction before the transaction reaches its commit point. However, these operations are typically recorded in the log on disk by force-writing before they are applied to the database, making recovery still possible. If a transaction fails after recording some changes in the database but before reaching its commit point, the effect of its operations on the database must be undone; that is, the transaction must be **rolled back**. In the general case of immediate update, both undo and redo are required during recovery, so it is known as the **UNDO/REDO algorithm**.

Transaction rollback

If a transaction fails for whatever reason after updating the database, it may be necessary to roll back or UNDO the transaction. Any data item values that have been changed by the transaction must be returned to their previous values. The log entries are used to recover the old values of the data items that must be rolled back. If a transaction T is rolled back, any transaction S that has, in the interim, read the value of some data item x written by T, must also be rolled back. Similarly, once S is rolled back, any transaction R that has read the value of some item y written by S must also be rolled back, and so on. This phenomenon is called **cascading rollback**. Cascading rollback, understandably, can be quite time-consuming. That is why most recovery mechanisms are designed so that cascading rollback is never required.

Figures 10.2(a), (b) and (c) show an example where cascading rollback is required. The read and write operations of three individual transactions are shown in figure 10.2(a). Figure 10.2(b) graphically shows the operations of different transactions along the time axis. Figure 10.2(c) shows the system log at the point of a system crash for a particular execution schedule of these transactions. The values of a, b, c, and d, which are used by the transactions, are shown to the right of the system log entries. At the point of system crash, transaction T3 has not reached its conclusion and must be rolled back. The write operations of T3, marked by a single * in figure 10.2(c), are the operations that are undone during transaction rollback.

Figure 10.2(a): The read and write operations of the three transactions

T1	T2	T3
read_item(a);	read_item(b);	read_item(c);
read_item(d);	write_item(b);	write_item(b);
write_item(d);	read_item(d);	read_item(a);
	write_item(d);	write_item(a);

Figure 10.2(b): Operations before the crash

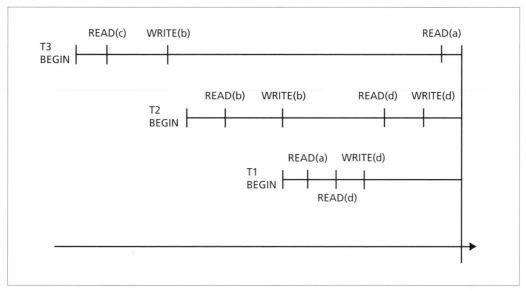

Figure 10.2(c): System log at point of crash

Log	a	b	c	d
	30	15	40	20
start_transaction(T3)				
read_item(T3, c)				
*write_item(T3, b, 15, 12)		12		
start_transaction(T2)				
read_item(T2, b)				
**write_item(T2, b, 12, 18)		18		
start_transaction(T1)				
read_item(T1, a)				
read_item(T1, d)				
write_item(T1, d, 20, 25)				25
read_item(T2, d)				
**write_item(T2, d, 25, 26)				26
read_item(T3, a)				
system crash				

* T3 is rolled back because it does not reach its commit point when system crash happens.

** T2 is rolled back because it reads the value of item b written by T3.

The rest of the write entries in the log are redone.

We must now check for cascading rollback. From figure 10.2(b) we see that transaction T2 reads the value B, which was written by T3. This can also be determined by examining the log. Because T3 is rolled back, T2 must also be rolled back. The write operations of T2, marked by ** in the log, are the ones that are undone. Note that only write operations need to be undone during transaction rollback. Read operations are only recorded in the log to determine whether cascading rollback of additional transactions is necessary.

10.6 Recovery techniques based on deferred update

Deferred update

The idea behind deferred update is to defer or postpone any actual updates to the database itself until the transaction completes its execution successfully and reaches its commit point. During transaction execution, the updates are recorded only in the log, and in the transaction workspace. After the transaction reaches its commit point and the log is force-written to disk, the updates are recorded in the database itself. If a transaction fails before reaching its commit point, there is no need to undo any operations, because the transaction has not affected the database in any way.

The steps involved in the deferred update protocol are as follows:

1. When a transaction starts, write an entry start_transaction(T) to the log.
2. When any operation is performed that will change values in the database, write a log entry write_item(T, x, old_value, new_value).
3. When a transaction is about to commit, write a log record of the form commit(T); write all log records to disk.
4. Commit the transaction; using the log to write the updates to the database, the writing of data to disk need not occur immediately.
5. If the transaction aborts, ignore the log records and do not write the changes to disk.

The database is never updated until after the transaction commits, and there is never a need to UNDO any operations. Hence, this technique is known as the NO-UNDO/REDO algorithm. The REDO is needed in case the system fails after the transaction commits, but before all its changes are recorded in the database. In this case, the transaction operations are redone from the log entries. The protocol, and how different entries are affected, can be best summarised as shown in figure 10.3.

Figure 10.3: How different entries are affected by deferred update protocol

Log entry	Log written to disk	Changes written to database buffer	Changes written on disk
start_transaction(T)	No	N/A	N/A
read_item(T, x)	No	N/A	N/A
write_item(T, x, old value, new value)	No	No	No
commit(T)	Yes	Yes	*Yes
checkpoint	Yes	Undefined	Yes (of committed transactions)

* Yes: writing back to disk may not occur immediately.

Deferred update in a single user environment

We will first discuss recovery based on deferred update in single user systems, where no concurrency control is needed. Hence we can understand the recovery process independently of any concurrency control method. In such an environment, the recovery algorithm can be rather simple. It works as follows. Use two lists to maintain the transactions: the **committed transactions list** which contains all the committed transactions since the last checkpoint, and the **active transactions list** (at most, one transaction falls in this category, because the system is a single user system). Apply the REDO operation to all the write_item operations of the committed transactions from the log, in the order in which they were written to the log. Restart the active transactions.

The REDO procedure is defined as follows: redoing a write_item operation consists of examining its log entry write_item(T, x, old_value, new_value) and setting the value of item x in the database to new_value. The REDO operation is required to be idempotent – that is, the same result will occur after the operation is applied more than once..

Notice that the transaction in the active list will have no effect on the database because of the deferred update protocol, and therefore is ignored completely by the recovery process. It is implicitly rolled back, because none of its operations were reflected in the database. However, the transaction must now be restarted, either automatically by the recovery process, or manually by the user.

The main benefit of the method is that any transaction operation need never be undone, as a transaction does not record its changes in the database until it reaches its commit point. The protocol is summarised in figure 10.4:

Figure 10.4: Deferred update protocol

Action	Entry in log	
	start_transaction(T)	commit(T)
Resubmit	Yes	No
Redo	Yes	Yes

Figures 10.5(a), (b) and (c) show an example of recovery in a single user environment, where the first failure occurs during execution of transaction T2, as shown in figure 10.5(b). The recovery process will redo the write_item(T1, D, 20) entry in the log by resetting the value of item D to 20 (its new value). The write(T2, ...) entries in the log are ignored by the recovery process because T2 is not committed. If a second failure occurs during recovery from the first failure, the same recovery process is repeated from start to finish, with identical results:

Figure 10.5(a): The read and write operations of two transactions

T1	T2
read_item(A)	read_item(B)
read_item(D)	write_item(B)
write_item(D)	read_item(D)
	write_item(D)

Figure 10.5(b): System log at the point of crash

start_transaction(T1)	
write_item(T1, D, 20)	
commit(T1)	
start_transaction(T2)	
write_item(T2, B, 10)	
write_item(T2, D 25)	system crash

Deferred update in a multi-user environment

For multi-user systems with concurrency control, the recovery process may be more complex, depending on the protocols used. In many cases, the concurrency control and recovery processes are interrelated. In general, the greater the degree of concurrency we wish to achieve, the more difficult the task of recovery becomes.

Consider a system in which concurrency control uses two-phase (basic 2-PL) locking, and prevents deadlock by pre-assigning all locks to items needed by a transaction before the transaction starts execution. To combine the deferred update methods for recovery with this concurrency control technique, we can keep all the locks on items in effect until the transaction reaches its commit point. After that, the locks can be released. This ensures strict and serialisable schedules. Assuming that checkpoint entries are included in the log, a possible recovery algorithm for this case is given below.

Use two lists of transactions maintained by the system: the committed transactions list which contains all committed transactions since the last checkpoint, and the active transactions list. REDO all the write operations of the committed transactions from the log, in the order in which they were written into the log. The transactions in the active list that are active, and did not commit, are effectively cancelled and must be resubmitted. The REDO procedure is the same as defined earlier in the deferred update in the single user environment. Figure 10.6 shows an example schedule of executing transactions.

Figure 10.6: Example of recovery in a multi-user environment

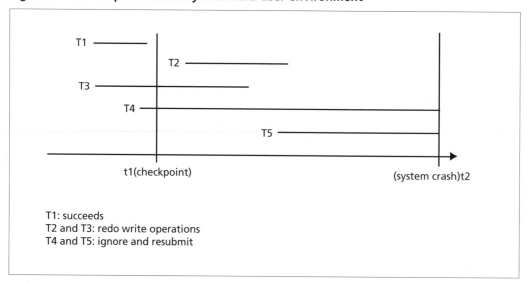

In figure 10.6, when the checkpoint was taken at time t1, transaction T1 had committed, whereas transactions T3 and T4 had not. Before the system crash at time t2, T3 and T2 were committed, but not T4 and T5. According to the deferred update method, there is no need to redo the write operations of transaction T1, or any transactions committed before the last checkpoint time t1. Write operations of T2 and T3 must be redone, however, because both transactions reached their commit points after the last checkpoint. Remember that the log is force-written before committing a transaction. Transactions T4 and T5 are ignored: they are effectively cancelled and rolled back because none of their write operations were recorded in the database under the deferred update protocol.

Transaction actions that do not affect the database

In general, a transaction will have actions that do not affect the database – such as generating and printing messages, or reports, from information retrieved from the database. If a transaction fails before completion, we may not want the user to get these reports, since the transaction has failed to complete. Therefore, such reports should be generated only after the transaction reaches its commit point. A common method of dealing with such actions is to issue the commands that generate the reports, but keep them as batch jobs. The batch jobs are executed only after the transaction reaches its commit point. If the transaction does not reach its commit point because of a failure, the batch jobs are cancelled.

Activity 10.1

Deferred update protocol

Given the operations of the four concurrent transactions in Table 1, and the system log at the point of system crash in Table 2, discuss how each transaction recovers from the failure using the deferred update technique. Give yourself some time to do this before reading the answer for this exercise.

Table 1: The read and write operations of four transactions:

T1	T2	T3	T4
read_item(A)	read_item(B)	read_item(A)	read_item(B)
read_item(D)	write_item(B)	write_item(A)	write_item(B)
write_item(D)	read_item(D)	read_item(C)	read_item(A)
	write_item(D)	write_item(C)	write_item(A)

cont...

Table 2: System log at the point of crash:

start_transaction(T1)	
write_item(T1, D, 20)	
commit(T1)	
checkpoint	
start_transaction(T4)	
write_item(T4, B, 15)	
commit(T4)	
start_transaction(T2)	
write_item(T2, B, 12)	
start_transaction(T3)	
write_item(T3, A, 30)	
write_item(T2, D, 25)	system crash

Activity 10.2

Recovery management using deferred update with incremental log

Look at the schedule, below, of the five transactions A, B, C, D, and E. Assume the initial values for the variables are a = 1, b = 2, c = 3, d = 4, and e = 5.

Using an incremental log with deferred updates, for each operation in each of the transactions, show:

1. The log entries.

2. Whether the log is written to disk.

3. Whether the output buffer is updated.

4. Whether the DBMS on disk is updated.

5. The values of the variables on the disk.

Discuss how each transaction recovers from the failure.

cont...

A	B	C	D	E	Log entries	Log to disk	Buffer changed	DBMS on disk changed	a	b	c	d	e
									1	2	3	4	5
start A													
read value a													
a:=a*2													
write value a													
commit A													
	start B												
	read value b												
	b:=b*2												
	write value b												
		start C											
		read value c											
		c:=c*2											
		write value c											
					checkpoint								
b:=0													
	write value b												
	commit B												
			start D										
			read value d										
			d:=d*2										
			write value d										
			commit D										
				start E									
				read value e									
				e:=e*2										
				write value e										
					FAILURE								

10.7 Summary

Following on from the previous chapter on transaction management and concurrency control, this chapter introduces recovery techniques and their importance in the management of large database systems. After reading this chapter, you will understand how system logs with before and after images, commit points and checkpoints are used to recover from different types of failures. The technique of rollback was also examined.

10.8 Review questions

Review question 10.1 Unfortunately, transactions fail frequently and this is due to a variety of causes. Discuss the different causes of transaction failures.

Review question 10.2 What is meant by a system log? Discuss how a system log is needed in a recovery process.

Review question 10.3 Discuss the actions involved in performing and writing a checkpoint entry.

Review question 10.4 Discuss how UNDO and REDO operations are used in a recovery process.

Review question 10.5 What is catastrophic failure? Discuss how a database can recover from catastrophic failure.

Review question 10.6 What is meant by transaction rollback? Why is it necessary to check for cascading rollback?

Review question 10.7 Compare deferred update with immediate update techniques by filling in the following blanks.

The **deferred update** techniques do not actually update the database until .... a transaction reaches its commit point; then the updates are recorded in the database. Before commit, all transaction updates are recorded in the local transaction workspace.

During commit, the updates are first recorded persistently in the ...., and then written to the .... If a transaction fails before reaching its commit point, it will not have changed the database in any way, so .... is not needed. It may be necessary to .... the effect of the operations of a committed transaction from the log, because their effect may not yet have been written in the database. Hence, deferred update is also known as .... algorithm.

In the **immediate update** techniques, the database may be updated by some operations of a transaction .... the transaction reaches its commit point. However, these operations are typically recorded in the log-on disk by ...., before they are applied to the database, making recovery still possible.

If a transaction fails after recording some changes in the database, but before reaching its commit point, the effect of its operations on the database must be .... ; that is, the transaction must be .... In the general case of immediate update, both .... and .... are required during recovery, so it is known as the .... algorithm.

Review question 10.8 Using your own words, describe the deferred update method for recovery management in a multi-user environment. Complete the following table to show how the deferred update protocol affects the log-on disk, database buffer, and database on disk:

Log entry	Log written to disk	Changes written to database buffer	Changes written on disk
start_transaction(T)			
read_item(T, x)			
write_item(T, x)			
commit(T)			
checkpoint			

10.9 Feedback on activities

Activity 10.1   T1 committed before the last checkpoint; its update has been successfully force-written to disk before the system crash. No action needs to be taken during the recovery process. T2 and T3 are ignored because they did not reach their commit points. They are in the active transaction list and will be resubmitted during the recovery process. T4 is redone because its commit point is after the last system checkpoint. As it is in the commit transaction list, its write operations will be redone. The following diagram will make things clearer.

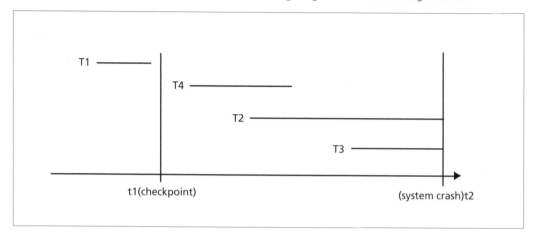

Activity 10.2

A	B	C	D	E	Log entries	Log to disk	Buffer changed	DBMS on disk changed	a	b	c	d	e
									1	2	3	4	5
start A					Start_transaction(A)	N	N	N	1	2	3	4	5
readvalue a					Read_item(A, a)	N	N	N	1	2	3	4	5
a:=a*2									1	2	3	4	5
writevalue a					Write_item(A, a, 1, 2)	N	N	N	1	2	3	4	5
commit A					Commit_transaction(A)	Y	Y	N	1	2	3	4	5
	start B				Start_transaction(B)	N	N	N	1	2	3	4	5
	readvalue b				Read_item(B, b)	N	N	N	1	2	3	4	5
	b:b*2								1	2	3	4	5
	writevalue b				Write_item(B, b, 2, 4)	N	N	N	1	2	3	4	5
		start C			Start_transaction(C)	N	N	N	1	2	3	4	5
		readvalue c			Read_item(C, c)	N	N	N	1	2	3	4	5
		c:=c*2							1	2	3	4	5
		writevalue c			Write_item(C, c, 3, 6)	N	N	N	1	2	3	4	5
					Checkpoint	Y	N	Y	2	4	6	4	5
	b:=0								2	4	6	4	5
	writevalue b				Write_item(B, b, 4, 0)	N	N	N	2	4	6	4	5
	commit B				Commit_transaction(B)	Y	Y	N	2	4	6	4	5
			start D		Start_transaction(D)	N	N	N	2	4	6	4	5
			readvalue d		Read_item(D, d)	N	N	N	2	4	6	4	5
			d:=d*2						2	4	6	4	5
			writevalue d		Write_item(D, d, 4, 8)	N	N	N	2	4	6	4	5
			commit D		Commit_transaction(D)	Y	Y	N	2	4	6	4	5
				start E	Start_transaction(E)	N	N	N	2	4	6	4	5
				readvalue e	Read_item(E, e)	N	N	N	2	4	6	4	5
				e:=e*2					2	4	6	4	5
				writevalue e	write_item(E, e, 5, 10)	N	N	N	2	4	6	4	5
					FAILURE								

The recovery activities can be summarised in the following table:

Transaction	No need for action – changes irrevocably made to the database	Redo	Undo	Re-presented
A	Yes			
B		Yes		
C				Yes
D			Yes	
E				Yes

Distributed database systems

OVERVIEW

In many organisations data is shared, often geographically. Typically, all personal computers are networked to support work-group computing and many previously (centralised) mainframe applications have been downsized for various reasons, including cost-effectiveness. Distributed databases are concerned with the efficient distribution of data across different platforms and networks. As far as users are concerned, the data is an integrated whole, even if it is geographically dispersed. Users may access a data item and be completely unaware that part of that data item resides on a machine in Tokyo, and that another component was recovered from Los Angeles.

Many of the issues considered in other chapters in this book require a degree of further consideration when translated into a distributed context. When it becomes a requirement to distribute data across a network, the processes of transaction processing, concurrency control, query optimisation, recovery, security and integrity control become significantly more involved. In this chapter we shall introduce some extensions to mechanisms which we have previously considered for non-distributed systems.

Learning outcomes On completion of this chapter, you should be able to:

- Describe the essential characteristics of distributed database systems

- Distinguish between client/server databases and distributed databases

- Understand the main design issues concerned with distributed DBMSs (fragmentation and replication).

11.1 Introduction

In previous chapters we assumed that databases are centralised where a single logical database is located at one site. We now discuss the concept and issues of **distributed database systems** where users can access data at both their own site, and remotely. We start by examining the various architectures for databases and show how distributed database systems have evolved from these earlier systems.

11.2 Centralised database

Figure 11.1: Centralised database

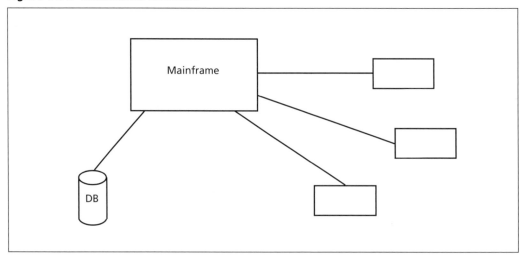

With this earlier architecture, all system components (i.e. the database and the DBMS) reside at a single mainframe computer or site. Users may be able to access the centralised database system remotely via terminals connected to the site; however, all the user interface processing, applications programs processing, as well as DBMS functionality, take place at the central site as in the figure 11.1.

Advantages:

- Cost – economies of scale (hardware, software and operations)
- Easier overall control over database (for backup, recovery and security).

Disadvantages:

- Data is not readily accessible to users at remote sites
- Data communication costs may be high
- The database system fails totally when the central system fails.

As the price of hardware fell, terminals were replaced with PCs and workstations. At first these were used just for interface processing, but gradually more of the processing was put on the user side. This led to client-side processing.

11.3 Client/server database

With client/server architecture we would expect many PCs and workstations, as well as a small number of mainframe computers, to all be connected by local area networks (LANs) and other types of computer networks. Application processing is divided (not necessarily evenly) between client and server. The client functions are performed on a separate computer from the database server functions. A client is a user machine and provides user interface and local processing capabilities. When the client requires functionality not available at the client, it connects to a server that provides additional functionality such as database access. This is shown diagrammatically as:

Figure 11.2: Client/server database

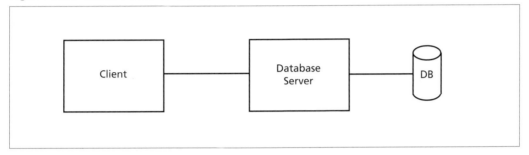

A client/server architecture is an example of a loosely coupled system which separates functions on specialised processors. The server and various clients may even run different operating systems. As the client functions are performed on a separate computer from the database server functions, neither the client nor the database server are complete application environments in themselves.

This approach is known as the **2-tier model of client/server computing**. This is because it is made up of the two types of component, **clients** and **servers**. It is also possible that a machine that acts as a server to some clients, may itself act as a client to another server. The distinction between a client and server machine is that the client is a device which initiates the connection, whereas the server is the device which accepts the connection.

Servers

The server is responsible for database storage, access and integrity checking, security, data dictionary maintenance and concurrent access management. Moreover, they also perform recovery and optimise query processing. The server controls access to the data by enforcing locking rules to ensure data integrity during transactions. The server can be a PC, mini- or mainframe computer and usually employs a multi-tasking operating system such as OS/2, Solaris, Mac OS X Server or Microsoft Windows Server.

The server software is responsible for local data management at a site, much like centralised DBMS software. A number of relational products have taken the SQL server approach. Clients submit SQL to the SQL server to manipulate or retrieve data. Since SQL is a relational standard, various different SQL servers, possibly provided by different vendors, can accept SQL commands. In this approach, the SQL server has also been called a **database processor** or a **back-end machine**. The server responds to queries from clients, checks the syntax of these commands, verifies the access rights of the user, executes these commands, and responds with desired data or error messages. The server hides the server system from the client and from the end user, so that the user is completely unaware of the server's hardware and software.

The server of a client/server system may also include the part of the DBMS software responsible for handling data storage on disk pages, buffering and caching of disk pages and other such functions.

Clients

This is the front-end of the client/server system. It handles all aspects of the user interface – it is the 'front-end' of the system since the client presents the system to the user. It can also provide PC-based application development tools to enter, display, query and manipulate data on the central server and to build applications. Examples of client operating systems are Microsoft Windows, OS/2, Mac OS X and Solaris.

Clients send database commands to the database server for processing (usually as SQL queries). The client manages the user interface. This includes the programming language interface functions, presenting data, and handling all interactions with local devices (printer, keyboard, screen, etc). The client has been called an **application processor** or a **front-end machine**. The client can be running any application system that is able to generate the proper commands to the server. For example, the application program might be written in Excel, a report writer, a sophisticated screen painter, or any fourth-generation language that has an application program interface (API) for the database engine. An API calls library routines that transparently manage SQL commands from the front-end client application to the database server. An API might work with existing front-end software, like a report generator, and it may include its own facilities for building applications. When APIs exist for several program development tools, there is considerable independence to develop client applications in the most convenient front-end programming environment, as well as drawing data from a common server database. APIs have evolved so that it is possible to have clients with different operating systems running applications against a common database.

Advantages of the client/server approach

Here are some of the advantages of the client/server approach over centralised or stand-alone processing:

- It allows companies to maximise the benefits of microcomputer technology, delivering impressive computing power at a fraction of the costs of mainframes
- Users do not have to retain copies of corporate data on their own PCs, which would become quickly out of date. They can be assured that they are always working with the current data stored on the server machine. As the data is in one place, there is improved control of backup, recovery and security
- Processing can be carried out on the machine most appropriate to the task. Data-intensive processes can be carried out on the server, whereas data entry validation and presentation logic can be executed on the client machine. This reduces unnecessary network traffic and improves overall performance
- Scalability – if the number of users of an application grows, extra client machines can be added (up to a limit determined by the capacity of the network or server) without significant changes to the server.

Disadvantages of client/server computing

Some disadvantages of the client/server approach:

- Operating database systems over a local area network (LAN) or wide area network (WAN) brings extra complexities of developing and maintaining the network. The interfaces between the programs running on the client and server machines must be well understood. This usually becomes increasingly complex when the applications and/or DBMS software come from different vendors

- Security is a major consideration. Preventative measures must be in place to protect data theft or corruption on the client and server machines and during transmission over the network.

11.4 Distributed database management systems

Figure 11.3: Distributed database management system

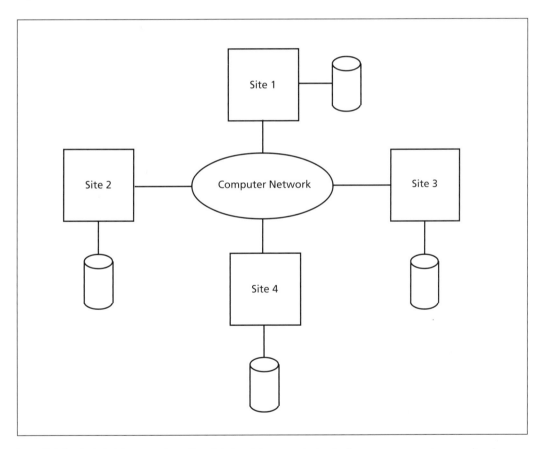

In a distributed database system the database is spread physically across computers or sites in different locations. These are usually connected with one another via high-speed networks or telephone lines. Typically, all personal computers are networked to support work-group computing, and many previously (centralised) mainframe applications have been downsized for various reasons, including for cost-effectiveness. Distributed databases are concerned with the efficient distribution of data across different platforms and networks.

A good working definition of a distributed database is that of C J Date (Date, 2002):

A **distributed database** consists of a collection of sites connected by some kind of communications network, in which:

Each site is a database system in its own right, but the sites have agreed to work together so that a user at any site can access data anywhere in the network exactly as if the data were all stored at the user's own site.

Note that the generally understood description of a distributed database system given here is rather different from the client/server systems we examined earlier in the chapter. In client/server systems, the data is not itself distributed; it is stored on a server machine and accessed remotely from client machines. In a distributed database system, however, the data is itself distributed among a number of different machines. Decisions not only need to be made about the way in which the data is to be distributed, but also about how updates are to be propagated over multiple sites.

The sites of a distributed database may be spread over a large area (such as Britain or the world) connected via a wide area network (WAN), or over a small area (such as a building or a campus) connected via a local area network (LAN). It is not uncommon for the computers to vary in both technical specification and function, depending upon their importance and position in the system as a whole. For example, there may be IBM mainframes, VAXs, SUN workstations, PCs, etc managed by different operating systems (such as VMS, UNIX, Windows NT). Each fragment of the database may be managed by a different DBMS (such as Oracle, Microsoft Access, O2).

As far as users are concerned, the data is an integrated whole, even if it is geographically dispersed. Users may access a data item and be completely unaware that part of that item resides on a machine in Tokyo, while another component was recovered from London. Users access the distributed database via applications. In a distributed database system, database applications running at any of the system's sites should be able to operate on any of the database fragments transparently (i.e. as if the data came from a single database managed by one DBMS). The software that manages a distributed database in such a way is called a **distributed database management system** (DDBMS).

Motivation for distributed database systems

So why have distributed databases become so desirable? There are a number of reasons that promote the use of a distributed database system. These can include such things such as:

- The sharing of data
- Local autonomy
- Data availability.

Furthermore, it is likely that the organisation which has chosen to implement the system will itself be distributed. By this we mean that there are almost always several departments and divisions within the company structure. An illustrative example is useful here in clarifying the benefits that can be gained by the use of distributed database systems.

Example scenario: banking system

Imagine a banking system that operates over a number of separate sites. For the sake of this example let us consider two offices, one in Piccadilly and another in Westminster. Account data for Piccadilly accounts is stored in Piccadilly, while Westminster's account data is stored in Westminster. We can now see that two major benefits are afforded by the use of this system: efficiency of processing is increased due to the data being stored where it is most frequently accessed, while an improvement in the accessibility of account data is also gained.

Functions of a distributed database management system (DDBMS)

A distributed DBMS coordinates the access to data at the various sites where the distributed database resides. A DDBMS is required to perform the following functions in addition to the normal functions of a DBMS:

- **Extended communication services:** to provide access to remote sites and allow the transfer of queries and data among them
- **Extended system catalog (global system catalog):** to store data distribution details; this can determine the location from which to retrieve requested data
- **Distributed query processing:** if necessary, translate the request at one site using a local DBMS into the proper request to another site using a different DBMS and data model
- **Extended concurrency control:** to maintain consistency of replicated data
- **Extended recovery services:** to be able to recover from crashes at a particular site and failure of communication links.

DDBMS transparencies

Date (1999) gives the 'fundamental principle' behind a truly distributed database:

> To the user; a distributed system should look exactly like a NON distributed system.

In other words, the system should make the distribution transparent to the user.

In order to accomplish this fundamental principle, a number of transparencies, which hide the implementation details, can be identified as objectives for a DDBMS:

- Location transparency
- Copy transparency
- Fragmentation transparency
- Transaction transparency
- Performance transparency
- Schema change transparency
- Local DBMS transparency.

Location transparency

A user can submit a query that accesses distributed objects without having to know where the objects are.

Copy transparency

The system supports the optional existence of multiple copies of database objects. Hence, if a site is down, users can still access database objects by obtaining one of the copies from another site, and the user does not need to know either that the data is replicated or the source of the data.

Fragmentation transparency

A relation (class) can be divided into multiple pieces and stored at multiple sites according to specified distribution criteria. For example, the following distribution criteria might control the placement of tuples from an Employee relation:

- EMPLOYEE where dept = "accounts" at London
- EMPLOYEE where dept <> "accounts" at New York

In this way the tuples of a relation can be distributed, and users can subsequently query the relation as if the data were not fragmented at all. In the example, a user can access the Employee relation unaware of its distribution.

Transaction transparency

A user can run an arbitrary transaction that updates data at any number of sites (i.e. a distributed transaction) and the transaction behaves exactly like a local one. Atomicity is maintained.

Performance transparency

This requires the DDBMS to perform as if it were a centralised DBMS. In order to achieve this, the DDBMS must be able to determine the most cost-effective strategy to execute a request. For example, if you have one million objects in New York and ten objects in London, you want to perform the join by moving the ten objects to New York and not vice versa. Performance transparency loosely means that a query can be submitted from any node in a distributed DBMS and it will run with comparable performance.

Schema change transparency

A user who adds or deletes a database object from a distributed database need make the change only once (to the distributed dictionary) and does not need to change the catalog at all sites that participate in the distributed database.

Local DBMS transparency

The distributed database system provides services without regard for which local DBMSs are actually managing local data. It hides the fact that the DBMSs at various sites may be different.

Advantages to distributed databases

There are numerous advantages to distributed databases. The most important of these are the following:

- Increased reliability and availability
- Local control
- Modular growth
- Lower communication costs
- Faster response.

Increased reliability and availability

When a centralised system fails, the database is unavailable to all. A distributed system continues to function at a reduced level even when a component fails. The reliability and availability will depend (among other things) on how the data is distributed.

Local control

Local groups exercise greater control over 'their' data, promoting improved data integrity and administration. At the same time, users can access non-local data when necessary. Hardware can be chosen for the local site to match local rather than other needs.

Modular growth

Suppose that an organisation expands to a new location and adds a new work group. It is often easier and more economical to add a local computer and its associated data to the distributed network than to expand a large central computer. Also, there is less chance of disruption to existing users than is the case when a central computer system is modified or expanded.

Lower communication costs

With a distributed system, data can be located closer to their point of use. This can reduce communication costs compared to a central system.

Faster response

Depending on how data is distributed, most requests for data by users at a particular site can be satisfied by data stored at that site. This speeds up query processing, because communication and central computer delays are minimised. It may also be possible to split complex queries and subqueries that can be processed in parallel at several sites, providing even faster response.

Disadvantages to distributed databases

The use of distributed database systems is not without its drawbacks. The main disadvantage is the added complexity that is involved in ensuring that proper coordination between the various sites is possible.

This increase in complexity can take a variety of forms:

- Software cost and complexity
- Processing overhead
- Data integrity
- Slow response.

Software cost and complexity

More complex software (especially the DBMS) is required for a distributed database environment. There is a greater potential for bugs. With a number of databases operating concurrently, ensuring that algorithms for the operation of the system are correct becomes an area of great difficulty.

Processing overhead

The various sites must exchange messages and perform additional calculations to ensure proper coordination among the sites. This is a considerable overhead not present in centralised systems.

Data integrity

A by-product of the increased complexity and need for coordination is the additional exposure to improper updating and other problems of data integrity.

Slow response

If the data is not distributed properly according to its usage, or if queries are not formulated correctly, response to requests for data can be extremely slow.

11.5 Distributing data: strategies

A significant problem in physical database design is deciding at which nodes (or sites) in the network to physically locate the data. Data distribution is designed so that as much as possible of the locally required data is held at the local node, while minimising replication and data communication costs. But, how should a database be distributed among the sites (or nodes) of a network?

This section is about the way decisions are taken on where to store data, and how many copies are to be kept in different places.

There are four basic data distribution strategies:

1. Centralised

All data is located at a single site. Although this simplifies the implementation, there are at least three disadvantages:

- Data are not readily accessible to users at remote sites
- Data communication costs may be high
- The database system fails totally when the central system fails.

2. Fragmented

With this approach, the database is divided into disjoint (non-overlapping) fragments. Each fragment (also called a partition) is assigned to a particular site. The major advantage of this approach is that data is moved closer to local users and so is more accessible.

3. Replicated

A full copy (or selective copies) of the database is assigned to more than one site in the network. This assignment maximises local access to data but creates update problems, since each database change must be reliably processed and synchronised at all of the sites.

4. Hybrid

With this strategy, the database is fragmented into critical and **non-critical fragments**. Non-critical fragments are stored at only one site, while critical fragments are stored at multiple sites.

Fragmentation

A system can support data fragmentation if a given stored relation can be divided up into pieces, or **fragments**, for physical storage purposes. In this case there is no replication. All data is divided between nodes in logical units. When fragmented, each fragment, which may be a single relation or set of relations, is held at the node with the highest activity with regard to that partition. Fragmentation is desirable for performance reasons: data can be stored at the location where it is most frequently used, so that most operations are purely local and network traffic is reduced.

A fragment can be any arbitrary subrelation that is derivable from the original relation, via **restriction** (horizontal fragmentation) and **projection** (vertical fragmentation) operations. Note that the conceptual object is unchanged (e.g. there is still just one table), but it is stored in different places.

Horizontal fragmentation

With horizontal fragmentation, some of the rows of a table (or relation) are put into a base relation at one site, and other rows are put into a base relation at another site. More generally, the rows of a relation are distributed to many sites.

Horizontal fragmentation example

A bank has many branches. One of the base relations is the 'Customer' relation. Table 11.1 is the format for an abbreviated version of this relation. For simplicity, the sample data in the relation applies to only two of the branches (Piccadilly and Westminster). The primary key in this relation is account number (ACCT No.). 'Branch name' is the name of the branch where customers have opened their accounts (and therefore where they presumably perform most of their transactions).

Table 11.1: Abbreviated version of Customer relation

ACCT No.	Customer name	Branch name	Balance
200	Jones	Piccadilly	1000.00
324	Smith	Westminster	250.00
426	Dorman	Piccadilly	796.00
153	Gray	Westminster	38.00
683	McIntyre	Piccadilly	1500.00
252	Elmore	Piccadilly	330.00
500	Green	Westminster	168.00

The next examples are the result of taking horizontal fragments of the Customer relation. Each row is now located at its home branch. If customers actually conduct most of their transactions at the home branch, the transactions are processed locally and response times are minimised. When a customer initiates a transaction at another branch, the transaction must be transmitted to the home branch for processing, and the response then transmitted back to the initiating branch (this is the normal pattern for persons using ATMs). If a customer's usage pattern changes (perhaps because of a move), the system may be able to detect this change and dynamically move the record to the location where most transactions are being initiated.

Table 11.2: Horizontal fragments of the Customer relation

Piccadilly Branch:

ACCT No.	Customer name	Branch name	Balance
200	Jones	Piccadilly	1000.00
426	Dorman	Piccadilly	796.00
683	McIntyre	Piccadilly	1500.00
252	Elmore	Piccadilly	330.00

Table 11.3: Horizontal fragments of the Customer relation

Westminster Branch:

ACCT No.	Customer name	Branch name	Balance
324	Smith	Westminster	250.00
153	Gray	Westminster	38.00
500	Green	Westminster	168.00

In summary, horizontal fragments for a distributed database have three major advantages:

- **Efficiency:** data is stored close to where it is used and separate from data used by other users or applications

- **Local optimisation:** data can be stored to optimise performance for local access
- **Security:** data not relevant to usage at a particular site is not made available.

Thus, horizontal fragments are usually used when an organisational function is distributed, but each site is concerned with only a subset of the entity instances (frequently based on geography).

Horizontal fragments also have two primary disadvantages:

- **Inconsistent access speed:** when data from several fragments is required, the access time can be significantly different from local-only data access
- **Backup vulnerability:** since data is not replicated, when data at one site becomes inaccessible or damaged, usage cannot switch to another site where a copy exists; data may be lost if proper backup is not performed at each site.

Vertical fragmentation

With vertical fragmentation, some of the columns of a relation are projected into a base relation at one of the sites, and other columns are projected into a base relation at another site (more generally, columns may be projected to several sites). The relations at each of the sites must share a common domain – the columns that define the primary key – so that the original table can be reconstructed.

Vertical fragmentation example

To illustrate vertical fragmentation, we use an application for the manufacturing company shown below in the 'Part' relation with 'Part no.' as the primary key. Some of the data is used primarily by manufacturing, while the other is used mostly by engineering. The data is distributed to the respective departmental computers using vertical fragmentation, as shown below. Each of the fragments shown is obtained by taking projections (that is, columns) from the original relation. The original relation in turn can be obtained by taking natural joins of the resulting fragments.

Table 11.4: Abbreviated version of Part relation

Part no.	Name	Cost	Drawing no.	Stock Level
P2	Widget	100.00	123-7	20.00
P7	Gizmo	550.00	621-0	100.00
P3	Thing	48.00	174-3	0.00
Pi	Whatsit	220.00	416-2	16.00
P8	Thumzer	16.00	321-0	50.00
P9	Bobbit	75.00	400-1	0.00
P6	Nailit	125.00	129-4	200.00

Table 11.5: Vertical fragments of the Part relation

Manufacturing:

Part no.	Name	Cost	Stock level
P2	Widget	100.00	20.00
P7	Gizmo	550.00	100.00
P3	Thing	48.00	0.00
Pi	Whatsit	220.00	16.00
P8	Thumzer	16.00	50.00
P9	Bobbit	75.00	0.00
P6	Nailit	125.00	200.00

Engineering:

Part no.	Drawing no.
P2	123-7
P7	621-0
P3	174-3
Pi	416-2
P8	321-0
P9	400-1
P6	129-4

In summary, the advantages and disadvantages of vertical fragments are identical to those for horizontal fragments. However, horizontal fragments support an organisational design in which functions are replicated, often on a regional basis, while vertical fragments are typically applied across organisational functions with reasonably separate data requirements.

Combinations of operations

To complicate matters further, there are almost unlimited combinations of the preceding strategies. Some data may be stored centrally, while other data is replicated at the various sites. Also, for a given relation, both horizontal and vertical fragments may be desirable for data distribution.

For example:

- Engineering parts, accounting, and customer data are each centralised at different locations
- Standard parts data are fragmented (horizontally) among the three locations
- The standard price list is replicated at all three locations.

The overriding principle in distributed database design is that data should be stored at the sites where they will be accessed most frequently (although other considerations, such as security, data integrity, and cost, are also likely to be important). The data administrator plays a critical and central role in organising a distributed database, in order to make it distributed, not decentralised.

Data replication

Data replication is the controlled duplication of data. A system supports data replication if a given stored relation – or, more generally, a given fragment – can be represented by many distinct copies or replicas, stored at many distinct sites. We can distinguish between **complete replication** where a complete copy of the database is maintained at each site (no fragmentation), and **selective replication** which is a combination of fragmentation and replication. The objective of this strategy is to have the advantages of the previous approaches without the disadvantages. However, this is subject to a good design.

There are two advantages to data replication:

- **Reliability** – if one of the sites containing the relation (or database) fails, a copy can always be found at another site
- **Faster and consistent access speeds** – applications can operate on local copies instead of having to communicate with remote sites.

There are also two primary disadvantages:

- **Storage requirements** – each site that has a full copy must have the same storage capacity that would be required if the data were stored centrally
- **Update propagation problem** – the major disadvantage of replication is that when a given replicated object is updated, all copies of that object must be updated – this is called the update propagation problem.

For these reasons, data replication is favoured where most transactions are read-only and where the data is relatively static, as in catalogues, telephone directories, train schedules and so on. CD-ROM storage technology has proved an economical medium for replicated databases. **Full replication** is where the whole database is replicated. **Partial replication** is where some data is replicated over several nodes – generally to achieve specific purposes, whether performance or recovery based.

Synchronous and asynchronous replication

As mentioned earlier, from the point of view of the user, a DDBMS should behave like a centralised DBMS. For example, as far as query processing is concerned, a user can ask a query of a database and be unaware of where the data is stored. When it comes to updates to data, transactions should appear to be atomic actions, regardless of data fragmentation and replication. With this view we refer to replication as **synchronous replication:** before an update transaction commits, it synchronises all copies of modified data. In other words, replicated data is updated immediately when the source data is updated, typically using the 2PL protocol that was discussed in Chapter 9. However, this method comes at a significant cost. Before an updated transaction can commit, it must lock all copies of the modified data. The lock requests may be at remote sites. These sites may be unavailable and there may be communication failures.

Another approach to data replication is known as **asynchronous replication**. This method is gaining in popularity for commercial DDBMSs. Copies of an updated transaction are updated only periodically. This means that a transaction that reads different copies of the same relation may see different values for short periods of time. This method violates location transparency: users must now be aware of which copy is being accessed and that copies may be inconsistent. This method is, however, acceptable in many situations. The data eventually will synchronise at all the replicated sites.

Activity 11.1

Distributed database design

Consider the following scenario:

A bank has its head office in Central London. It has two branches, one in East Finchley and the other in Brent Cross. Each customer account belongs to one branch only. Currently, the company has one database located in the Head Office. Customers at branches access this database via a communication network for whatever data they need.

One of the relations in this centralised database system is the Account relation, where data about the accounts is kept. The attributes of the Account relation are: the account number (Acc no.), account type (Acc type), the customer's identification (assume Name), the branch where the account is held, the current balance for the account (Balance) and an indicator which lets Head Office know if the publicity (information on updates to regulations, interest rates etc) for a particular account type for a customer has been sent out. An instance of the Account relation is given below:

Acc no.	Acc type	Name	Branch	Balance	Publicity
191688	002	Jones	Brent Cross	2000	yes
779865	005	Smith	East Finchley	600	no
158756	002	Green	East Finchley	8	yes
125467	007	White	East Finchley	10000	no
124678	005	Black	Brent Cross	150	yes

The bank has decided to move to a distributed database system where each of the sites has its own database. Propose a fragmentation design of the Account relation that reflects the distribution of the company's sites and their functionality. Justify your proposal.

11.6 Summary

This chapter introduced the student to distributed database systems. It opened with a comparison with other architectures, namely centralised databases and client/server systems. Distributed database transparencies were described, followed by a discussion of distributed database system advantages and disadvantages. Students were then introduced to various approaches to distributed database design, namely, vertical and horizontal fragmentation and replication.

11.7 Review questions

Review question 11.1 Explain what is meant by the 2-tier model of client/server computing.

Review question 11.2 Why is it sometimes said that client/server computing improves the scalability of applications?

Review question 11.3 What additional security issues are involved in the use of a client/server system, compared with a traditional, centralised, mainframe database accessed via dumb terminals?

Review question 11.4 Distinguish between the terms 'fragmentation' and 'replication' in a distributed database environment.

Review question 11.5 Describe the main advantage and disadvantage of synchronous replication.

11.8 Feedback on activity

Activity 11.1 A number of solutions are acceptable. For example, the relation is first fragmented vertically. The first fragment (Acc no., Acc type, Publicity), is stored at the Head Office. The second fragment (Acc No., Name, Branch, Balance) is then horizontally fragmented to two groups of tuples. The ones where Branch = 'Brent Cross' will be stored in Brent Cross, whereas those where Branch = 'East Finchley' will be stored in East Finchley.

In the vertical fragmentation, the attribute Acc no. is included in both the fragments, so that the original relation can be reconstructed. Note that it may also be necessary to replicate the Account type, and to hold this at the 'branch fragments', depending on the functions performed at the branch.

Web database connectivity

OVERVIEW

Database technology has been around for a long time. For many organisations, database systems are an essential and integral part of their everyday operation. Prior to the advent of the Internet, these systems have only been accessible through company-based local area networks (LANs), or wide area networks (WANs). Now, the Internet has opened up new opportunities for developing and disseminating innovative database applications, and has made legacy systems available via the same paradigm. A multinational company, for example, can create a web-based database application to enable the effective sharing of information among offices around the world. A book company, such as Amazon, or computer company, such as Dell, can reach a world-wide audience that can order their goods, track the status of orders and pay for the goods online without leaving their PC. Via the web, a database application can be made available, interactively, to users and organisations anywhere in the world.

In this chapter, we examine the impact that the web brings to the development and deployment of database applications. We will study the most commonly used approaches for creating and operating web databases, and discuss related issues such as dynamic updating of web pages online. In keeping with all aspects of web technology, which has been evolving at a considerable pace since it was first proposed in 1989, there are multiple, and sometimes conflicting ways of performing similar tasks.

The first part of this chapter introduces the concept and need for **web database connectivity**. This includes a discussion on the differences between traditional client/server and web-based applications and an examination of **dynamic web pages** and the role they play in web-based applications. We then look at the hardware and software architecture, in terms of a **3-tier model**, that is appropriate for both traditional and web-based applications. Next, each of the layers (components) of the architecture is looked at in depth, including **client-side database access** and **server-side database access**. As each layer is discussed, the concepts and approaches for **web server** management, **application logic** development and **database connectivity** are introduced. Lastly, the Extensible Markup Language (XML) is introduced.

Learning outcomes   On completion of this chapter, you should be able to:

- Distinguish between traditional and web-based database connectivity

- Understand the requirements for connecting database systems to the web

- Describe the 3-tier architecture, and functional components or layers, within the model which forms the essential building block for web database applications

- Identify the differences between client-side and server-side database access

- Critically compare a number of approaches that might be used to build a web-enabled database

- Describe some of the features of XML

12.1 Differences between traditional client/server and web-based applications

Web-based database applications use a new type of client/server technology. Some of the traditional client/server database techniques, which we looked at in Chapter 11, are still adopted. However, because of the incorporation of the web technology, there are important differences as set out in table 12.1.

Table 12.1: Traditional vs web server comparison

Traditional client/server applications	Web-based applications
Platform-dependent	Platform-independent
Client is natively compiled and therefore has fast execution speed	Client is an interpreter (e.g. HTML, Java, Java Script) and therefore is slower
Installation necessary	No need for installation
Complex client; high maintenance cost	Simple client; minimum maintenance
New, unfamiliar interface for users	One common, familiar interface across applications
Rich, custom GUI constructs possible	Limited set of GUI constructs; custom ones add to download time
Difficult to integrate with existing applications	Easy to integrate
Difficult to add multimedia	Easy to add multimedia
Persistent connection to database	Non-persistent connection

Platform independence

Web client logic (operating within any web browser) is platform-independent and does not require modification to be run on different operating systems. Traditional database clients, on the other hand, are frequently platform-specific, and extensive porting effort is required to support multiple platforms. This is arguably one of the most compelling reasons for building a web-based client/server database application.

Interpreted applications

Web client logic is written in interpreted languages (e.g. HTML and Java). This has an adverse effect on performance. In many applications, however, this is a price worth paying to gain the advantage of platform independence. Time-critical applications may not be good candidates to be implemented on the web.

No need for installation

Another benefit of web database applications is that the need for installing special software is eliminated on the client's side. It is pretty safe to assume that the clients have already had a web browser installed, which is the only piece of software needed for the clients to run the applications. All web client logic (i.e. the HTML page) is automatically retrieved from the web servers when required.

Simple client

As a client needs just a browser to run a web-based database application, the potential complications are minimised.

Common interface across applications

Again, because there is no need for specialised software, users have the benefit of using a browser for possibly different applications.

Limited GUI (graphical user interface)

This is one area in which web-based database applications may fall short. Highly customised application interfaces and highly interactive clients may not translate well as web applications. This is because of HTML limitations. At the moment, HTML forms do not offer an extensive feature set, and GUI developers can resort to client-side scripting (e.g. JavaScript) or applets to provide better user interfaces. This can be complex, adds to downloading time, and degrades performance (although raw client power is still being doubled every two years through more powerful PCs).

Integrate with other applications

Because of the benefit of being platform-independent, different applications that adhere to the HTML standard can be integrated without many difficulties.

Multimedia support

HTML already provides easy-to-use constructs to present and manipulate multimedia contents, such as image files, and, with browser extensions (e.g. plug-ins), audio and video files.

Non-persistent connection to database

Persistent database connections are highly efficient data channels between a client and the DBMS, and, therefore, are ideal for database applications. However, web-based applications do not have this benefit. A web-based client maintains its connection to a database only as long as is necessary to retrieve the required data, and then releases it. Thus, web application developers must address the added overhead for creating new database connections each time a client requires database access.

12.2 Web database connectivity

The term 'web database connectivity' describes the connection between a client machine and a remote database via the World Wide Web. Such a connection allows a web browser user to connect with a remote database, to both access and update the database content. Access and update of the database is, as with traditional systems, controlled by a layer of application logic. This is provided by the designers and developers of the database system. However, the manner in which a database connection is provided via the web, and the architecture and components that make up the solution, is very different from the traditional one and is the subject of this chapter.

In the first instance, web database connectivity is initiated through a web browser that understands HTML. In the second instance, web database connectivity involves database interaction via web servers on remote websites and results in 'dynamic' web pages that are returned to the browser user.

Static web pages

We will first of all consider the situation when a fixed HTML page with the standard '.html' file extension is requested:

- A web browser passes a URL reference to a remote website via the http protocol
- The web server on the website looks up the URL reference and retrieves the corresponding HTML file that is passed back, again via the http protocol, to the web browser
- The web browser displays the HTML page to the user.

This is an example of static web page access. What the end user sees remains the same (unless the author puts an updated version of the HTML file on the server).

Dynamic web pages

The alternative to a static web page is a dynamic web page. The content of a dynamic web page is generated each time it is accessed, and it is server-side processing that handles the generation.

The flow is as follows:

- A web browser passes a URL reference to a remote website via the http protocol
- The web server sees that the URL reference is not a static '.html' reference but is a process or file reference with a different extension type
- The web server invokes an associated process, based on the URL name and extension type, that is responsible for generating the required HTML file

- The associated process generates the HTML file, accessing (and updating if necessary) one or more databases
- The HTML file is returned to the web server and is passed back, again via http protocol, to the web browser
- The web browser displays the HTML page to the user.

A conceptual diagram of this flow, including access to static HTML files, is shown in figure 12.1.

Figure 12.1: Dynamic HTML generation

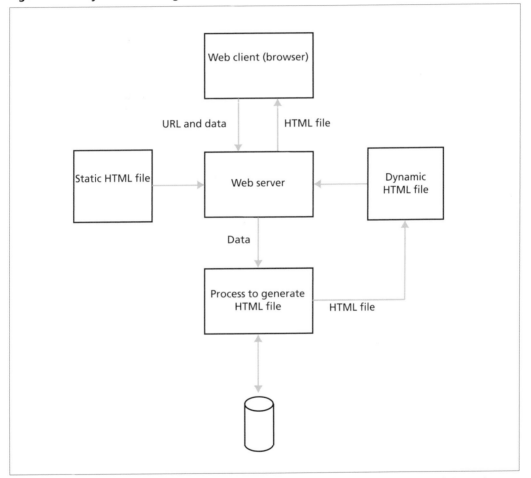

The need for web database connectivity is a natural extension of early limitations of the web. Initially, as we have already seen, websites were file-based where each document was stored in a separate HTML file. When items in a collection were to be presented on the web, a separate web page was created for each item or grouping of items. Such pages were difficult to organise and almost impossible to keep up to date and consistent over time. Increasingly, the huge volume and structure of data on the web warranted storing and organising into databases, and then generating web pages based on these databases. Any website that presents information about a collection of 'like items' is a candidate for using a web database. These items could be goods for sale, information about courses and modules at a university, or film clips. Organisations are now rapidly building new database applications, or changing existing ones, to take advantage of the web technologies.

Process to generate HTML file

What is the HTML generation process itself? What type of process is it? How does it get user input? What computer language is the application logic written in? How are underlying databases accessed and updated? In practice, there are multiple technologies addressing these questions, each handling the problem in slightly different ways.

Common Gateway Interface program (CGI program)

A type of HTML generation process, and the one that has been around for the longest time, is a CGI program (often called a CGI script). A CGI program is identified by the URL passed from a web browser and it communicates with the web server via the CGI protocol (Common Gateway Interface protocol). CGI programs can be written in a number of languages, including C and Java, though very often they are written in the Perl scripting language, hence the name CGI script. The logic of a CGI program generates the entire HTML file that is returned to the web browser.

Java Servlets

Java Servlets perform a similar function to CGI programs. Java Servlets are Java programs that generate entire HTML files.

HTML 'template' approach

A further approach, typified by a number of technologies including Active Server Pages, Java Server Pages and Coldfusion Markup Language, involves template HTML files that are identified by the URL. The template files (with various extensions such as .aspx, jsp, cfm as described later in this chapter) are a mixture of HTML code and programming (or 'scripting') code. The HTML code in the template forms the basis of the HTML document passed back to the web browser user, while the programming code specifies the logic that generates the remaining parts of the HTML page. This is illustrated in figure 12.2.

Figure 12.2: HTML generation from template

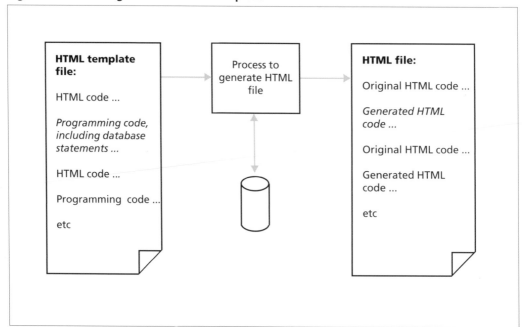

Example of HTML template and generated file

The programming code can be based around proprietary HTML tags (as is the case with Coldfusion template files). Alternatively, it can be written as a server-side scripting language (such as server-side JavaScript or server-side VBScript), or written in pure Java. An example of a Coldfusion template page and its dynamically generated HTML file is given below in figure 12.3. Here, a database called 'MDX University' is accessed, and the data items, module codes and titles are retrieved from the database. These are placed in an HTML file for subsequent display by a web browser.

Figure 12.3: Coldfusion template page example and generated HTML file

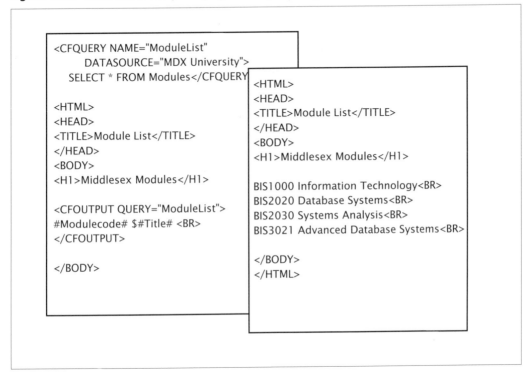

12.3 Web connectivity architecture

Business systems, whether or not they are delivered via the web, must have components that handle the user interface, the application logic and the database access and update. In a classic mainframe environment, most of these were packaged within the mainframe themselves. As we saw in Chapter 11, this gradually moved to a 2-tier client/server architecture, in which the user interface and some of the application logic was housed on a client machine (typically a PC), with the majority of the application logic and the database being on a server machine. Most business systems nowadays are built around a three-tier architecture that supports better distribution of processing, scalability and robustness.

3-tier architecture

There are three levels in the 3-tier architecture, as shown in figure 12.4.

Figure 12.4: 3-tier architecture

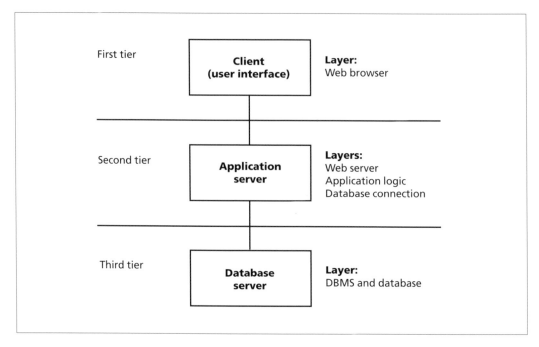

The first tier is the client machine that contains user interfaces. In a web-based system the client machine typically runs a web browser. The middle tier is the application server that provides application logic and data processing functions. In a web-based system, the application server runs the web server, which is a software component rather than a hardware one. The third tier, running on a separate server called a database server, contains the actual database management system (DBMS).

There may be variations on this theme in any particular implementation of a website. For example, there may be multiple, and possibly distributed, application server machines for multiple applications, and there may be multiple database servers each supporting a different database system within the organisation's operation.

Layers within the 3-tier model

Referring again to the 3-tier architecture diagram (figure 12.4), there are a number of functional components, or layers, that form essential building blocks for web database applications. These layers are summarised below and then described in more detail in subsequent sections:

- **Web browser layer:** this is in the first tier of the 3-tier model. One of the best-known browsers is Internet Explorer (IE) from Microsoft, which runs only under Windows. There are now a number of browsers competing with IE, including Firefox which is free, cross-platform and developed by Mozilla

- **Web server layer:** this is in the second tier of the 3-tier model. As with the web browser, there are a number of web server options. Microsoft provides a web server known as IIS (Internet Information Services) ,running exclusively on Windows-based operating systems (such as XP and Vista). There are also a number of 'freeware' or 'shareware' systems, such as

Apache, which has become the most popular web server product. Coldfusion sells a web server that supports its HTML extensions and, more recently, a number of web servers have appeared within transaction and session managers that are becoming the engines of eCommerce websites. Examples are WebSphere from IBM, and WebLogic from BEA Systems

- **Application logic layer:** this is in the second tier of the 3-tier model. The application logic layer is where the specifics of any web-based application are housed, containing all the business and data processing logic that makes up the application. It is this layer that is most important from an application developer's point of view, since this is where the features and functions of the application are built using the available web-based technologies. Examples of such technologies are CGI programs, Active Server Pages, ASP.NET, Java Servlets and Java Server Pages

- **Database connection layer:** this is in the second tier of the 3-tier model. The database connection layer is the set of communication protocols and APIs (application program interfaces) between the application logic and the database systems that hold all the data for an organisation. At one extreme, database connection can be provided through the native interfaces offered by the database management system(s) being used. However, this is not an ideal approach as it limits portability of the application, both from a hardware and software perspective. A preferred approach is to introduce a measure of database independence, through connection interfaces such as ODBC (open database connectivity) and JDBC (Java database connectivity)

- **Database layer:** this is in the third tier of the 3-tier model. The database layer holds the DBMS and the database(s), such as the Oracle DBMS, Microsoft Access and other DBMS solutions. This layer is not discussed further in this chapter.

12.4 Web browser layer

The browser is the client of a web database application and it has two major functions. First, it handles the layout and display of HTML documents. Second, it executes client-side extension functionality such as Java (in the form of Java Applets), client-side scripting, ActiveX (a Microsoft technology to extend a browser's capabilities) and plug-ins. An additional function of a web browser is to manage cookies, which are a way to overcome the stateless nature of the http protocol. Cookie functions are described later in this section. Currently, the most popular browsers are Microsoft Internet Explorer (IE), FireFox Web Browser from Mozilla, Safari (developed by Apple) and Opera (popular for use on mobile devices). They have their own advantages and disadvantages with respect to web database applications:

- All support Java and JavaScript; IE also fully supports ActiveX and the VBScript scripting language (which is similar to Visual Basic)
- FireFox is supported on numerous platforms, whereas IE runs only on Microsoft systems (such as Windows XP and Vista)
- IE offers compatibility with other Microsoft products, and can easily be integrated with existing tools such as Word, Excel and PowerPoint. The drawback is that IE is heavily dependent on the Windows platforms and other Microsoft proprietary systems
- ActiveX is designed to extend the functionality of IE, and works only on Windows platforms and Macintosh System 7+
- All support XML (Extensible Markup Language), which is an open way to describe both the data structure and actual content of information displayed to an end-user.

Browsers are also responsible for providing forms for the collection of user input, packaging the input, and sending it to the appropriate server for processing. For example, input can include registration for site access, guest books and requests for information. HTML, Java Applets, scripting languages (JavaScript, VBScript) and ActiveX (for IE) may be used to implement forms.

Browsers, or more specifically the HTML pages rendered by browsers, most commonly access remote databases indirectly through the web server, application logic and database connectivity components. That is, access is indirect. Browsers can, via scripts and ActiveX controls, directly access local databases (those on the client machine). Browsers can also, via applets, ActiveX controls or plug-ins, directly connect to and access remote databases. This may be required when integrating a company's legacy applications into the web browser environment, but is not typical of most eCommerce systems accessed via the Internet.

In addition, some non-web applications, particularly if the GUI front-end is developed in a language such as Java, can be launched and run from within a browser environment, and operate in exactly the same way as if run from the operating system environment. Again, this might be due to integration of legacy systems but these will not be true web-based database applications.

Client-side scripting

Client-side scripting, in either JavaScript or VBScript, is embedded in standard HTML pages. It is used primarily to make the web page interface with the end-user more interactive. Objects within a web page can be dynamically moved, hidden or highlighted, user input can be received and validated, and user events (e.g. mouse over object) can be listened for. Scripts are programming languages in their own rights with computational, formatting and conditional capabilities, as well as methods to interact with applets and ActiveX controls.

Client-side scripting can reduce the load on the remote web server, for example, by doing input validation. This avoids having to use multiple web server requests to manage invalid data. Scripting can also reduce the load on the database server. For example, a web client request can result in a single database query on the server side that obtains a number of items (e.g. books by a given author). These items are then packaged into a JavaScript array or an XML document and are transmitted back to the client to be browsed locally.

Applets

An applet is a small bit of Java code that is downloaded from a web server host when referenced by an applet tag within a web page. Being Java programs, applets operate on any browser platform that supports a Java Virtual Machine, and can do most things that a Java program can do, including access and connection to remote databases. Such connections bypass the http protocol and web server path typically used for web database access, and make use of available connection mechanisms for standard Java programs. These include direct socket connections to databases via DBMS net protocols (such as SQL*Net for Oracle), and approaches such as Java DataBase Connectivity (JDBC), Open DataBase Connectivity (ODBC) and Remote Method Invocation (RMI).

Applets, working in this manner, do have an advantage over server-side solutions: they can be in full control over the user transaction and can utilise whatever transaction management capabilities are offered by the database management systems they connect to. Applets can also be used to lessen the load on the server-side processors, as they can be responsible for more of the application functionality. In practice, because of major concerns about remote programs creating havoc on a client's local machine, the Java applet package has in-built security constraints. One such constraint allows only connection to a database running on the server machine from which the applet was originally downloaded. Other constraints prohibit access to local files, invoking other programs and finding out local identities (e.g. usernames, passwords).

ActiveX controls

ActiveX is the name for a set of technologies and services based on Microsoft's Component Object Model (COM). An ActiveX control is a software component that performs a given function or set of functions. Typically, an ActiveX control is used to extend the functionality of a web browser, but controls are also used extensively in Microsoft's own web server systems (e.g. Internet Information Server – IIS).

Within a web page, controls can be used for almost anything a web page developer wants to do, from enhanced GUI, access to local or remote databases, database searches, graphical displays, multimedia file display, video and audio presentation and online games. As with applets, if an ActiveX control is used to access a remote database from within a web page, then the standard 'http/' web server path is bypassed. ActiveX controls have less in-built security mechanisms than applets, and can make use of the same database connection protocols such as direct sockets and ODBC. Any organisation or individual can develop controls, and there are more than a thousand available today. You can go to URL references such as http://www.active-x.com to look at the possibilities for yourself.

Note, of course, that ActiveX controls operate only on a Microsoft-compatible operating environment.

Plug-ins

Plug-ins are software programs that extend the capabilities of a browser in a specific way – giving you, for example, the ability to play audio samples or view video movies from within your browser. They are similar in concept to an ActiveX control, but must be separately installed before they can be used. Plug-ins can operate like any stand-alone applications on the client side.

Cookies

Cookies are not in the same category as applets, ActiveX controls and plug-ins, in that they do not offer mechanisms to connect to remote databases. However, they are an important web application concept as they support session persistence for a local web browser client connecting to a remote web-based application and database. Before we discuss what cookies are, we firstly need to look at why session persistence (overcoming the stateless nature of the http protocol) is necessary.

In a typical web application the client makes a request via the http protocol, which the web server honours by returning a dynamically generated web page. Once the page is returned, the web server and the web application have no further knowledge of the client, but the 'transaction' that the client is trying to do may not be complete. As an example, the end user may be trying to buy one or more items in an eCommerce transaction, filling up a 'shopping cart' before completing the purchase. This involves multiple web browser/web server interactions.

Cookies are small bits of textual information that a web server sends back to the browser for storage locally. On the next interaction (i.e. http request) the web browser returns the cookie information to the server, which can then use the stored information to continue the transaction. The information stored in a cookie by a web application can be anything that the web application needs to identify the end user and/or transaction. For example, a cookie can hold a user identity/password, and the current state of his/her shopping cart.

Cookies have a number of properties, including 'expiry date'. They can exist across multiple visits to a website. They also provide convenience to the user by remembering, for example, the user registration details, so that the user does not need to key in identity and password each time they visit a site. Cookies are not the only approach to session persistence, but they are one of the more widely used approaches. Other approaches include extending the URL data and using 'hidden' form fields.

12.5 Web server layer

The web server layer is responsible for receiving client requests via the http protocol, for initiating appropriate action for each request, and for passing the end results back to the client. In its simplest form, a web server merely retrieves the static HTML file identified by a URL and sends it back to the web browser. No database interaction is required. Web servers became more sophisticated when CGI programs were introduced. In this case, the web server initiates the CGI program named in the URL, passes parameters to the program via the CGI protocol and receives the generated HTML file. The generated file is then transmitted to the web browser client, as shown in figure 12.5.

Figure 12.5: CGI processes

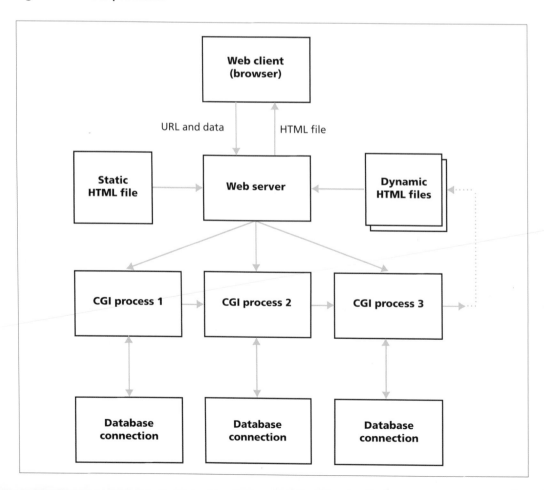

There are problems with the CGI approach. In the first instance, each and every client request results in a new process being spawned. Then, if database interaction is required (and it very often will be), each new process has the overhead of logging onto and off the database management system. Finally, there is no form of transaction management that, if present, would allow more complex transactions perhaps over multiple databases to be handled. As a result, web server vendors have added capabilities to support more efficient passing of parameters between the server and the called processes, using, for example, multiple threads. One multi-thread process is spawned per named URL, and each client request is managed as a thread of this process. Database logon and other process overheads are done once rather than many times. Typical examples of web server extensions are provided by Netscape and Microsoft, through NSAPI, their Netscape Server application program interface (API) and Internet Information Server API (ISAPI) extensions respectively.

More recently, web servers have evolved into more complicated and more fully functioned components called application servers. Application servers offer, in addition to the web server role, transaction and session management, access to multiple data sources and better security. Transaction management provides two-phase commit and rollback across multiple databases, such that either all of an end user's transaction completes, or none of it does, ensuring the integrity of the transaction. Session management can keep the user session open across a number of separate http request/response actions, thereby minimising the user and database logon overhead.

These application servers also support scalable solutions through distributed computing, combining technologies such as CORBA (Common Object Request Broker Architecture), EJB (Enterprise Java Beans) and others. Typical examples are IBM's WebSphere and BEA's WebLogic. A conceptual diagram of such a solution is shown in figure 12.6.

Figure 12.6: Application server processes

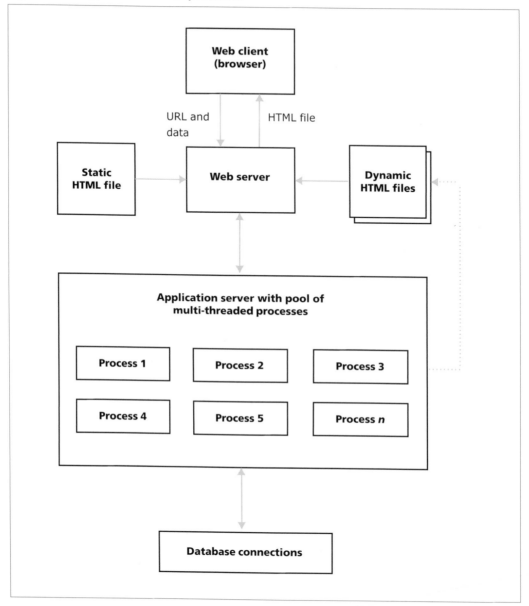

Many web servers support standard URL file access and CGI programming. Increasingly, they should also support Java-based connectivity solutions such as Java Servlets and Java Server Pages. Microsoft's web servers, such as those operating on the Windows XP and Vista environments, also support Microsoft-specific scripting languages, such as VBScript, and Microsoft-specific HTML templates, such as ASP.NET (those with .aspx file extensions). There are some 3rd party web servers that also support .aspx files in a Unix (i.e. non-Microsoft) operating system environment.

12.6 Application logic layer

The application logic layer is the part of a web database application with which a developer will spend the most time. It is responsible for:

- Receiving and validating the input from the user request
- Collecting data for a query (e.g. an SQL statement)
- Preparing and sending the query to the database via the database connection layer
- Retrieving the results from the connection layer
- Formatting the data for display – most commonly in the shape of an HTML file
- Passing the data for display back to the web server layer.

Most of the application's business rules and functionality will reside in this layer, either in the form of server-side scripting logic (e.g. in JavaScript, VBScript, Perl or other scripting language) or Java code (packaged as Java Servlets or within Java Server Page templates). The browser client displays data as well as forms for user input, whereas the application logic component compiles the data to be displayed and processes user input as required. In other words, the application logic generates HTML that the browser renders. Also it receives, processes and stores user input that the browser sends.

As we have seen earlier, when we introduced the application logic layer, there are multiple ways in which it can be coded. Some solutions fall into the Microsoft camp; others tend towards the Sun and Java camp. Some are very proprietary, while others have been dominated by the early emergence of the CGI protocol standard. There is no 'right' way, and the application developer is free to pick and choose the approach that best fits the organisation for which they work. This will, of course, be heavily influenced by existing IT and IS strategy.

Application layer approaches

Some of the more popular approaches are summarised in table 12.2:

Table 12.2: Example approaches to application logic layer

Approach	Type*	URL reference	Scripting language	Database connection	Comment
CGI Script	All HTML is generated	File has .cgi extension or in cgi-bin directory	Primarily Perl but also many others including C, C++, Java and even Cobol	Native database API, CGI's DBI API** (Database Independent API)	
ASP.NET	HTML template	File has .aspx extension	Current C++, C#, VB.NET and others	ADO.NET (Microsoft Active Data Objects) which typically connects to ODBC	• Runs on any browser on any platform • Example given later in chapter (example web database display)
Java Server Pages	HTML template	File has .jsp extension	Java	JDBC (plus other Java approaches) for processing ODBC– (via ODBC-JDBC Bridge)	• JSP files are automatically generated into Java Servlets • Advantage over servlets is that the number of print statements are minimised (i.e. a servlet has to generate all the HTML)
Java Servlet	All HTML is generated	Java program	Java	JDBC (plus other Java approaches) ODBC (via ODBC-JDBC Bridge)	

cont...

Approach	Type*	URL reference	Scripting language	Connection database	Comment
Coldfusion	HTML template	File has .cfm extension	Coldfusion Markup Extension tags	Native database API, ODBC	• Linked to the Coldfusion web server from Allaire Corporation • Example given at the start of this chapter (see figure 12.3)
PHP Hypertext	HTML template	File has .php3 extension	PHP Hypertext Preprocessor scripting language	Native database API, ODBC	• Freely supported, as part of the Apache Software Foundation
Web Server Extension API (e.g. Microsoft's Internet Database Connector approach within Microsoft's ISAPI web server)	HTML template	File has .idc extension	Standard HTML in a file with .htx extension, plus database query specified in .idc file	ODBC plus others	Netscape offers a similar approach with its NSAPI

* Type

    = HTML template if script embedded in an HTML template file referenced by the URL

    = All HTML is generated if all the resulting HTML is generated by the referenced URL file

** Database-independent API

12.7 Introduction to ASP.NET

ASP, the Microsoft technology used for website development, has been around for some time. It is not a language: rather it is a framework that lets you combine one of a number of scripting languages plus other software components.

ASP has now been superseded by ASP.NET which is quite a different technology from the original ASP. ASP.NET is a part of the .NET Framework. The .NET Framework is a development environment which allows developers to create Windows-based applications using different programming languages and extensive libraries of pre-coded solutions. Microsoft maintains that applications created using the .NET framework 'are easier to build, manage, deploy, and integrate with other networked systems'. (**http://msdn.microsoft.com/netframework/**)

An ASP.NET file has extension .aspx. To develop ASP.NET web sites, IIS must be installed in your computer. This is the Microsoft server or engine that drives the ASP.NET (and ASP) websites. An ASP.NET program runs inside IIS.

ASP.NET web pages are developed using HTML and a .NET scripting language such as VB.NET, C# (sharp) or J#. .An ASP.NET file can contain, for example, text, HTML tags, SQL, XML and server scripts written in the languages just mentioned. Scripts in an ASP.NET file are executed on the server, and can contain any valid expressions, operators, statements and procedures. An ASP.NET file can be used to access a database from a web page.

The original ASP technology had limitations. With ASP, the code contains a mixture of HTML and other executable code such as VBscript. It was criticised as being difficult to read and maintain – the executable code and the HTML are mixed together in a 'spaghetti-like' fashion. One major difference between the original ASP and ASP.NET is that with the latter the executable code is kept separate from the HTML.

ASP.NET web pages

ASP.NET is a technology which includes several other technologies. It is NOT a programming language like C# or VB.NET but requires a programming language like C# (C sharp) or VB.NET to write the code. Examples of the technologies that an ASP.NET file might contain are described below:

- **HTML:** hypertext markup language is a simple language used to develop web pages; mark up tags tell the web browser how to display the page

- **Server-side scripting:** programming scripts in an ASP.NET file are executed on the server. To display dynamic content in the ASP.NET website, you must use a scripting language such as VB.NET C#, C++ or Jscript. Server-side scripting is a language which can be used for dynamically editing, changing or adding any content to a web page. VB.NET is a version of MS's programming language Visual Basic – it is the full Visual Basic, unlike VBScript and is the default scripting language for ASP.NET

- **SQL (Structured Query Language):** SQL statements are used to retrieve and update data in a database

- **ADO.NET (ActiveX Data Object):** programming interface to access data in a database

- **XML (Extension Markup Language):** used to describe both the data structure and actual content of information displayed to an end user. We will discuss XML later in this chapter.

ASP.NET server controls

ASP.NET comes with a set of controls that is purported to make web development easier. Server controls tags are understood and processed by the server. They have solved the 'spaghetti-code' problem described above by moving the logic which affects the tags away from the tags themselves, thus allowing us to write cleaner code. You can identify a server control tag by the fact that they contain a runat="server" attribute. There are three kinds of server controls:

- **HTML server controls:** these closely resemble their corresponding HTML tags

- **Web server controls:** such as Label, Textbox, Button, Listbox, Datagrid

- **Validation server controls:** used to validate user inputs from a web page.

How browsers understand ASP.NET

A browser can understand html (also client-side scripts such as Javascript): it does not know ASP.NET. You can, however, use web development technologies such as ASP.NET to develop web sites but what is happening behind the scenes is that ASP.NET is used to dynamically generate the html. The html is then sent from web server to the browser.

As an example we could request a web address such as the following (the Microsoft Search Facility requesting a search on 'olympics london'):

http://search.msdn.microsoft.com/search default.aspx?siteId=0&tab=0&query=olympics%20london

- The browser will make a request for this page to the web server

- The web server examines the request and understands that it is for an ASP.NET page called default.aspx. Next the web server hands over the request to the ASP.NET service running as part of the web server

- The ASP.NET service loads the page default.aspx. This code read the parameter called query which contains the text 'olympics london'. The corresponding content is then retrieved from the database. It then embeds this data into the page and returns the modified page back to the web server

- The web server returns the dynamically generated page to the browser as pure html.

ASP.NET examples

We now will look at ASP.NET components and controls using some examples. All examples assume a basic understanding of HTML. If you wish to try these out for yourself, you can run ASP.NET on your own PC without an external server. To do that, you must install Microsoft's Internet information server (IIS) on your PC. For information about installing the ASP.NET and the IIS server, see the 'W3Schools' website **(www.w3schools.com/default.asp)** where you will find a number of tutorials for web-building. In particular, look at the ASP.NET tutorial – here it is explained early on how to install IIS and run ASP.NET on a number of Windows platforms. Creating these examples involves four fundamental steps:

- Create an ASP.NET file using a text editor or an editor such as Visual Studio.NET which can help you develop web pages.
- Add code to read the Access database and write corresponding HTML
- Copy the ASP.NET file and the database onto the web server
- Run the page from a browser and view the results.

Example 12.1: HTML

The basic difference between an html page and an ASP.NET page is that they have different file extensions. You could simply change the extension of an html file to make it an ASP.NET page. For example, the html code below could either be held with extension .htm or .aspx (the ASP.NET extension) and the displayed results would be identical.

Coding	Display result

`<! -- simple HTML example -- >`
`<html>`
`<body>`
 	
`This is what is displayed in your Browser: Enjoy your day!`
 	
`</body>`
`</html>`
	This is what is displayed in your Browser: Enjoy your day!

By examining the file extension, the web server understands what type of file it is and decides how to process it. If the extension is .htm the browser will request an HTML page from the server and the server will send the page to the browser without making any changes; on the other hand, if the extension is .aspx, the server will process any executable code, before the result is sent back to the browser. In example 12.1 there is no executable code – i.e. it is a static web page.

Example 12.2: With executable code

Coding

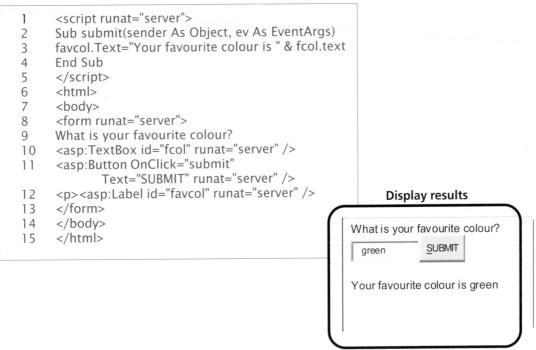

```
1    <script runat="server">
2    Sub submit(sender As Object, ev As EventArgs)
3    favcol.Text="Your favourite colour is " & fcol.text
4    End Sub
5    </script>
6    <html>
7    <body>
8    <form runat="server">
9    What is your favourite colour?
10   <asp:TextBox id="fcol" runat="server" />
11   <asp:Button OnClick="submit"
             Text="SUBMIT" runat="server" />
12   <p><asp:Label id="favcol" runat="server" />
13   </form>
14   </body>
15   </html>
```

Display results

What is your favourite colour?

green   SUBMIT

Your favourite colour is green

On examination of example 12.2 you will notice that there are two parts to the code: the script (or executable code) and the html.

- **Line 1** The runat attribute in line 1 indicates that this script block will contain server-side code.
- **Lines 2 and 11** The OnClick event (line 11) fires when the user clicks the left mouse button on the object (Submit button). ASP.NET will automatically call the subroutine submit (line 1) and execute the code inside it.
- **Line 8** All the web controls must be places within the <Form> </Form> tags.
- **Lines 8, 10, 11 and 12** The example above uses four server controls. By adding the runat="server" attribute to the html element, we indicate that the html element should be treated as a server control and processed on the server. Without this attribute, html elements are treated as text.
- **Lines 10, 11 and 12** Textbox, button and label are examples of web controls provided by ASP.NET to help in the development of complex web pages. Label controls are used to display text in the web page.

Note that if the above example is run from a browser you cannot view the ASP.NET code; if you try to view the source code (VIEW SOURCE) all you will see is plain html. This is because the scripts are executed on the server before the result is sent to the browser.

Example 12.3: Connecting to a database

ADO stands for ActiveX Data Objects and is automatically installed with Microsoft IIS. It is a programming interface for accessing and manipulating data in a database. ADO is imbedded in the ASP.NET pages.

In this example we access the bus depots' database built using Microsoft Access. We want to display the drivers and their depots. The datagrid control is used to display data in tabular form.

ASP.NET DataGrid Web control example

```
1    <%@ Import Namespace="System.Data.OleDb" %>

2    <script runat="server">
3    sub Page_Load
4    dim dbconn,sql,dbcomm,dbread
5    dbconn=New OleDbConnection("Provider=Microsoft.Jet.OLEDB.4.0;data
     source=" & server.mappath("/db/busdepot.mdb"))
6    dbconn.Open()
7    sql="Select * from BusDriver bd, Depot d where bd.dNo=d.dNo"
8    dbcomm=New OleDbCommand(sql,dbconn)
9    dbread=dbcomm.ExecuteReader()
10   driverdepot.DataSource=dbread
11   driverdepot.DataBind()
12   dbread.Close()
13   dbconn.Close()
14   end sub
15   </script>

16   <html>
17   <body>
18   <asp:datagrid id="driverDepot" runat="server"
19   BorderColor="black" BorderWidth="1"
20   CellPadding="3" CellSpacing="0"
21   Font-Name="Verdana" HeaderStyle-BackColor="#c0c0c0" />
22   </body>
23   </html>
```

Result:

bdNo	bdName	bdSalary	pcvDate	bd.dNo	d.dNo	dName	dAddress
001	Jane Brown	1800	09-02-85	101	101	Holloway	Camden Road
007	James Bond	1500	09-01-99	102	102	Hornsey	High Road
008	Maggie May	2200	09-01-00	102	102	Hornsey	High Road
009	Jack Jones	1400	09-08-08	101	101	Holloway	Camden Road
010	Peter Piper	3500	09-06-04	104	104	Islington	Upper Street
011	John Peel	2000	09-02-05	102	102	Hornsey	High Road

- **Line 1**   Here we specify the data provider, i.e a bridge between an application and a data source that can be used to access, retrieve and manipulate data from the databases. We can use the OleDb provider for database sources including MS Access, Oracle, Sybase. (There is a separate provider available for SQL Server)

- **Lines 2 and 18** <script runat="server"> – see example 12.2

- **Line 3** Page_Load is an example of an event. Another is the OnClick event in the previous example.The Page_Load event fires when a page loads (i.e., ASP.NET will automatically call and execute the Page_Load subroutine)

- **Lines 4, 5** Here we have declared a number of strings including the connection string 'dbconn'. The connection string points to an MS Access bus drivers' database.

- **Line 6** We open a connection to the database specified in the connection string
- **Line 7** The SQL statement needed to access our data is assigned to a string variable 'sql'
- **Line 8** We create an OleDbCommand object 'dbcomm'. This command object is used to execute sql statements and uses the connection opened by the OleDbConnection object. When issuing a SELECT statement, a set of records is returned from the database and made available to the script
- **Line 9** We now need to iterate through the set of returned records and process them. A data reader (OleDbDataReader) object is created called 'dbread'. This represents a stream of database records returned from the SELECT statement issued through the OleDbCommand object. A data reader is created by using the ExecuteReader() method of the OleDbCommand object
- **Lines 10 ,11** The next step is to assign the DataReader object (dbread) to the DataSource property of the DataGrid and then call the DataBind method.
- **Lines 12, 13** Close both the data reader and database connection
- **Line 18** Under ASP.NET a typical method of working with a data reader is to bind it to one of the listing controls: asp:Repeater, asp:DataList, or asp:DataGrid. In the example script above we bind the data reader to a DataGrid control which has the id value of 'driverDepot'.The DataGrid control displays tabular data and optionally supports selecting, sorting, paging, and editing the data.

12.8 Database connection layer

This is the component that actually links a database to the web. The connection layer within a web database application must accomplish a number of goals. It has to provide access to the underlying database, and it also needs to be easy to use, efficient, flexible, robust, reliable and secure. The database connection layer for a web database application is not different in principle to database connectivity for traditional client/server systems. In fact, the same approaches can be adopted, ranging from embedded database commands, through native database APIs to more open database APIs such as ODBC and JDBC.

Embedded database commands

The traditional way of providing database connectivity was to embed database commands within the programming language in which the application was constructed. The command set would be both database vendor specific, and programming language specific. Typically, a pre-compiler would be run before the compilation process, to translate the database commands into language-specific database function calls. Access to relational databases also started this way, though the ISO standards body introduced some standards. For example, the keywords 'EXEC SQL' normally started each database command. Again, each database/ programming language combination required the corresponding pre-compiler. A simple C program to access all the rows of a BusDriver table might look like the code in example 12.4:

Example 12.4: Embedded SQL

```
/* Program to access BusDriver table */
#include <stdio.h>
#include <stdlib.h>
EXEC SQL INCLUDE sqlca;
Main()
{
/* Connect to database */
EXEC SQL CONNECT 'application_database';
/* Query database */
EXEC SQL SELECT * from BusDriver;
Process query results ...
/* Disconnect from database */
EXEC SQL DISCONNECT;
```

As we have already discussed, the code in example 12.4 does not result in portable applications.

Native database APIs

Some database vendors improved upon the embedded database command approach by providing application program interfaces (APIs) to interact with their systems. Essentially, the APIs consist of a collection of functions, or object classes, that provide source code access to the databases. These functions enable the application developer to:

- Connect to the DBMS
- Create an SQL statement and send it to the DBMS
- Check for success
- For a query, retrieve each resultant row with call
- Disconnect from the DBMS.

Again, the APIs tended to be database specific, thus the name 'native database APIs', and therefore the result is code that is not immediately portable between operating platform and/ or database vendor.

Open database API: ODBC

The ODBC standard (open database connectivity), pioneered by Microsoft, is an open database API that has been very successful in overcoming the problems of native database APIs. ODBC is not tied to any specific vendor, and drivers are available for over fifty DBMSs. ODBC provides:

- A library of function calls to connect to, access, update and disconnect from a database
- A representation of data type
- A standard set of error codes
- A standards-based SQL syntax.

ODBC has been ported to most popular computer platforms, including Windows, UNIX and Macintosh, and is so ubiquitous that you may be using it without knowing it. For example, database access within ASP.NET is commonly conducted using active data objects (ADO), but ADO.NET is merely an abstraction above ODBC.

Similarly, open database connectivity from Java programs (using JDBC as discussed in the next section) often uses ODBC to connect to specific database types. To illustrate how ODBC works, we will use pseudocode rather than a real programming language (such as VBScript or server-side JavaScript), as in example 12.5:

Example 12.5: ODBC

```
1.     /* Specify use of ODBC API */
2.     use ODBC;
3.     /* Connect to database */
4.     Connection ("mydatabase");
5.     /* Issue selection statement */
6.     SqlStatement("SELECT * FROM BusDriver);
7.     /* Process resultant records */
8.     .....
9.     /* Close database connection and finish
10.    EndConnection("mydatabase");
11.    End;
```

Notes:

- **Line 2** We indicate that the ODBC API is to be used
- **Line 4** We connect to a specific database 'mydatabase', referring to the database as a string. If we wished to, we could dynamically connect to one of a number of databases governed by an input parameter, or to more than one database. Each database that we refer to in this way will have been registered to the operating environment that we are running in, as a data source with a given data name source (DNS). That is, 'mydatabase' will have been registered as a known DNS. In fact, the data source does not have to be a relational database, but we will be using SQL to access and update it
- **Line 5**, and those following, should be self-explanatory.

When the above program is executed, the ODBC driver manager process linked to the program automatically loads the appropriate ODBC driver, which then becomes a client of the database engine. This is shown in figure 12.7, in which two databases are being accessed (Oracle and Microsoft Access) through their respective ODBC drivers.

Figure 12.7: ODBC architecture

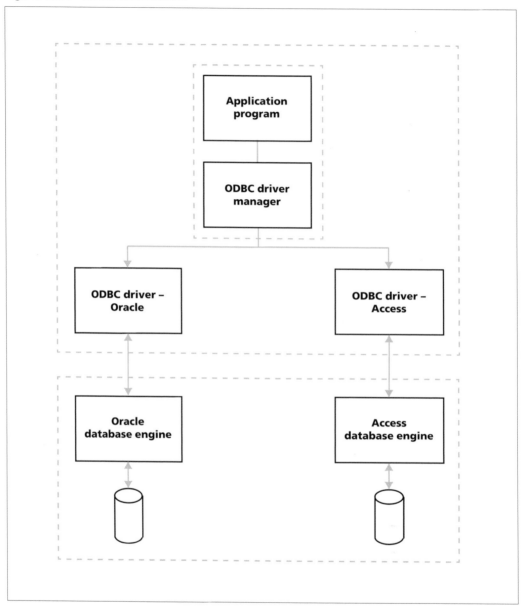

ODBC drivers are available from many sources and for many operating platforms. Typically, a database vendor (such as Oracle) will provide the drivers. The drivers are responsible for providing a level of indirection for the application program's interface to the database. Therefore a driver's role includes translation of database requests (in SQL) into the command set of the specific database (which may not have an SQL interface), and translation of result sets and error conditions into the standard form.

One proviso, the drivers must be available on the machine that the application program is running on. The database engine that the driver connects to can be on the same machine, or on a separate database server machine. The beauty of the above arrangement is that the application is fully portable across any machine environment that supports ODBC. Also, one application can connect to multiple databases simultaneously if necessary, and the application program can dynamically establish the database to connect to at run time.

Open database API: JDBC

The JDBC database connection (JDBC unofficially stands for Java database connectivity) operates in a very similar way to the ODBC connection, but for Java programs. In a JDBC connection, the level of indirection is firstly provided by the set of classes and interfaces that is included within the java.sql package. A Java program uses these classes and interfaces to establish database-independent connections and access. In turn, a specific JDBC package is dynamically loaded to interact with a specific database. This is shown in figure 12.8.

Figure 12.8: JDBC architecture

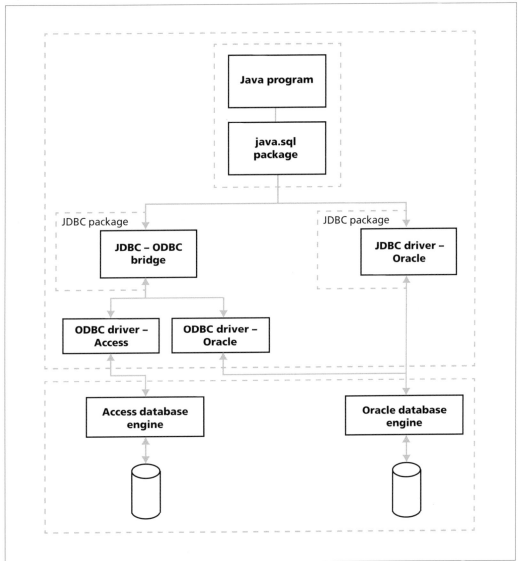

The diagram in figure 12.8 shows, on the left-hand side, a JDBC package that uses a JDBC-ODBC bridge for the connection. The bridge then uses appropriate ODBC drivers to connect to Access and Oracle databases respectively. On the right-hand side of the diagram, the JDBC package supports a direct connection to an Oracle database. Again, the database vendors, or third parties, supply the JDBC packages (the JDBC drivers). The JDBC-ODBC bridge approach makes use of the many existing drivers available with ODBC, and ensures wide Java connectivity to many types of databases.

12.9 Introduction to XML

Data on the web does not often conform to the classic database structures such as relational or object-oriented. Such data is sometimes termed semistructured, i.e. the data has some structure but does not fit into a fixed schema. With the advent of the web, a new technology was required for data communication and exchange of web data. XML (extensible markup language) is a web-based standard for describing many different kinds of data: it is a data description language used for storing and sharing data.

XML is used extensively as a format for web document storage and processing. It can be used to encode data, for saving it onto storage media and for transmitting it across a network. For such documents, XML describes how they are organised, not how they are presented. In contrast HTML is the primary language used to develop web pages – it tells the web browser how to display the page. When data is stored in XML format, at some point the XML will be transformed into another format – for example, HTML, Word or PDF, depending on its use. So data in a relational database might be imported to an XML file, transmitted and stored as XML on a web server and displayed by a brower in table format (i.e. HTML format).

XML was adopted by the standards body, W3C (World Wide Web Consortium) in 1998 and is a simplified version of a general data description language known as SGML (Standard Generalised Markup Language). Since its introduction it has steadily been gaining in importance; by the late 1990s, many software vendors began to integrate XML into their products.

Example 12.6: XML (1)

An XML file (stored with extension .xml) describes the structure of data (in the form of tags with angled brackets, similar to HTML tags). In addition the file contains the data, as in a database. Unlike HTML which has a fixed collection of tags, XML is more flexible and allows user-defined tags.

Consider the sample XML document for data related to the bus depot company that we examined earlier:

```
<?xml version="1.0" ?>
<MDXBuses>
  <Depot dNo="101">
    <dName>Holloway</dName>
    <dAddress>Camden Road</dAddress>
  </Depot>
  <Depot dNo="102">
    <dName>Hornsey</dName>
    <dAddress>High Road</dAddress>
  </Depot>
</MDXBuses>
```

The code above shows how XML can be used to define data in the MDX Bus Company, for the Holloway and Hornsey depots. All their data records (for bus drivers, cleaners, routes and so on) can be defined in this way and this can be stored on web servers and shared by different depots and departments in the company and outside agencies.

Note one major difference between data in XML form and a relational (or object-oriented) schema is that in the former case the structure and data are mixed together, whereas with the latter these are kept separate. XML is more understandable to users: the term 'self-describing' is used in this context.

Elements

The second line of code in the example above defines the root element of the document – the root element in the example is MDXBuses. An element is a nested piece of text of the form <startTag>.....<endTag>. Note that unlike HTML, XML tags are case sensitive.

Content

The text between the opening and closing tags is called the content. So for example in the XML above an example of content is 'Camden Road', between the <dAddress> and </dAddress> tags.

Attributes

An opening tag can have attributes. Attributes are alternatives to creating elements within other elements. For example, in the XML above, the depot numbers (dNo) is coded as an attribute:

```
< Depot  dNo="101">
```

Here 'dNo' is an attribute which belongs to the element depot and has a value of '101'. Alternatively attributes can usually always be represented by elements instead of attribute:

```
<Depot>
<dNo>101</dNo>
.......
</Depot>
```

Well-formed documents

There are two levels of correctness of an XML document: well formed and valid. Valid XML is discussed in the next section. If an XML parser successfully processes an XML document, the document is said to be well-formed. A well-formed document conforms to all of XML's syntax rules. For example, if a start-tag appears without its corresponding end-tag, it is not well formed. Parsers are discussed later in this chapter.

Document Type Definitions

Document Type Definitions (DTDs) are part of the XML standard. An XML document can have an optional DTD which determines the document structure. It can be specified as part of the document itself or as a separate file with extension .dtd. The latter is probably the most common method. In this case we need to specify the DTD file inside the XML document. For example:

```
<!DOCTYPE  MDXBuses SYSTEM "MDXBuses.dtd">
```

An XML document that conforms to its DTD is said to be valid, i.e. it conforms to some semantic rules. The DTD is just one method of defining these rules.

Below we show a DTD which is consistent with the XML document above:

```
<!ELEMENT MDXBuses (Depot*)>
<!ELEMENT Depot(dName, dAddress)>
<!ELEMENT dName (#PCDATA)>
<!ELEMENT dAddress (#PCDATA)>
<!ATTLIST Depot dNo CDATA #REQUIRED >
```

An ELEMENT statement is used to specify the rules for the elements in the XML document. For example <!ELEMENT MDXBuses (Depot*)> states that the element MDXBuses contains zero or more occurrences of element Depot. Where the asterisk is not present, this means that the occurrence is once only. #PCDATA is used for the base elements and indicates that these are character strings. The way the rules have been set up above means that a depot must have one name and one address. If we are to allow the situation where data is missing – for example, if an address were not known – then we could include a '?' with the field to indicate optionality:

<!ELEMENT Depot(dName, dAddress?)>

We can also specify which elements may have attributes. In the XML code in example 12.6, dNo is an attribute and is included in the Document Type Definitions as such:

<!ATTLIST Depot dNo CDATA #REQUIRED >

Attributes can be specified as optional or mandatory – in this case #REQUIRED means that dNo is mandatory (i.e. a value must always be provided). Other possibilities are #IMPLIED (optional) and #FIXED (a default value is used).

XML parsers

To process an XML document, a program called an XML parser is required. The parser is built into a browser. Parsers check the XML syntax. An example parser is Internet Explorer's inbuilt parser, which reads XML into memory and converts it into an XML DOM object. DOM (Document Object Model) defines a standard way for accessing and manipulating web documents. When XML documents are parsed by a DOM-based parser, their data is placed in a tree-like structure. Diagrammatically, this process can be represented as:

Figure 12.9: Parsing an XML document by a DOM-based parser

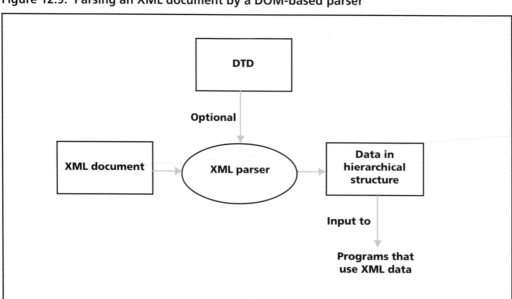

Example 12.7: XML (2)

The XML document above can be extended to cover all elements relevant to the Bus Depot
Company. Below we have introduced the bus drivers (only one driver in this example):

```xml
<?xml version="1.0" ?>
<!DOCTYPE  MDXBuses SYSTEM "MDXBuses.dtd">
<MDXBuses>
    Depots>
        <Depot  dNo="101">
            <dName>Holloway</dName>
            <dAddress>Camden Road</dAddress>
        </Depot>
        <Depot  dNo="102">
            <dName>Hornsey</dName>
            <dAddress>High Road</dAddress>
        </Depot>
    </Depots>
    <BusDrivers>
        <BusDriver bdNo ="001">
            <bdName>Jane Brown</bdName>
            <bdSalary>1800</bdSalary>
            <pcvDate>09-feb-1985</pcvDate>
            <dNo>101</dNo>
        </BusDriver>
    </BusDrivers>
</MDXBuses>
```

Example 12.8: XML (3)

As we saw earlier in this chapter the purpose of HTML is to control the display of static data in
a web page. XML looks somewhat like HTML but does not control the display. The XML files
can be stored separately from the HTML files and XML file can be imported into an HTML
document, so that HTML can be used for information display in combination with XML. XML
can also be embedded in an HTML file as in the example below, where we display the depots'
names and addresses within a table:

```html
<html>
<body>

<xml id="xmldoc">
    <MDXBuses>
        <Depot dNo="101">
            <dName>Holloway</dName>
            <dAddress>Camden Road</dAddress>
        </Depot>
        <Depot dNo="102">
            <dName>Hornsey</dName>
            <dAddress>High Road</dAddress>
        </Depot>
    </MDXBuses>
</xml>
```

...cont/

```
<table border =1 datasrc="#xmldoc">
    <thead>
    <tr>
        <th>Depot name </th><th>Address</th>
    </tr>
    </thead>
    <tr>
        <td><span datafld="dName"></span></td>
        <td><span datafld="dAddress"></span></td>
    </tr>
</table>
</body>
</html>
```

This results in the following output when the html file above is opened from a browser;

Depot name	Address
Holloway	Camden Road
Hornsey	High Road

XML-related technologies and query languages

Besides DTDs discussed above, there are a number of other technologies relating to XML which are used in the development of XML applications. Some of these are listed below:

- XSL and XSLT - eXtensible Stylesheet Language (Transformation). XSL defines how XML document data is displayed on the screen (similar to CSS for HTML but more powerful). A subset of XML, XSLT is concerned with the transformation from one XML document to another (text-based) document, such as HTML

- XSD (XML Schema Definition) is used to verify that the XML is valid. This is a more powerful alternative to DTDs

- XML query languages including XPath, XQuery, SQL/XML (extension of SQL).

Advantages of XML

These include:

- XML is fairly simple but at the same time has a rich syntax
- It is flexible language and extensible: new tags can be defined by users to meet particular requirements. XML tags can be reused by many applications
- Its hierarchical structure makes it suitable for most (but not all) types of documents
- The strict syntax makes the necessary parsing algorithms simple, efficient, and consistent
- A large set of software tools can be used alongside XML
- XML can be used to create new markup languages. Many hundreds have been created including CML (Chemical Markup Language for managing chemical information), MathML (developed by W3C for describing mathematical notations) and WML (Wireless Markup Language used in specifying user interface and content for narrowband devices, including mobile phones and pagers)
- As well as textual data, XML can be applied to images, sound and video data
- It is platform-independent.

12.10 Summary

This chapter introduced concepts relating to connecting a database to the World Wide Web. The 3-tier architecture and layers within the 3 tiers, which form the building blocks for connecting a database to the web, were described. A variety of methods for extending client-side functionality, for creating the application logic layer and for connecting to the database were described, as was XML, the web-based standard for data communication and exchange.

12.11 Review questions

Review question 12.1 What is meant by web database connectivity?

Review question 12.2 What is a dynamic web page?

Review question 12.3 What are the three general approaches to server-side processing?

Review question 12.4 How can a 3-tier client/server architecture be used to implement a web database application?

Review question 12.5 The 3-tier architecture consists of five layers. What are they? Briefly discuss the function of each.

Review question 12.6 Name four ways that a browser can be extended to implement client-side processing.

Review question 12.7 Explain the role of an application server and list the main activities conducted within the application logic layer.

Review question 12.8 There are many ways in which the application logic layer can be coded, and this will depend on what best fits the target organisation. Give five examples of scripting languages that can be used.

Review question 12.9 What is the fundamental difference between an ASP.NET and an HTML file?

Review question 12.10 An ASP.NET file consists of a number of components. Identify some of them and explain what they are used for.

Review question 12.11 Identify ways in which Coldfusion, ASP.NET and JSP can connect to databases.

THE BUS DEPOTS' DATABASE

Middlesex Transport is responsible for running a fleet of buses throughout North London. The buses are housed in one of three depots: Holloway, Hornsey and Islington. Each depot is identified by its depot number; in addition, the depot name and address are recorded.

Each bus is identified by its registration number. Details of the buses' models are also held, for example Routemaster and Spirit of London. The buses run on various routes which are described by their starting and finishing point, for example Camden Town/Hendon. Each route is identified by its route number. Only buses from particular depots will travel on a particular route, so, for example, only buses from the Islington depot will travel on the Camden Town/Hendon route. Buses are classified by various types such as doubledecker, bendy-bus etc. There are restrictions on some bus types for some of the routes, for example those with low bridges may exclude doubledecker buses, and bendy-buses may be unable to operate around some corners. For this reason, buses are designated to particular routes.

The bus company employs bus drivers to operate the buses and cleaners who help maintain them. Both the bus drivers and cleaners work at one particular depot. Drivers and cleaners have an employee number, name, and salary. In addition, the company holds information on the date that the driver passed his/her PCV (Passenger Carrying Vehicle) driving test.

For cleaning purposes, the depots are organised with cleaners being responsible for a number of buses; each bus has one cleaner who is particularly responsible for that bus. In the case of bus drivers, they can only drive buses where they have completed training for that type of bus, and the date when training is completed is recorded. In addition, bus drivers can only drive buses where they have had practice on a route.

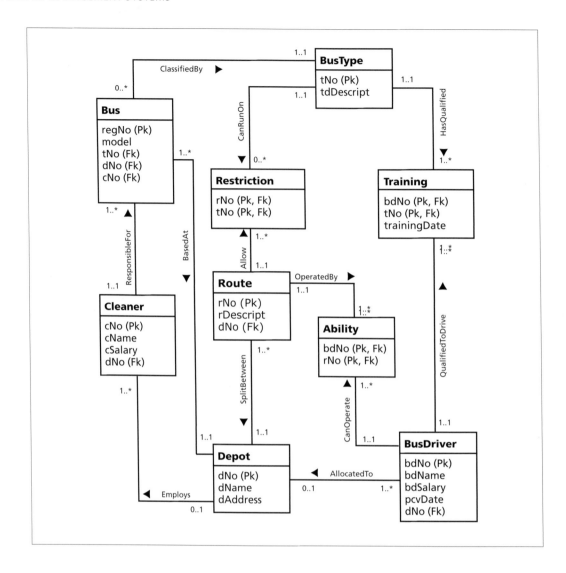

The Depot table

describe depot;

Name	Null?	Type
DNO	NOT NULL	VARCHAR2(5)
DNAME		VARCHAR2(20)
DADDRESS		VARCHAR2(20)

select * from Depot;

DNO	DNAME	DADDRESS
101	Holloway	Camden Road
102	Hornsey	High Road
104	Islington	Upper Street

The BusType table

describe bustype;

Name	Null?	Type
TNO	NOT NULL	VARCHAR2(5)
TDESCRIPT		VARCHAR2(20)

select * from bustype;

TNO	TDESCRIPT
1	double-decker
2	metrobus
3	midibus
4	bendy bus
5	open top

The BusDriver table

describe busdriver;

Name	Null?	Type
BDNO	NOT NULL	VARCHAR2(5)
BDNAME		VARCHAR2(20)
BDSALARY		NUMBER(6,2)
PCVDATE		DATE
DNO		VARCHAR2(5)

select * from busdriver;

BDNO	BDNAME	BDSALARY	PCVDATE	DNO
001	Jane Brown	1800	09-FEB-85	101
006	Sally Smith	1750	09-MAR-96	
007	James Bond	1500	09-JAN-99	102
008	Maggie May	2200	09-JAN-00	102
009	Jack Jones	1400	09-AUG-01	101
010	Peter Piper	3500	09-JUN-04	104
011	John Peel	2000	09-FEB-05	102

The Cleaner table

describe cleaner;

Name	Null?	Type
CNO	NOT NULL	VARCHAR2(5)
CNAME		VARCHAR2(20)
CSALARY		NUMBER(6,2)
DNO		VARCHAR2(5)

select * from cleaner;

CNO	CNAME	CSALARY	DNO
110	John	2550	101
111	Jean	2500	101
112	Betty	2400	102
113	Vince	2800	102
114	Jay	3000	102
115	Doug	2000	102
116	Geeta	4000	

The Route table

describe route;

Name	Null?	Type
RNO	NOT NULL	VARCHAR2(5)
RDESCRIPT		VARCHAR2(30)
DNO		VARCHAR2(5)

select * from route;

RNO	RDESCRIPT	DNO
10	Tottenham/Angel	102
11	Islington/Highgate	102
6	Camden/Golders Green	101
7	Finchley/Tottenham	101
8	Hendon/Muswell Hill	101

The Bus table

describe bus;

Name	Null?	Type
REGNO	NOT NULL	VARCHAR2(10)
MODEL		VARCHAR2(20)
TNO		VARCHAR2(5)
DNO		VARCHAR2(5)
CNO		VARCHAR2(5)

select * from bus;

REGNO	MODEL	TNO	DNO	CNO
A123ABC	Routemaster	1	101	110
D678FGH	Volvo 8700	2	101	110
D345GGG	Volvo 8500	1	101	112
H259IJK	Daf SB220	3	102	114
P200IJK	Mercedes 709D	2	102	113
P300RTY	Mercedes Citaro	4	102	113
R678FDS	Daf SB220	1		110

The Ability table

describe ability;

Name	Null?	Type
BDNO	NOT NULL	VARCHAR2(5)
RNO	NOT NULL	VARCHAR2(5)

select * from ability;

BDNO	RNO
001	6
001	7
001	8
007	10
007	6
008	10
008	11
009	7

The Training table

describe training;

Name	Null?	Type
BDNO	NOT NULL	VARCHAR2(5)
TNO	NOT NULL	VARCHAR2(5)
TRAININGDATE		DATE

select * from training;

BDNO	TNO	TRAININGDATE
001	1	09-JAN-06
001	2	09-JAN-06
006	2	09-FEB-06
007	1	09-FEB-06
007	2	09-FEB-06
007	3	09-MAR-06
008	2	09-MAR-06
008	3	09-MAR-06
008	4	09-APR-06
009	3	09-APR-06
009	4	09-MAY-06
011	1	09-MAY-06
011	2	09-MAY-06
011	3	09-JUN-06
011	4	09-JUN-06
011	5	09-JUN-06

The Restriction table

describe restriction;

Name	Null?	Type
RNO	NOT NULL	VARCHAR2(5)
TNO	NOT NULL	VARCHAR2(5)

select * from restriction;

RNO	TNO
10	1
10	2
10	3
10	4
11	1
11	2
11	3
11	4
6	1
6	2
6	3
6	4
7	1
7	2
8	3
8	4

Answers to review questions

1   Answers to review questions

Answer to review question 1.1

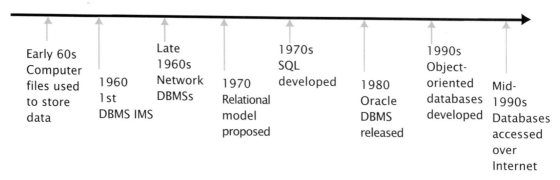

Answer to review question 1.2

Advantage of shared files: inconsistencies should not develop as only one copy of a file to update.

Disadvantages: not efficient, as a shared file would only be available to one application at a time, i.e. simultaneous access of the data by different users is not possible; not effective in providing data for planning and control of an organisation.

Answer to review question 1.3

With shared files, only one copy of each file is made available.

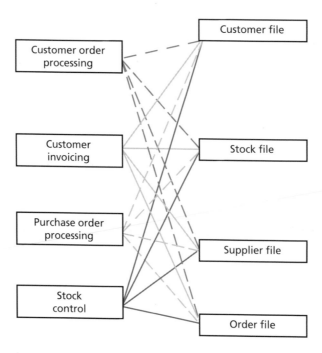

Answer to review question 1.4

The following are examples of the kind of data that might be held:

- **A library**
  Borrower (borrowerId, name, address); BookTitle (isbn, title, publisher, value); BookCopy (copyId, dateAcquired); Loan (borrowerId, isbn, copyId, dateOut, dateDue, dateBack); Author (authorId, authorName)

- **A hospital**
  HospitalWorker (staffId, name, address, position); Patient(patientId, type, generalPractitioner, medicalHistory, admissionDate, ward, nextOfKin), Ward (name, numberOfbeds, sisterInCharge); Operation (patientId, staffOperating, date, details)

- **A university**
  UniversityWorker(staff id, name, address, position, room, extension); Student (studentId, name, address, dateOfBirth, termAddress, LocalAuthority, countryOfDomicile), Course (courseId, name, coreModules); Module (id, name, prerequisites)

- **A manufacturing company**
  Staff (staff id, name address, position), Customer (id, name, address, contact person) Supplier (id, name, address, contact person), CustomerOrder (id, date, customer, orderDetail), Stock (item, quantity, reOrderLevel)

Answer to review question 1.5

Data can be defined as numerical, character or other facts which can be recorded in a form suitable for processing by a computer.

A **database** has the following characteristics:

- a collection of persistent, related data stored on computer storage medium and arranged for speedy search and retrieval
- it is managed by a piece of software called a database management system (DBMS)
- it is integrated data for access by many applications
- generally there is only one copy of each item of data although there may be controlled repetition of some of the data
- the data is independent of the programs which use the data.

A **database system** is made up of a number of related components including:

- the data
- the people involved in designing, creating, maintaining and using the data
- the computer hardware
- the DBMS
- the applications programs written by programmers to create, update and query the database.

Answer to review question 1.6

Compare the search engine definitions with those in this chapter.

Answer to review question 1.8

Databases offer **logical database independence**, in that users are shielded from changes to the conceptual schema (the global view of the data). It is therefore possible to alter the conceptual schema without affecting user views. So, for example, existing user views and applications should not be affected if a new table is added to the database.

Physical data independence: the conceptual schema also shields users from changes to the physical schema. The specification of the physical structure (including how the data is stored on disk and the access methods) is stored separately and is independent of the application programs that use the data. So if a database is moved to a different storage device or indexes are created for tables in a database, the change should not affect the user views or the conceptual schema.

2   Answers to review questions

Answer to review question 2.1

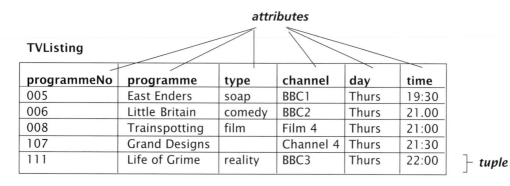

* Example of **domains**

  'programme': all valid characters

  'day': Mon - Sun

  'time': valid times

* The **degree** of a relation is the number of **attributes** it contains (6)

* The **cardinality** of a relation is the number of **tuples** it contains (5)

Answer to review question 2.2

Relations are linked together in the relational model using foreign keys. For example, if we wish to link instances of employees stored in an employee relation, with the records of their departments, stored in a department relation, we would place the primary key of each department (for example, department number) into the record of the employee working in that department (where it will become the foreign key). In that way we can then identify in which department each employee is located.

Empolyee

empNo	name	deptNo	office
005	Jane Smith	101	A12
109	Pierre Cellard	103	B33
111	Fred Jones	101	D155

Department

deptNo	departName
101	Finance
103	Personnel

Answer to review question 2.3

Primary keys:

- Book Title: isbn (note that the attribute 'title' is not a good choice for the primary key in the Book Title relation as, in reality, different books can have the same title)

- Book Copy: isbn, bookCopyId

Answer to review question 2.4

StudentLoan

studentNo	isbn	bookCopyId	loanDate	dueDate	dateBack
25005	0-88-123456	1	12-12-06	01-03-07	02-03-07
25005	0-88-123456	2	01-03-07	21-03-07	18-03-07
26008	0-33-543216	1	01-03-07	01-03-07	
26107	0-88-123456	3	01-03-07	01-03-07	

- Relation names are unique: name StudentLoan should be the only table with this name

- Attribute names are unique within each relation: studentNo, isbn, bookCopyId, loanDate, dueDate, dateBack

- A cell of a relation contains atomic values: all cells contain single values

- Attribute values in a column are all from the same domain: column 1 contains student numbers only, column 3 are dates only, etc

- Each tuple is unique: there are no duplicate rows. As a student can borrow a number of books and as books can be borrowed more than once, the identifiers for these are repeated in the relation, but no two rows contain the same date

- The order of attributes is not significant

- The order of tuples is not significant.

Primary key: studentNo, isbn, bookCopyId, loanDate

You might have identified the primary key as the composite studentNo, isbn and bookCopyId. However, if a student borrows the same book more than once then that combination will no longer be unique. So the primary key should include the loanDate (or dueDate) as well. (Possibly the time should be included if it is likely that a borrower borrows the same book more than once within one day.)

Answer to review question 2.5

- **Entity integrity violation:** filmNo cannot be null (Trainspotting)
- **Referential integrity violation:** director number (directorNo) 101 in the Film relation does not exist in Director relation

Note that, in Film relation, it is possible for the foreign key (directorNo) to be null (Pulp Fiction) and, in the Director relation for the 4th row (Mamet) to exist in the relation without a film directed by this director.

Answer to review question 2.6

a) List each book title and value

R1= Project over BookTitle [title, value]
Resulting relation R1:

title	value
Great Expectations	15.00
Little Dorrit	9.99
Martin Chuzzlewit	12.50
Dombey and Son	7.99
Oliver Twist	15.00

b) List all book title details for books valued over £10

R1= Restrict from BookTitle where value>10
Resulting relation R1:

isbn	title	publishNo	value
0-88-123456	Great Expectations	1001	15.00
0-10-876543	Martin Chuzzlewit	4302	12.50
0-66-974145	Oliver Twist	1001	15.00

c) List isbns, book titles, copy ids and dates acquired for books in the library

R1= BookTitle Join BookCopy where BookTitle isbn = BookCopy isbn
R2= Project over R1 [isbn, title, copyId, dateAcquired]
Resulting relation R2:

isbn	title	copyId	dateAcquired
0-88-123456	Great Expectations	1	12-12-06
0-88-123456	Great Expectations	2	12-12-06
0-88-123456	Great Expectations	3	05-05-07
0-33-543216	Little Dorrit	1	12-01-06
0-10-876543	Martin Chuzzlewit	1	01-07-06
0-07-123678	Dombey and Son	1	06-06-06
0-07-123678	Dombey and Son	2	06-06-06

d) List book titles, copyId, dateAcquired, borrower name and the dates the books were borrowed and returned (dateOut, dateBack) for each loan made by borrower 1001

R1 = Book-Title Join Book-Copy where Book-Title isbn = Book-Copy isbn
R2 = Loan Join R1 where R1 isbn = Loan isbn and R1 copyId = Loan copyId
R3 = Borrower Join R2 where R2 borrowerNo = Borrower borrowerNo
R4 = Restrict from R3 where borrowerNo = '1001'
R5= Project over R4 [title, copyId, dateAcquired, name, dateOut, dateBack]

Resulting relation R5:

title	copyId	dateAcquired	name	dateOut	dateBack
Great Expectations	1	12-12-06	Jo	03-06-07	03-07-07
Martin Chuzzlewit	1	01-07-06	Jo	03-06-07	03-07-07
Dombey and Son	2	06-06-06	Jo	03-06-07	03-07-07

Answer to review question 2.7

a) List title, author and year of all books which are either written by Dickens or published after 1850 or both

S1=Union BooksByDickens with BooksPublishedAfter1850
S2= Project over S1 [title, author, yearOfPublication]

Resulting relation S2:

title	author	yearOfPublication
Great Expectations	Charles Dickens	1861
Little Dorrit	Charles Dickens	1857
Dombey and Son	Charles Dickens	1848
Martin Chuzzlewit	Charles Dickens	1844
Oliver Twist	Charles Dickens	1839
The Europeans	Henry James	1877
The Moonstone	Wilkie Collins	1868
Armadale	Wilkie Collins	1866

b) List details of all books written by Dickens and (at the same time) published after 1850 for books values at greater than £12

> **S1= Intersection BooksbyDickens and BooksPublishedAfter1850**
> **S2= Restrict from S1 where value>12**
> Resulting relation S2:

isbn	title	author	publish erNo	yearOf Publication	value
0-88-123456	Great Expectations	Charles Dickens	1001	1861	15.00

c) List the isbn, title and year of publication of all books published after 1850 but not written by Dickens

> **S1= Difference BooksPublishedAfter1850 and BooksByDickens**
> **S2= Project over S1 [isbn, title, yearOfPublication]**

isbn	title	yearOfPublication
0-22-876543	The Europeans	1877
0-32-765435	The Moonstone	1868
0-33-768646	Armadale	1866

3   Answers to review questions

Answer to review question 3.1

Examples of entities for a Library Application.

- **Entity** can be defined as a group of logically associated data items identified by a unique key (Examples: Book, Borrower, Loan)

- **Attribute** can be defined as a property or characteristic of an entity about which there is a need to record data; attributes for Book are isbn (international standard book number), title, publisher, datePublished

- A **relationship** is an association between entities that is operationally significant to the organisation. Relationship between Book, Borrower and Loan could be:

  - Borrower makes a Loan

  - Loan made for a Book

- A **candidate key** is a unique and irreducible identifier for the entity – there may be more than one candidate key. In the Library application, candidate keys for Borrower could be borrowerNo or the composite key (name, address)

- A **primary key** (Pk) is an attribute (or combination of attributes) with the property that, at any given time, no two entity occurrences contain the same values for that attribute (or combination of attributes). One candidate key is chosen as the primary key. In the Library application, the primary key for Borrower could be borrowerNo.

- A **foreign key** (Fk) is used in the Relational model – it is an attribute in a relation which is also the primary key in another relation (for example a borrowerNo may be a primary key in a Borrower relation and a foreign key in a Loan relation)

- A **composite key** is a key that consists of more than one attribute. For example, in the Loan entity the primary key could be the composite of borrowerNo, isbn, copyNo, dateOfLoan. Note that the attribute copyNo (e.g. serial number 1, 2 ,3, etc) is needed as there may well be more than one copy of a book title held in the libarary. Also the date is included because a borrower could borrow the same copy of a book more than once. The time of loan would also have to be included in the primary key if we assume that the borrower might borrow the same copy of a book more than once on the same day.

Answer to review question 3.2

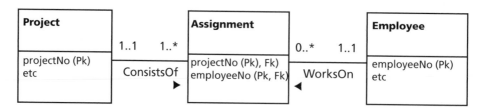

- One project consists of 1 or more assignments

- One assignment relates to one project

- One employee works on zero or more assignments

- One assignment is worked on by one employee.

Answer to review question 3.3

The relation diagram:

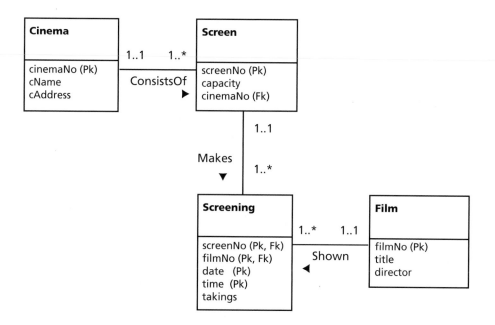

Answer to question 3.4

The relation diagram for the Bus Depots' database:

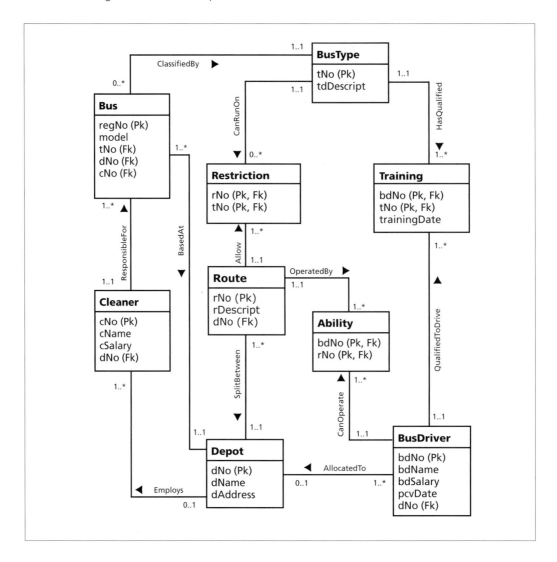

Answer to review question 3.5

The relation diagram:

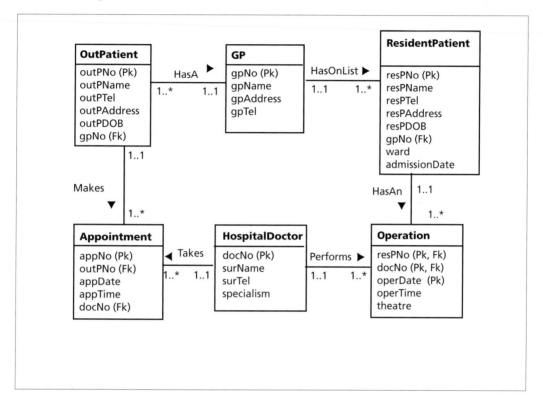

Answer to review question 3.6

An access path is the path of the logical connections that has to be followed in order to retrieve the required information. The access path for the query is: OutPatient - GP - ResidentPatient - Operation - hospitalDoctor.

4 Answers to review questions

Answer to review question 4.1

Normalisation is a formal bottom-up technique for producing a set of relations for an enterprise, given its data requirements. The technique involves a series of steps each of which corresponds to a specific normal form with known properties. The steps involve primary keys and the identification of functional dependencies. As normalisation proceeds, the relations become less vulnerable to insertion, deletion and update anomalies.

Answer to review question 4.2

- **Redundancy:** for example the customer name, telephone number, etc are repeated for each customer number in the relation

- **Update anomalies:** as a consequence of the redundancy, we could update the customer name in one tuple, while leaving it fixed in another

- **Deletion anomalies:** if we delete a booking for a particular customer, we might lose all the information about that customer

- **Insertion anomalies:** the inverse to deletion anomalies: we cannot record a new customer in our table unless there exists a booking for that customer.

Answer to review question 4.3

Relation in un-normalised form:

custNo	cust Name	cust Tel	booking Date	service Type	service	date Required	eNo	eName	Per hr £	hrs
111	J Smith	980 2223	11.08.08.	01	Baby-sitting	16.08.08	01	Issa Ahmed	7	5
			18.09.08	02	Dog walking	30.09.08	02	Ben Brown	10	1
144	G Best	678 4455	18.09.08	01	Baby-sitting	12.09.08	02	Ben Brown	7	3
•	•	•	•	•	•	•	•	•	•	•

Answer to review question 4.4

The primary key is **custNo, bookingDate, serviceType**

Answer to review question 4.5

A relation is in 1NF, if and only if, all domains contain only atomic or single values – i.e. all repeating groups of data are removed. A repeating group is a group of attributes that occurs a number of times for each record in the relation.

1NF determinancy diagram:

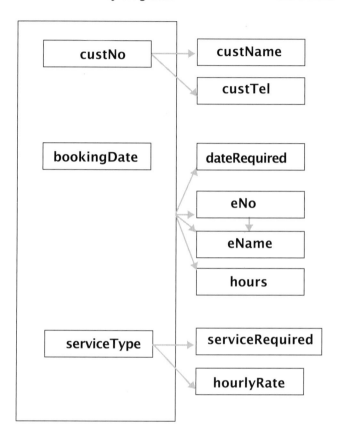

Answer to review question 4.6

custNo	cust Name	cust Tel	booking Date	service Type	service	date Required	eNo	eName	Per hr £	hrs
111	J Smith	980 2223	11.08.08.	01	Baby-sitting	16.08.08	01	Issa Ahmed	7	5
111	J Smith	980 2223	18.09.08	02	Dog walking	30.09.08	02	Ben Brown	10	1
144	G Best	678 4455	18.09.08	01	Baby-sitting	12.09.08	02	Ben Brown	7	3
•	•	•	•	•	•	•	•	•	•	•

Answer to review question 4.7

A relation is in 2NF if it is in 1NF and all non key attributes are dependent on the whole of the primary key and not part of it. If an attribute determines only part of a multi-valued key, remove it to a separate table.

2NF determinacy diagram:

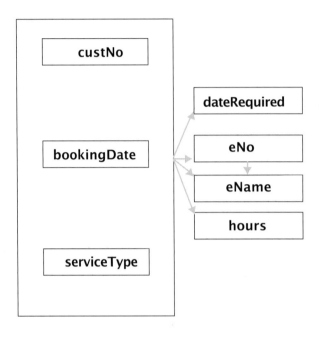

Answer to review question 4.8

The partial dependencies are removed, thus we have:

custNo	custName	custTel
111	J Smith	980 2223
112	G Best	678 4455
•	•	•

serviceType	serviceRequired	hourlyRate
01	Baby-sitting	7
02	Dog walking	10
•	•	•

custNo	bookingDate	serviceType	dateRequired	eNo	eName	hrs
111	11.08.08	01	16.08.08	01	Issa Ahmed	5
111	18.09.08	02	30.09.08	02	Ben Brown	1
•	•	•	•	•	•	•

Answer to review question 4.9

A 3NF relation is in 2NF and also every non-key attribute must be non-transitively dependent on the primary key. Another way of saying this is that a relation is in 3NF if all its non-key attributes are directly dependent on the primary key. Transitive dependencies are resolved by creating new relations for each entity.

3NF determinacy diagram (Service and customer diagram as before):

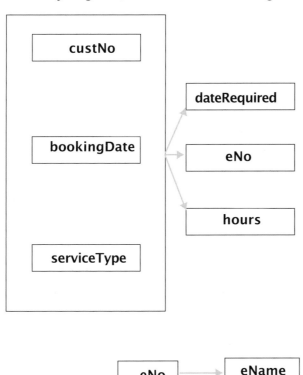

Answer to review question 4.10

custNo	bookingDate	serviceType	dateRequired	eNo	hrs
111	11.08.08	01	16.08.08	01	5
111	18.09.08	02	30.09.08	02	1
o	o	o	o	o	o

eNo	eName
01	Issa Ahmed
02	Ben Brown
o	o

All other relations as above.

Answer to review question 4.11

A relation is in 3NF if it is in 2NF and all non-key attributes are non-transitively dependent on the primary key. Thus the process involves looking for transitive dependences and, where these are found, making a separate relation for these attributes transitively dependent on the primary key. BCNF concerns overlapping candidate keys. The process involves checking to make sure that all the determinants in a table are candidate keys. Where a determinant is found not to be a candidate key, then it is separated out to form another relation.

Answer to review question 4.12

Well-normalised design tends to perform poorly when subjected to large volumes of transactions. For this reason, there are trade-offs to be made between how much normalisation is carried out and the performance response of the implemented system.

5   Answers to review questions

Answer to review question 5.1   SQL includes in the CREATE TABLE statement the optional clause:

constraint constraint_name primary key(pk_no)

which specifies the primary key. This is used to ensure **entity integrity**.

The entity integrity rule states that no attribute which forms part of the primary key of a relation can accept null values. This is achieved in SQL by stating the primary key in the clause as above and by defining the key attribute 'pk_no' as NOT NULL.

Answer to review question 5.2   SQL includes in the CREATE TABLE statement the optional clause:

constraint constraint_name foreign key(fK_no) references table_name(pk_no)

The constraint states the foreign key (fK_no) in a table, and the referenced table's primary key [table_name(pk_no)]. It is used to ensure **referential integrity**. This rule states that the database must not contain any unmatched foreign key values.

Answer to review question 5.3   If the complete set of relational algebra operators can be implemented then it is relationally complete.

Answer to review question 5.4   Restriction is achieved by including a WHERE clause in the SELECT statement (e.g. where cname = 'Bill'). Projection: in the SELECT clause of a SELECT statement (e.g. select dNo, dName).

Answer to review question 5.5   This requires us to list driver number, name and depot where James Bond is based. Code with aliases:

```
select bd.bdNo, bdName, dName
from BusDriver bd, depot d
where bd.dNo = d.dNo
and bdName = 'James Bond';
```

Answer to review question 5.6   The code is incorrect – it does not list the buses that cleaner Vince is responsible for. To do this we would need to include the join condition:

and bus.cNo = cleaner.cNo;

The code, as given, illustrates relational algebra PRODUCT, where the result is every bus and cleaner whether the cleaner is associated with the bus or not.

Answer to review question 5.7   Aggregate functions are functions which are applied to sets of rows in a table. They return a single value. For this type of query, SQL provides the aggregate functions min, max, avg, sum and count.

Answer to review question 5.8   An inner join retrieves data only from those rows where the join condition is met; any unmatched rows are ignored. With an outer join, unmatched rows are included as well as matched rows. Oracle's SQL provides the LEFT OUTER JOIN, the RIGHT OUTER JOIN and the FULL OUTER JOIN operators.

Answer to review question 5.9   A GROUP BY clause groups the data from the selected tables and returns groups of rows. It produces a single summary row for each group, so that for example aggregates (e.g. avg, min, max) of the grouped data can be retrieved.

Restrictions: each item in the select-list must be single-valued per group. The words GROUP BY are followed by one or more data items, specifying the categories into which the data is to be grouped.

Answer to review question 5.10   The HAVING keyword is used to filter groups out of the results set of a query, in the same way that the WHERE clause is used to filter rows. The HAVING clause is optional, and must always follow and relate to a GROUP BY clause, in the same way that the WHERE clause is optional, and must always relate to a SELECT statement.

Answer to review question 5.11   Give the name of the doctor, the title of the diagnosis, the number of times the doctor made the diagnosis, the total estimated cost and total estimated admission days for each doctor for each standard diagnosis, where that doctor has made diagnoses for that standard diagnoses with a total estimated cost greater than £1000.

Answer to review question 5.12   GROUP BY and ORDER BY perform similar functions. However, there is one major difference in that the GROUP BY is specifically designed to group identically defined data. On the other hand, the function of ORDER BY is to sort the data into a particular order.

Answer to review question 5.13   This is not possible because, in relational databases, rows are inserted in no particular order. You can only request rows using valid SQL features, such as ORDER BY.

6   Answers to review questions

Answer to review question 6.1   List the buses by registration number which are based at the same address as the bus with registration number 'P200IJK'.

Table Bus b1 is to find the bus with registration number 'P200IJK'. Table Depot d1 is used to find the depot where this bus is based with its location. Table Depot d2 is used to find depots at the same location. Finally table Bus b2 is used to find the registration numbers of buses based at these depots.

Answer to review question 6.2

```
Select  regNo
From  Bus
Where dNo in
        (select dNo
         from Depot
         where dAddress in
                (select dAddress
                 from Depot
                 Where dNo in
                        (select dNo
                         from Bus
                         where regNo= 'P200IJK')));
```
Both queries give output:

REGNO
H259IJK
P200IJK
P300RTY

Answer to review question 6.3   The statements **are** equivalent.

The first query is the natural join of the two tables, so only includes rows from each table that have a match on the other. The result is to identify those cleaners who are responsible for buses of model Daf.

The second query does the same thing more directly, searching for a cleaner identifier in the list of cleaners who are responsible for buses of model Daf.

Answer to review question 6.4   The statements **are not** equivalent.

The first query does NOT make sense. It asks for the number and name of any cleaner such that there is a different cleaner that is responsible for buses of model Daf. Since two different cleaners have buses for which they are responsible, then this is true for all cleaners, so the result will be the numbers and names of all cleaners.

The second query is 'sensible' SQL. For each cleaner, a check is made to see if that cleaner is responsible for buses of model Daf, and if the cleaner is not, then that cleaner (no. and name) is included in the result, i.e.: lists all those cleaners not responsible for buses of model Daf.

Answer to review question 6.5   Give the name of each patient who was never treated during an admission by the doctor who admitted him/her on that occasion.

Answer to review question 6.6   This gives the names of patients who have been admitted to every hospital.

It can be thought of as looping for each hospital within each patient. The inner loop returns a row if there is any hospital where there is no admission row for that patient at that hospital (NOT EXISTS true). If any row has been assembled by the end of the cycle, the outer NOT EXISTS is false, so the patient is eliminated.

Answer to review question 6.7   Under most circumstances it will give the correct answer. If there is incorrect data in the database, it may give misleading results. The relational algebra divide solution is a better solution, as it checks for the existence for each patient's admission to each hospital.

Answer to review question 6.8   Views are used for a number of reasons:

- To enforce security by hiding data from certain users

- To simplify complex queries by providing intermediate answers which are dynamically updated and can be reused as input

- As input to utilities such as report generators.

```
create view HollowayBuses
as          select regNo, model, d.dNo
            from Bus b, Depot d
            where b.dNo = d.dNo
            and dName = 'Holloway';
```

This creates a view of registration numbers, models and cleaner number for buses based at Holloway. The view name is then incorporated into a select-statement in the normal way. For example:

```
Select distinct cName
from HollowayBuses h, Cleaner c
where h.dNo = c.dNo;
```

This gives the names of cleaners who look after buses based at the Holloway depot.

Answer to review question 6.9   PL/SQL is an extension to SQL. It includes high-level programming features such as block structure, variables, constants, types, assignment statement, conditions, loops, procedures and functions.

Answer to review question 6.10   PL/SQL is grouped into units called blocks. Blocks can be stand alone or nested. A block is divided into three parts. The declaration section consists of types, constants, variables, exception and cursor declarations. At the end of this section, subprograms (procedures and functions), if any, are declared. The executable commands section contains the program statements. The exception section is for exception handling.

It has the following structure:

```
declare
<declarations section>
begin
<executable commands>
exception
<exception handling>
end;
```

Answer to review question 6.11   In PL/SQL a SELECT INTO statement can be used if the query returns one – and only one – row. Cursors are provided when more than one row is returned. This allows rows of a query result to be accessed one row at a time. The cursor acts as a pointer to a particular row of a query result.

Answer to review question 6.12   Stored procedures, containing SQL or PL/SQL statements, allow one to move code that enforces business rules from the application to the database. Some of the most important advantages of using stored procedures are summarised as follows:

- The code can be stored once for use by different applications. Since the procedural code is stored within the database and is fairly static, applications may benefit from the reuse of the same queries within the database

- The use of stored procedures can make the application code more consistent and easier to maintain. This principle is similar to the good practice in general programming, in which common functionality should be coded separately as procedures or functions

- Because the processing of complex business rules may be performed within the database, significant performance improvement can be obtained in a networked client/server environment.

Answer to review question 6.13   A trigger defines an action the database should take when some database-related event occurs. They are associated with a single table within the database and are specific to an UPDATE, INSERT or DELETE operation or a combination of these against rows in the table. The database stores triggers in the same way that it stores normal data. They are automatically executed whenever a specified event occurs and a condition is satisfied.

Answer to review question 6.14

- For example, integrity of the database can be enforced before an event instead of after. If we wish to disallow overdrafts in a bank database, a trigger could be set up that rolls back a transaction if a balance field goes negative

- A trigger might reject updates to a price greater than 50%

- They can be used to recalculate ongoing tallies – for example, in an employee relation containing salary and department triggers an Insert/Delete/Update of an employee relation can be used to maintain the total salary bill for each department. Note that using triggers is not the only way to maintain summary data and may not be the best way.

Answer to review question 6.15   Because of their flexibility, triggers may supplement database integrity constraints. However, they should not be used to replace them. When enforcing business rules in an application, you should first rely on the declarative constraints available with the DBMS (e.g. in Oracle within the CREATE Table statement). Triggers should only be used to enforce rules that cannot be coded through declarative constraints. This is because the enforcement of the declarative constraints is more efficient than the execution of user-created triggers.

Answer to review question 6.16   The foreign key constraint is often used for ensuring the referential integrity among parent and child tables. However, the foreign key constraint can enforce only standard integrity rules. When other non-standard rules have to be enforced as well, appropriate triggers need to be created instead of using the foreign key constraint. Some possible non-standard rules are:

- Cascade updates (cascade update means update all related dependent objects as well as the specified object.)

- Set the foreign key column to NULL on updates and deletes

- Set a default value to the foreign key column on updates and deletes.

It must be noted that if triggers are to be used, then for each of the integrity rules (standard and non-standard), one or more triggers may need to be created to perform appropriate actions. Also, the foreign key constraint must not be declared when creating the corresponding tables; otherwise, the triggers will not work, because the standard foreign key constraint will override the trigger actions.

7   Answers to review questions

Answer to review question 7.1

a. Select pNo, pName

from Part p, Shipment sp, Supplier s

where p.pNo = sp.pNo

and sp.sNo = s.sNo

and city = 'Manchester';

b.

```
F1= Part Join Shipment where Part pNo = Shipment pNo
F2= F1 Join Supplier where F1 sNo = Supplier  sNo
F3= Restrict from F2 where city = 'Manchester'
F4 = Project over F3 [pNo, pName]
```

In the solution above, note that Shipment and Part are joined first; followed by Supplier; next, city has been restricted to Manchester after the join.

Alternatively:

c. Select pNo, pName

from Part p, Shipment sp, Supplier s

where city ='Manchester'

and s.pNo = sp.pNo

and sp.sNo = p.sNo

```
F1 = Restrict from Supplier where city = 'Manchester'
F2 = F1 Join Shipment where F1 sNo = Shipment sNo
F3 = F2 Join Part where F2 pNo = Part pNo
F4 = Project over F3 [pNo, pName]
```

In this solution, the Supplier table is restricted; followed by a join to Shipment; followed by a join to Part.

Answer to review question 7.2   A software optimiser is superior to a human optimiser because:

- A software optimiser would have access to a huge amount of statistical information kept in the system catalog and not available to programmers (e.g. the cardinality of each domain, the cardinality of each table, and the number of times each different value occurs in each column)

- A software optimiser can assess many more different forms of query than a human optimiser would be inclined to, or capable of doing

- A software optimiser can embody the best optimising practices.

Answer to review question 7.3   Optimisation is required if a DBMS is to perform a query in a reasonable period of time. Queries can be written in different ways, many of them inefficient. It is the job of the optimiser in the DBMS to take a query and transform it into a version that can be executed efficiently. The larger a database becomes, the greater the need for an optimiser. As many databases may contain over a million records, even a modest improvement in efficiency would have a dramatic effect on response times.

Answer to review question 7.4   Heuristic optimisation involves substituting relational algebra expressions with more efficient expressions, using equivalence-preserving transformation rules. This results in more efficient evaluation and may include the reordering of expressions, or removing of redundant or useless operations. The transformation rules are not independent of each other: given a particular expression to transform, the application of one rule might generate an expression that is susceptible to transformation after the application of another rule. The optimiser applies transformation rules until it finally results in an acceptable version of the query.

Answer to review question 7.5   In this example, assume we have started the process with the following tree:

Answer to review question 7.6   Perform restriction as early as possible; therefore, push the restriction operator as far down the tree as possible:

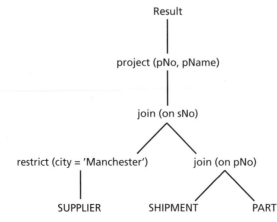

Answer to review question 7.7   In the example, SUPPLIER is the only table to be restricted, so we exchange PART and SUPPLIER. Remember that the tree is executed from the bottom right-hand side, so the first join is now a join from SUPPLIER to SHIPMENT:

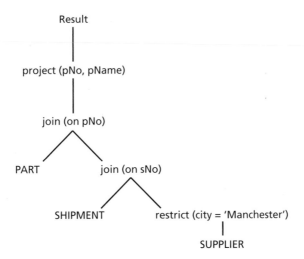

Answer to review question 7.8

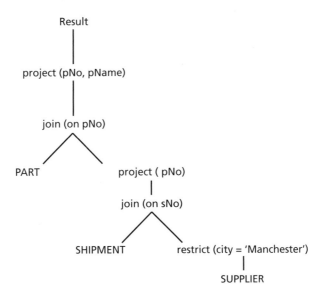

Remember that a project cannot be simply moved down the tree. When a projection is preceded by a join, it is possible to push the projection down before the join. As the projection is pushed down the tree it may acquire new attributes, therefore the original projection must be performed after the join.

Here, we have pushed the attribute pNo down the tree before the join. In order to push the projection further down the tree, the projection has to acquire a new attribute, sNo, so that the join (on sNo) can be performed. The original projection (pNo, pName) is still performed after the join.

Here, we have succeeded in reducing the cardinalities of the intermediate relations:

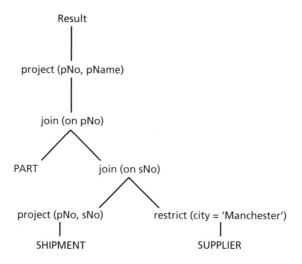

Answer to review question 7.9

    F1 = Restrict from Supplier where city = 'Manchester'
    F2 = Project over Shipment [pNo, sNo]
    F3 = F1 Join F2 where F1 sNo = F2 sNo
    F4 = F3 Join Part where F3 pNo =Part pNo
    F5 = Project over F4 [pNo, pName]

Answer to review question 7.10   Example rules:

- Perform restriction as early as possible

- Rearrange leaf nodes, if necessary, so that the leaf with the most restrictive restriction operates first

- Perform projection as early as possible – under certain conditions projection may be commuted with a Cartesian product or join. However, a projection cannot be simply moved down the tree. When a projection is preceded by a join, it is possible to push the projection down, before the join, but the projection may acquire new attributes. Therefore, the original projection must be performed after the join. This is worthwhile only if the cardinalities of the intermediate relations are reduced

- Perform restrict before project by commuting (exchanging) restrict with project.

Answer to review question 7.11   The following rules make expressions simpler:

- Combine a cascade of restrictions into one restriction

- Combine a cascade of projections into one projection.

The following rule involves rewriting the query in a less computationally demanding form:
- Any restriction condition is converted into conjunctive normal form.

8 Answers to review questions

Answer to review question 8.1

CAD/CAM	Relational
Data may have many types, each with a small number of instances	Typically, a database consists of a smallish number of relations (usually tens rather than hundreds) but relations may contain thousands of tuples. For example, consider a database for a university
Designs are often very large, with many subdesigns	Each attribute in a relation is atomic and cannot be broken down further
The design evolves through time	Typically, a conventional relational database is relatively static
Updates can be far-reaching – one change may affect a large number of design objects	Updates to a relational schema usually affect only a small number of other, related relations
Various versions of designs must be maintained, with many staff working on these versions at the same time. There needs to be version control and the final product must be consistent and coordinated	Maintaining versions or the evolution of objects (schema evolution) is not so important for traditional database applications

Answer to review question 8.2   Classes for university personnel department. Your answer should list classes such as the following:

- Employee
- Job
- Department.

Objects that are instances of university personnel system. Your answer should list instances with typical attributes such as the following:

- Class Employee: with name attribute values such as 'Jo Bloggs', 'Jane Smith', 'Nimesh Patel'
- Class Job: with jobFunction attribute values such as 'manager', 'cleaner', 'lecturer', 'professor', 'administrator'
- Class Department: with departmentTitle attribute values such as 'Computing Science', 'Biology', 'Mechanical Engineering', 'Performing Arts', 'Social Science'.

Answer to review question 8.3

- Embed OO database language constructs in a conventional host language
- Provide OODBMS libraries to an OO programming language
- Extend an existing language (SQL) with OO capabilities.

Answer to review question 8.4   Messages are the means by which objects communicate with one another. Messages are passed between objects in order to convey information, and to request an object to perform a particular function. Methods are fragments of program code that are the part of objects that enable them to perform actions. The details of methods are not visible outside of the object. When a message is received by an object requesting that a particular action be performed, this will be enacted by the object executing one or more of its methods. The result of the action will, in many situations, be conveyed back to the requesting object via a message.

Answer to review question 8.5   The main advantages of inheritance are:

1. **Reusability:** through the inheritance mechanism, the characteristics of an object can be made available to other objects. Depending on the system, this may involve both state (data) and behaviour (methods) of objects.

2. **Extensibility:** another aspect of the mechanism is that it provides a natural means of developing a modelled system. As new features, data or program code are added, these can be defined in terms of new objects, which inherit the already tested characteristics of the earlier part of the system.

Answer to review question 8.6

1. An 'object' is a uniquely identifiable entity, which contains the attributes that describe both the state of a 'real world' object and the actions that are associated with it.

2. An 'attribute' is a property that describes some aspect of an object. Attributes have values, which have a simple or complex structure and are stored within the object.

3. 'Object identity' is a unique identity for each independent object stored in the database. The value of the OID is not visible to the external user but is used internally by the system to identify each object uniquely.

4. A 'complex object' is an object that contains other objects.

Answer to review question 8.7

OODBSs OIDs	RDBSs primary keys
They are efficient: OIDs require little storage within a complex object	Need to use inefficient joins to retrieve data
As the user cannot modify them, the system can ensure entity and referential integrity more easily and users do not need to maintain referential integrity	Can be modified by the user
They help locate objects quickly as the OIDs point to an actual address or to a location within a table that gives the address of the referenced object	Do not relate to the actual address
They do not depend upon the data contained in the object in any way. This allows the value of every attribute of an object to change, but for the object to remain the same object with the same OID	Primary key is one (or more) attribute in the relation and is subject to change – may be subject to integrity violations

Answer to review question 8.8 Eight features which apply to OO concepts:

- OODBMSs should allow complex objects
- Encapsulation must be supported
- Classes must be supported
- The DML must be computationally complete
- Classes must be able to inherit from their ancestors
- Dynamic binding must be supported
- The set of data types must be extensible
- Object identity must be supported.

Answer to review question 8.9 Generalisation involves the identification or abstraction of the common properties of a number of classes into a superclass. With generalisation, all properties of a generalised type (superclass) can be inherited downwards to subclasses of entities. These subclasses may also have some properties pertinent to only that subclass. Also the inheritance of specific properties can be explicitly disallowed. With generalisation, the cardinality of the relationships is always one-to-one.

Inheritance and super-/subclasses are key ideas of OODB systems. Each object in an OODB is an instance of a class, and classes are related to each other via inherited relationships.

Answer to review question 8.10 The new superclass 'Organisation' is created by extracting a common structure (and behaviour) by generalising the two classes in class Organisation, with instance variables companyName, address and telephoneNo. Thus we have (note that system types such as characters and numbers have been omitted):

```
class Organisation
  properties
        companyName
        address
        telephoneNo;

class Supplier inherits Organisation
  properties
        Sno
        contactPerson
        balanceOwing;

class Customer inherits Organisation
  properties
        Cno
        balanceOwed;
```

Answer to review question 8.11 (i)

Relation diagram for object-oriented schema:

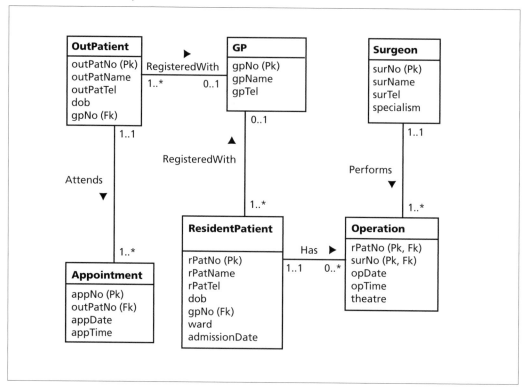

Answer to review question 8.11 (ii)

```
class Person
 properties
       name
       tel;

class Patient inherits Person
 properties
       patientNo
       dob
       generalPractitioner        GP;

class ResidentPatient inherits Patient
 properties
       ward
       admissionDate
       patOperations         set [ surg:          Surgeon
                             opDate
                             opTime
                             theatre                          ];
```

cont...

```
class OutPatient inherits Patient
  properties
        outPatAppointments              set [Appointment];

class GP inherits Person
  properties
        gpNo
        patients                        set [Patient];

class Surgeon inherits Person
  properties
        surNo
        specialism;

class Appointment
  properties
        outPat                          OutPatient
        appDate
        appTime;
```

A number of answers are acceptable. An alternative three-tier hierarchy could be the top tier containing Person, the middle tier Patient and Doctor, and the bottom tier the two types of patients and the two types of doctors. Also Appointment could be included as a structured attribute in the OutPatient class. Operations (patOperations) have been included in the ResidentPatient class to illustrate structured types. Alternatively, they could have been included in the Surgeon class, or retained as class Operation.

Answer to review question 8.11 (iii) The following solution assumes the 'alternative' three-tier solution to part (ii) and includes the Operations class.

Object-oriented database schema:

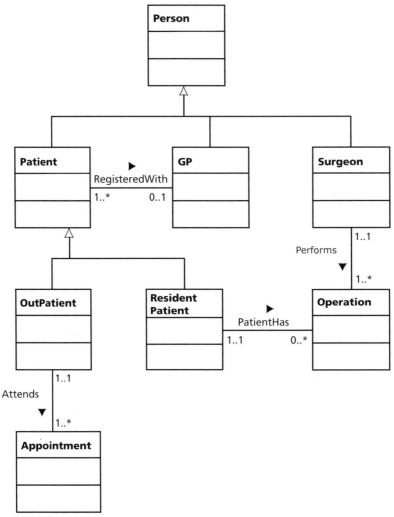

Answer to review question 8.12 (i)

```
Create or replace type DepartmentType as object
(deptno            varchar2(10),
deptname           varchar2(20),
depthead           varchar2(20) );

Create or replace type EmployeeType as object
(eno               varchar2(10),
ename              varchar2(20),
department         DepartmentType,
presentposition    varchar2(20) );
```

Note use of 'replace' which replaces previous versions of EmployeeType.

Answer to review question 8.12 (ii)

```
Create table Employee of EmployeeType;
Create table Department of DepartmentType;
```

ADTs provide the structure which will be used when objects are inserted into an object table. They are the building blocks on which object tables can be created. ADTs cannot be queried, in the same way that the built-in data types in Oracle such as number and varchar2 cannot be queried. Object tables are the elements which are queried, and these are established using a combination of base data types such as varchar2, date, number and any relevant ADTs as required.

Answer to review question 8.12 (iii) Employee type as before:

```
Create or replace type EmployeeType as object
(eno                varchar2(10),
 ename              varchar2(20),
 department         DepartmentType,
 presentposition    varchar2(20) );
```

To use this ADT as the basis for a nested table we now need to create a new ADT thus:

```
Create or replace type EmployeeNT as table of EmployeeType;
```

The Project table is now created containing a nested table of type EmployeeNT:

```
Create table Project
(projectNo          varchar(6),
 description        varchar(20),
 days               number,
 employees          EmployeeNT)
 nested table employees store as EmployeeNT_tab;
```

Answer to review question 8.13

```
Create type GradesType as object
(grade        number );
```

We now create the varying array:

```
Create type GradesVA as varray(10) of GradesType;
```

Now we create a Student table which includes a varying array of type GradesType for its grades column:

```
Create table Student
(registrationNo         char(10),
 name                   varchar2(50),
 email                  varchar2(50),
 grades                 gradesVA);
```

9   Answers to review questions

Answer to review question 9.1 A transaction is a logic unit of work on the database that is either completed in its entirety or not done at all.

A transaction is concerned with accessing or changing the contents of a database and may be the entire program, a portion of a program or a single command. A transaction has a clear start and finish. The assumption is that it will start its execution on a consistent database and, if it runs to completion, then the transaction is said to be committed, and the database will be in a new consistent state. Once a transaction is committed, then the transaction manager knows that the database is in a consistent state again, and all of the updates made by that transaction can now be made permanent. If the changes are made permanent, then the database has reached a new synchronisation point. The other possibility is that the transactions do not commit satisfactorily (i.e. do not reach their end). In this case the transaction is aborted and the incomplete transaction is rolled back. The database is then restored to the consistent state it held before the transaction was started by the transaction manager.

Answer to review question 9.2 The acronym ACID indicates the properties of any well-formed transactions. Any transaction that violates these principles will cause failures of concurrency.

- **Atomicity:** a transaction is an atomic unit of processing; it is either performed in its entirety or not performed at all. A transaction does not partly happen

- **Consistency:** the database state is consistent at the end of a transaction

- **Isolation:** a transaction should not make its updates visible to other transactions until it is committed; this property, when enforced strictly, solves the temporary update problem, and makes cascading rollbacks of transactions unnecessary

- **Durability:** when a transaction has made a change to the database state, and the change is committed, this change is permanent and should be available to all other transactions.

Answer to review question 9.3

- **Lost update problem** – two transactions access the same database items (x) and have their operations interleaved in a way that makes the value of some database item incorrect

- **Uncommitted dependency problem** – occurs when one transaction can see intermediate results of another transaction before it has committed

- **Inconsistent analysis problem** – occurs when a transaction reads partial results of other incomplete transactions.

Answer to review question 9.4

1. **Dirty read** – data may be made available to one transaction from another before completion of the second transaction. If the second transaction does not complete successfully, and the original data is restored, the first transaction may continue with inaccurate data.

2. **Serial schedule** – a schedule S is serial if for every transaction T participating in the schedule, all of the operations of T are executed consecutively in the schedule.

3. **Serializability** – serializability identifies those executions of transactions guaranteed to ensure consistency. If a set of transactions executes concurrently, we say that the schedule is correct if it produces the same results as some serial execution. The objective of serializability is to find non-serial schedules that allow transactions to execute concurrently without interfering with one another. The result should be the same as if the database state had been produced by a serial execution. It is essential to guarantee serializability in order to ensure database correctness.

Answer to review question 9.5

S (shared locks or read): if a transaction has a read lock on a data item, it can read the item but not update it. It is permissible for more than one transaction to hold read locks simultaneously on the same item. If a read lock is requested on an item that already has a read lock on it, the request is granted; otherwise it has to wait.

X (exclusive or write): if a transaction has a write lock on a data item, it can both read and update the item. This transaction has excusive access to the data item. Other transactions must wait until the lock is released.

Answer to review question 9.6 A transaction is said to follow the basic two-phase locking protocol if all locking operations (read_lock, write_lock) precede the first unlock operation in the transaction. Such a transaction can be divided into two phases: an expanding (or growing) phase, during which new locks on items can be acquired, but none can be released; and a shrinking phase, during which existing locks can be released but no new locks can be acquired.

It can be proved that if every transaction in a schedule follows the two-phase locking protocol, the schedule is guaranteed to be serializable, because the protocols will prevent interference among different transactions. The lost update, uncommitted dependency and inconsistent analysis problems will not happen if 2PL is enforced. However, basic 2PL is prone to deadlock.

Conservative 2PL is a deadlock-free protocol. It requires all transactions to lock all the data items it needs in advance. If at least one of the required data items cannot be obtained, then none of the items are locked. Rather, the transaction waits and then tries again to lock all the items it needs. This solution further limits concurrency.

Answer to review question 9.7 Deadlock is the situation where one transaction is waiting for a resource which is locked by another transaction. This transaction, in turn, is waiting for a resource which is locked by the first transaction (or possibly yet another transaction).

10 Answers to review questions

Answer to review question 10.1   The practical aspects of transactions are about keeping control. There are a variety of causes of transaction failure. These may include:

1. **Concurrency control enforcement:** the concurrency control method may abort the transaction, to be restarted later, because it violates serializability, or because several transactions are in a state of deadlock.

2. **Local error detected by the transaction:** during transaction executions, certain conditions may occur that necessitate cancellation of the transaction (e.g. an account with insufficient funds may cause a withdrawal transaction from that account to be cancelled). This may be done by a programmed ABORT in the transaction itself.

3. **A transaction or system error:** some operation in the transaction may cause it to fail, such as integer overflow, division by zero, erroneous parameter values or logical programming errors.

4. **User interruption of the transaction during its execution** (e.g. by issuing a control-C in a VAX/VMS or UNIX environment).

5. **System software errors** that result in abnormal termination or destruction of the database management system.

6. **Crashes due to hardware malfunction** resulting in loss of internal (main and cache) memory (otherwise known as system crashes).

7. **Disk malfunctions** such as read or write malfunction or a disk read/write head crash. This may happen during a read or write operation of the transaction.

8. **Natural physical disasters and catastrophes** such as fires, earthquakes or power surges, sabotages, intentional contamination with computer viruses, or destruction of data or facilities by operators or users.

Answer to review question 10.2   The system log contains information about the start and end of each transaction, plus any updates which occur in the transaction. It keeps track of all transaction operations that affect the values of database items. This information may be needed to recover from transaction failure. The log is kept on disk. Thus, the majority of the log is not affected by failures, except for a disk failure or catastrophic failure. In addition, the log is periodically backed up to archival storage to protect against the effect of such catastrophic failures. The types of entries that are written to the log are described below – in these entries, T refers to a unique transaction identifier that is generated automatically by the system and used to uniquely label each transaction:

- **start_transaction(T):** this log entry records that transaction T starts the execution

- **read_item(T, x):** this log entry records that transaction T reads the value of database item x

- **write_item(T, x, old_value, new_value):** this log entry records that transaction T changes the value of the database item x from old_value to new_value. The old value is sometimes known as a **before image of x**, and the new value is known as an **after image of x**

- **commit(T):** this log entry records that transaction T has completed all accesses to the database successfully and its effect can be committed (recorded permanently) to the database

- **abort(T):** this records that transaction T has been aborted
- **checkpoint:** this is an additional entry to the log. The purpose of this entry will be described in the next review question answer.

Because the log contains a record of every write operation that changes the value of some database item, it is possible to undo the effect of these write operations of a transaction T, by tracing backward through the log and resetting all items changed by a write operation of T to their old_values. We can also redo the effect of the write operations of a transaction T, by tracing forward through the log and setting all items changed by a write operations of T to their new_values.

Answer to review question 10.3   This activity asked you to list all actions taken when a checkpoint entry is written in the system log:

- Suspending executions of transactions temporarily
- Writing (force-writing) all modified database buffers of committed transactions out to disk
- Writing a checkpoint record to the log
- Writing (force-writing) all log records in main memory out to disk.

Answer to review question 10.4

- **UNDO:** if a transaction crash does occur, then the recovery manager may undo transactions (that is, reverse the operations of a transaction on the database). This involves examining a transaction for the log entry write_item(T, x, old_value, new_value), and setting the value of item x in the database to old_value. Undoing a number of write_item operations from one or more transactions from the log must proceed in the reverse order from the order in which the operations were written
- **REDO:** is achieved by examining a transaction's log entry; and for every write_item(T, x, old_value, new_value) entry, the value of item x in the database is set to new_value. Redoing a number of transactions from the log must proceed in the same order in which the operations were written.

    It is only necessary to redo the last update of x from the log during recovery, because the other updates are overwritten by this last redo.

Answer to review question 10.5   *Catastrophic failure* is extensive damage to a wide portion of the database, such as disk malfunctions, read or write malfunction or a disk read/write head crash. This may happen during a read or write operation of the transaction, and can be caused by natural physical disasters and catastrophes such as fires, earthquakes or power surges, sabotage, intentional contamination with computer viruses, or destruction of data or facilities by operators or users.

The main technique used to handle catastrophic failures, including disk crash, is that of **database backup**. The whole database and the log are periodically copied. In case of a catastrophic system failure, the latest backup copy can be reloaded, and the system can be restarted.

Answer to review question 10.6   If a transaction fails, for whatever reason, after updating the database, it may be necessary to roll back or UNDO the transaction. Any data item values that have been changed by the transaction must be returned to their previous values. The log entries are used to recover the old values of data items that must be rolled back.

If a transaction T is rolled back, any transaction S that has, in the interim, read the value of some data item x written by T must also be rolled back. Similarly, once S is rolled back, any transaction R that has read the value of some item y written by S must also be rolled back, and so on. This phenomenon is called **cascading rollback**. If cascading rollback is not checked, it may lead to an inconsistent database state. For example, when T is rolled back, S and R must also be rolled back, otherwise uncommitted dependency problems occur.

Answer to review question 10.7   The **deferred update** techniques do not actually update the database until after a transaction reaches its commit point; then the updates are recorded in the database. Before commit, all transaction updates are recorded in the local transaction workspace.

During commit, the updates are first recorded persistently in the log, and then written to the database. If a transaction fails before reaching its commit point, it will not have changed the database in any way, so UNDO is not needed. It may be necessary to REDO the effect of the operations of a committed transaction from the log, because their effect may not yet have been written in the database. Hence, deferred update is also known as the NO-UNDO/REDO algorithm.

In the **immediate update** techniques, the database may be updated by some operations of a transaction before the transaction reaches its commit point. However, these operations are typically recorded in the log-on disk, by force-writing, before they are applied to the database, making recovery still possible.

If a transaction fails after recording some changes in the database, but before reaching its commit point, the effect of its operations on the database must be undone; that is, the transaction must be rolled back. In the general case of immediate update, both UNDO and REDO are required during recovery, so it is known as the UNDO/REDO algorithm.

Answer to review question 10.8   Use two lists of transactions maintained by the system: the **committed transactions list** which contains all committed transactions since the last checkpoint, and the **active transactions list**. REDO all the write operations of the committed transactions from the log, in the order in which they were written into it. The transactions in the active list that are active and did not commit are effectively cancelled and must be resubmitted.

The REDO procedure is defined as follows: redoing a write_item operation consists of examining its log entry write_item(T, x, old_value, new_value), and setting the value of item x in the database to new_value. The REDO operation is required to be idempotent:

Log entry	Log written to disk	Changes written to database buffer	Changes written on disk
start_transaction(T)	No	N/A	N/A
read_item(T, x)	No	N/A	N/A
write_item(T, x)	No	No	No
commit(T)	Yes	Yes	*Yes
checkpoint	Yes	Undefined	Yes (of committed transactions)

*Yes: writing back to disk may not occur immediately.

11 Answers to review questions

Answer to review question 11.1 The 2-tier model of client/server computing refers to the arrangement where the processing of an application is distributed across two types of machines:

- **Servers:** that handle the database functions of the application
- **Clients:** that handle the data entry and display and simple input validation tasks of the application.

In more complex applications, the way in which the processing is distributed between the two types of machines will vary depending on the power of the machines, volume of network traffic, etc. There may be a number of client and server machines within any given network, though usually each server will support a number of client machines. It is possible in the 2-tier system to have a server which also behaves as a client with respect to another server machine.

Answer to review question 11.2 The client/server model provides a scalable solution because, within the limits of the available network and server machines, new client machines can be added to the network. In this way, more users can be added to the system.

Answer to review question 11.3 It is possible for data to be downloaded to client machines and taken away either on the machine or on other storage media such as disks or CD-ROMs. This is a major issue which needs to be addressed within organisations using client/server systems, requiring the development of policies about what data can be downloaded, and whether or not to allow removable storage media to be used on client machines.

A further major issue is the possibility of viruses being introduced to the system via client machines. Once more, policies need to be developed and enacted in order to establish protection against the introduction of viruses; these policies might disallow the introduction of external programs and data files by users via client machines.

Answer to review question 11.4

- **Fragmentation:** refers to the splitting up of relations in order that they may be stored in a distributed manner across a number of machines within the distributed system. The fact that the data itself is distributed distinguishes this type of system, known as a distributed database system, from a client/server system, in which only the processing is distributed. Relations may be fragmented horizontally and/or vertically
- **Replication:** refers to the process of keeping a number of distinct copies of data up to date although it is distributed across a network. Updates made at one of the sites containing data are propagated or replicated to other sites. A range of strategies are available to the designer to choose how updates will be propagated across the network.

Factors that will influence this choice include:

- How up to date it is necessary for the data to be in order for users at different sites to perform their tasks effectively

- The peak and average volumes of update transactions
- The amount of data updated by each transaction
- The available network bandwidth.

Answer to review question 11.5   The main advantage of synchronous replication is that it maintains all replicas of the data in synchronisation. This means that regardless of which site a person is using, they are guaranteed to be working with the most up-to-date version of the data.

The disadvantage of this approach is the overhead of the extra messages and data that needs to be transferred across the network in order for this synchronous updating process to take place. The effect of this extra network traffic is that the times to perform update transactions are increased.

12   Answers to review questions

Answer to review question 12.1 Web database connectivity is the connection between a client machine and a remote database via the World Wide Web. Such a connection allows a web browser user to connect to a remote database, to both access and update the database content.

Answer to review question 12.2 A dynamic web page is one whose contents are generated each time it is accessed. As a result, a dynamic web page can respond to user input from the browser by, for example, returning data requested by the completion of a form, or returning the result of a database query. A dynamic page can also be customised by, and for, each user. Once a user has specified some preferences when accessing a particular site or page, the information can be recorded, and appropriate responses can be generated according to those preferences.

Answer to review question 12.3

- Common Gateway Interface program (CGI program)
- Java Servlets
- HTML 'template' approach.

Answer to review question 12.4 In the 3-tier client/server architecture, the first tier is the client which contains user interfaces. In a web-based system the client machine typically runs a web browser. The second tier is the application server that provides application logic and data processing functions. In a web-based system the application server runs the web server, which is a software component rather than a hardware one. The third tier contains the actual DBMS, which may run on a separate server called a database server.

Answer to review question 12.5 A web database application should comprise the following five layers:

1. **Browser layer:** the browser is the client of a web database application, and it has two major functions. First, it handles the layout and display of HTML documents. Second, it executes the client-side extension functionality such as Java, JavaScript, and ActiveX (a method to extend a browser's capabilities).

2. **Web server layer:** this is the software component. It is responsible for receiving client requests via the http protocol, for initiating appropriate action for each request, and for passing the end results back to the client.

3. **Application logic layer:** most of the application's business rules and functionality will reside in this layer. The browser client displays data as well as forms for user input, whereas the application logic component compiles the data to be displayed and processes user input as required. In other words, the application logic generates HTML that the browser renders. Also, it receives, processes, and stores user input that the browser sends.

4. **Database connection layer:** the database connection layer provides a link between the application logic layer and the DBMS.

5. **Database layer:** this is the place where the underlying database resides within the web database application.

Answer to review question 12.6 Client-side scripting, in either JavaScript or VBScript; plug-ins; ActiveX controls (IE only); Java applets.

Answer to review question 12.7 An application server is a machine which is placed between the database server and client machines, in a client/server environment. It is used to provide a centralised point for the processing of application or business logic. It is used to relieve the load on the client and database server machines, enabling them to be used solely for interfacing, and data-intensive tasks respectively. Main activities:

- Receiving and validating the input from the user request
- Collecting data for a query (e.g. an SQL statement)
- Preparing and sending the query to the database via the database connection layer
- Retrieving the results from the connection layer
- Formatting the data for display; most commonly in the shape of an HTML file, and passing the data for display back to the web server layer.

Answer to review question 12.8

- CGI script (e.g. Perl)
- ASP.NET (Microsoft)
- Java Server Pages
- Java Servlet
- Coldfusion.

Answer to review question 12.9 The difference between an ASP.NET and an HTML file:

- When a browser requests an HTML file, the server returns the file
- When a browser requests an ASP.NET file, the web server passes the request to the ASP.NET engine. The ASP.NET engine reads the ASP.NET file, line by line, and executes the scripts in the file. Finally, the ASP.NET file is returned to the browser as plain HTML.

Answer to review question 12.10

- **HTML:** (Hypertext Markup Language); markup tags tell the web browser how to display the page
- **Server-side VBScript**: Scripts in an ASP.NET file are executed on the server. VBScript is a version of MS's programming language 'Visual Basic'. Server-side scripting is a language which can be used for dynamically editing, changing or adding any content to a web page. Also responds to user queries, or data submitted from HTML forms. Default scripting language for ASP.NET
- **SQL (structured query language):** SQL statements are used to retrieve and update data in a database
- **ADO (ActiveX data object):** programming interface to access data in a database.

Answer to review question 12.11

Approach	DB connection
Coldfusion	Native database API, ODBC
ASP.NET	Microsoft Active Data Objects (ADO.NET),which typically connects to ODBC
Java Server Pages	JDBC (plus other Java approaches)

Atkinson, Malcolm P, Bancilhon, Francois, DeWitt, David J, Dittrich, Klaus R, Maier, David and Zdonik, Stanley B, *The Object-Oriented Database System Manifesto*, DBLP, **http://dblp.uni-trier.de, 1989.**

Booch G, Rumbaugh J and Jacobson, I, *The Unified Modelling Language, User Guide*, 2nd edition, Addison Wesley, 2005.

Beynon-Davies P, *Database Systems*, 3rd edition, Palgrave, 2004.

Bowman J, Emerson L and Darnovsky M, *The practical SQL using Structured Query Language*, Addison Wesley, 2000.

Buyens J, *Web Database Development, Step by Step*, Microsoft, 2000.

Chen P P, The entity relationship model - towards a unified view of data, *ACM Transactions on Database Systems*, 1(1): 9-36, 1976.

Codd E F, *Further normalization of the database relational model, Database Systems*. Ed.Rustin, Prentice Hall, 1972.

Codd E F, Extending the relational database model to capture more meaning, *ACM Transactions on Database Systems*, 4(4): 397-434, 1979.

Codd E F, Data Models in Database Management, *ACM SIGMOD Record* 11, 1981.

Connolly, T and Begg, C, *Database Systems, A Practical Approach to Design, Implementation & Management*, Pearson Education Ltd, 4th edition, 2005.

Date, C J, *Introduction to Database Systems*, 7th edition, Addison Wesley, 2002.

Date, C J, Where SQL falls short, *Datamation*, Volume 33, Issue 9, 1987.

Deitel, H, Deitel P and Neto T, *eBusiness and eCommerce: How to Program*, Prentice Hall, 2001.

Eaglestone, B and Ridley M, *Web Database Systems*, McGraw-Hill, 2001.

Hall, M, *Core Servlets and JavaServer Pages*, 2nd Edition, Prentice-Hall, 2004.

Howe, A, *Data Analysis for Database design*, 3rd Edition, Edward Arnold, 2000.

International Standards Organisation *ISO/IEC 9075-14:2006 SQL XML-Related Specifications (SQL/XML)* **www.iso.org/iso/iso_catalogue/catalogue_tc/catalogue_detail.htm?csnumber=38647**

Kent, W A, Simple Guide to Five Normal Forms in Relational Database Theory, *Communications of the ACM* 26(2) 1983.

Kiper, M, Bernstien, A and Lewis, P, *Database Systems: An Application Oriented Approach*, 2nd edition, 2005.

Khoshafian, S and Abnous, R, *Object orientation: concepts, languages, databases, user interfaces*, John Wiley & Sons, Inc., 1990.

Kusnetzky, D and Olofson, C W, *Oracle 10g: Putting Grids to Work*, White Paper by IDC sponsored by Oracle, 2004.

Jarke, M and Koch, J, Query optimization in database systems, *ACM Computer Surveys*, Volume 16, Issue 2,1984.

Loney K and Koch G, *Oracle9i: The Complete Reference*, Osborne McGraw-Hill, 2002.

Microsoft's .NET
http://msdn.microsoft.com/en-us/library/default.aspx
http://msdn.microsoft.com/netframework/

Microsoft's ASP.NET
www.asp.net/

... and for code samples
http://code.msdn.microsoft.com/default.aspx?SiteEntry=gdn

Morrison J, Morrison M and Conrad R, *Guide to Oracle 10g*, Thomson, 2006.

Oracle Corp *Oracle Database 11g*
www.oracle.com/technology/products/database/oracle11g/index.html

Oracle's SQL and PL/SQL User's Guide and Reference
www.oracle-doku.de/oracle_10g_documentation/

Oracle Corp *Oracle 9i Application Developer's Guide - Object Relational Features*, 2002.

Ramakrishnan R and Gehrke J, *Database Management Systems*, 3th edition, McGraw-Hill Science Engineering, 2002.

Riccardi, G, *Principles of Database Systems with Internet and Java Applications*, Addison Wesley, 2001.

Silberschatz A and Korth H, Sudarshan S, *Database System Concepts*, 4th edition, McGraw-Hill, 2002.

Smith W, *Systems Building with Oracle*, Palgrave Macmillan, 2004.

Sunderraman R, *Oracle 9i Programming*, Addison Wesley, 2004.

Umanath, N and Scamell, R, *Data modelling and database design*, Thomson, 2007.

Watson R, *Data Management Databases and Organizations*, 3rd edition, Wiley 2002.

W3 Schools (SQL, ASP.NET & XML)
www.w3schools.com/default.asp